# New Perspectives on Hegel's Philosophy of Religion

# New Perspectives on Hegel's Philosophy of Religion

*edited by David Kolb*

**State University of New York Press**

Published by
State University of New York Press, Albany

© 1992 State University of New York

For information, address State University of New York Press,
State University Plaza, Albany, N.Y., 12246

Production by Marilyn P. Semerad
Marketing by Fran Keneston

**Library of Congress Cataloging-in-Publication Data**

New perspectives on Hegel's philosophy of religion    [editor] David
    Kolb.
        p.    cm.
    Includes index.
    ISBN 0-7914-1437-X (hard.) — ISBN 0-7914-1438-8 (pbk.)
    1. Hegel, Georg Wilhelm Friedrich, 1770-1831—Contributions in
philosophy of religion.   2. Religion—Philosophy—History—19th
century.   I. Kolb, David.
B2949.R3N48   1992      _75403_                                92-23739
200'.1—dc20                                                    CIP

10   9   8   7   6   5   4   3   2   1

# Contents

# Contents

# Editor's Introduction

*David Kolb*

This is an exciting time for Hegel's philosophy of religion. With the publication of the new critical edition of Hegel's lectures on the subject, readers have for the first time the opportunity see more accurately what Hegel said and how he connected his topics. Previous editions had run together material from different years; now we can compare and contrast the different sequences of lectures. We can follow the unity of the different treatments and the changes in Hegel's thought. With the appearance of the excellent English translation of the lecture series (and the one-volume presentation of the 1827 lectures) this resource has become available to readers in other fields. Interest in Hegel's thought on religion has grown and old impressions have had to be revised.

Hegel's discussions of religion are intellectually profound and historically informed. They challenge standard theological and philosophical pieties. With the new edition the field is open for discussion; whether we end up agreeing with Hegel or not we will all learn from the investigation.

This book presents current essays on Hegel's philosophy of religion. They include global interpretations of Hegel's stance toward religion and the relation of religion and philosophy, examinations of Hegel's treatment of particular points of religious imagery or doctrine, and historical comparisons of Hegel with other thinkers.

Despite the variety of subjects addressed in these essays, one set of issues comes up again and again: the relation of religious practices and representations to philosophical concepts. What happens to religious images and symbols when the thinker interprets them philosophically? For Hegel, does religion provide only material to be taken up into philosophy where imagistic presentations are left behind? Or do the religious symbols retain their independent richness and validity as a source of thought? Does philosophy supplant religion or complement it? Hegel's famous pronouncements on the subject prove to be themselves challenges to interpretation, and the contributors to this volume do not agree.

These issues concerning the relation of religion and philosophy speak not only to historical questions of Hegel-interpretation, but also to our own attempts to understand our situation and our world today. Do we live in a time which can be only addressed by science and abstract concepts? Have our self-analyses and self-reflection so distanced us from earlier modes of communication that we can only relate to traditional symbols by taking them from the closeness of tradition into the strange public intimacy of rational validity, which is supposed to touch us at the anonymous level where we define ourselves as knowing subjects? Since the Enlightenment and the Romantic reaction to it the modern world has been struggling with the relation of the different modes of knowing. Hegel tried to define a position that was neither Enlightenment distance nor Romantic subjectivity; his theories about religion (and art) play a crucial role in this regard. These essays explore those theories and different ways of reading our position as rational subjects in a world that seems at times to exceed rationality and at times to be thoroughly disenchanted.

There is a related contemporary issue: Hegel insists that there is a final unifying systematic language in which spirit speaks its world to itself. Much is written today against any such proposal that would counter the multiplicity of perspectives and the privilege of difference. In various ways the authors of these essays wonder what kind of total language Hegel was proposing, and whether its relations to other kinds of discourse might be more subtle than at first appears.

In the first essay Walter Jaeschke, editor of the new German edition of the Lectures on the Philosophy of Religion, argues for a dominant relation of philosophy over religion, and discerns an "end of religion" thesis in Hegel's lectures that is somewhat parallel to his famous claims about the end of art. Martin de Nys replies to Jaeschke's views with an interpretation claiming a mutual interdependence of religion and philosophy and the continuing validity of religious symbols and doctrines within the philosophical synthesis. Similarly, Stephen Rocker argues that within the system philosophy must turn back to religion for its own nourishment. Robert Williams examines the current relation of philosophy to religion and Hegel's notion of tragedy, exploring the possibility a non-foundationalist theology based on Hegel.

Martin Donougho probes the relations between myth and philosophy; he discusses the received ways of discussing myth and mythology at the time Hegel was writing, and examines the work of Friedrich Creuzer, a friend of Hegel whose methods of studying myth influenced Hegel and provided a stimulus for Hegel's own distinctive views on symbolism and early religion. Louis Dupré shows how in the different lecture series Hegel shifted his structure for interpreting the place of the historical religions, and explores the resistance of these religious traditions to the kind of unification that Hegel wanted to achieve.

In his presidential address to the Hegel Society, John Burbidge examines Hegel relation to traditional Christianity; he adduces evidence that Hegel's experience and thought were deeply Christian, but that the movement of that thought in today's world would lead Hegel beyond standard Christianity. Burbidge's paper discusses Hegel's connection with Christian mysticism; two other papers discuss that relation in more detail. Cyril O'Regan studies the complex connections and differences between Hegel's philosophy and the mysticism of Meister Eckhart. Clark Butler argues for a reading of Hegel's logic of God as an updated version of the heretical Joachimite Christianity of the late middle ages.

Stephen Dunning studies how despite initial hostility Hegel finally reconciles speculative generality with the resistant particularity of religious belief and practice. The issue of particularity is brought up again in other essays. William Desmond gives a close reading of Hegel on the classic problem of evil; he concludes that Hegel's nuanced treatment still remains inadequate to the singularity of evil and of our response to it. Sarah Lilly Heidt examines Hegel's treatment of the individual and community, bringing recent French criticisms to bear on the degree to which Hegel's notion of community might be repressive in itself, and yet also foreshadow our world of shattered community and nomadic individuals. In a somewhat more optimistic vein, Michael Vater studies the relation of religious and political/social community in Hegel; by examining the ways Hegel mediates the immediacy of religion he brings the essays full circle to the theme Walter Jaeschke introduced, by suggesting the passing away of specifically religious community into the social whole.

## References and Abbreviations

Because they are referred to so frequently in these essays, two works of Hegel (the *Encyclopedia* and the *Lectures on the Philosophy of Religion*) receive special treatment to facilitate references.

The *Encyclopaedia of the Philosophical Sciences* of 1830 is designated by "E" followed by the paragraph numbers (e.g., E §43); the paragraph numbers are found in all editions and translations. A "z" or "a" following the number refers to the comments (*Zusätze*) or the additions (from lecture material) following the main text of the paragraph.

References to the *Lectures on the Philosophy of Religion* are made as follows:

"LPR" followed immediately by a page number designates a page in the new one-volume edition of the 1827 lectures (*Lectures on the Philosophy of Religion: One Volume Edition, The Lectures of 1827*, ed. Peter C. Hodgson [Berkeley: University of California Press, 1988]).

"LPR" followed by one or more modifiers and a page number designates a page in the new three volume edition of the lectures. The modifiers can indicate which series of lectures (1821, 1827, 1831), which volume (I, II, III) and which language (E or G). When reference is made to both German and English editions, a "/" separates them; the second reference is usually abbreviated.

In citing the language, "E" refers to *Lectures on the Philosophy of Religion*, Vols 1-3, ed. Peter C. Hodgson, trans. R. F. Brown, Peter C. Hodgson, and J. M. Stewart (Berkeley: University of California Press, 1984-87). "G" refers to *Vorlesungen über die Philosophie der Religion*, Vols. 1-3, ed. Walter Jaeschke (Hamburg: Meiner, 1983-85)

References to all other works, including all other works of Hegel, are made in the end notes which follow each essay according to the different editions and abbreviations chosen by the authors of the essays. In these cases also, when references are made to both the German and English editions of a work by Hegel a "/" separates the two references with the German reference preceding the English.

The index at the end of the book includes proper names mentioned in the text and notes, and some general topics, but not omnipresent topics such as God, religion, Christianity, or Hegelian terms of art such as spirit, reason, absolute, or the stages of the dialectic.

# 1

# Philosophical Theology and Philosophy of Religion

*Walter Jaeschke*

H egel's philosophy begins by pronouncing the death of God, and ends with the insight into the end of religion. On the road, however, that leads from this experience of the death of God to this insight into the end of religion it unfurls a philosophical theology and a philosophy of religion of a spiritual and intellectual level far surpassing that of any other philosophy of religion. But in order to comprehend to what extent a philosophical theology and a philosophy of religion can issue from experience of the death of God and terminate in insight into the end of religion it is necessary to proceed to a detailed explanation concerning these four concepts.

## The Death of God

The pronouncement of the death of God met the same fate that is the customary lot of other concepts too, once they are encapsulated in catchwords and become known to a wider public. To use Lessing's expression, which was also taken over by Hegel, it became a wax nose which any rogue can mold to his own face at will. What Hegel meant is distorted to the point that he is alleged, in pronouncing the death of God, to have been protesting against the way in which the living God of the Bible is forcibly cabined and confined in contemporary metaphysics. But even leaving aside such tendentious assertions, whose character as deliberate misrepresentations is all too plain, it is possible to distinguish several—at least five—different meanings of this pronouncement in Hegel's texts. Of these meanings I would here like to draw attention to only one, that offering a diagnosis of his time.

1

In its original, classic formulation Hegel's pronouncement considers the significance of the death of God on the basis of the way in which the thought of God was treated by the philosophy of his day. But this does not refer for instance to modern metaphysics in general but rather to the current of opinion that in Hegel's days had rejected that metaphysics and declared it obsolete—the so-called "reflective philosophy of subjectivity," that is to say the philosophy of Kant, Jacobi and Fichte, or at any rate the early Fichte, as with the benefit of hindsight it is now necessary to add. In referring to the death of God Hegel is characterizing the assertion made at the end of the Enlightenment to the effect that God is unknowable. A God who is not known Hegel declares to be a dead God—for a God about whom nothing more can be said has no further significance, whether for life or for philosophy. And this is also the case if God becomes the object of moral postulates or of immediate knowledge, i.e., of the individual religiously inclined person's assurances. For the line of argument whereby God is constituted a postulate is weak in the extreme, whereas if God is taken back into immediate knowledge God can be made whatever one chooses: each individual can testify what he or she likes about God, without there being the remotest prospect of a basis of understanding. So the expression "death of God" does not actually refer to the death of God but to the status of the idea of God in regard to the theoretical situation in Hegel's time. It expresses the decline of contemporary philosophy, which affirms its own inability any longer to conceive the idea of God and, what is more, presents the ready acknowledgement of its incapacity as the hallmark of intellectual honesty.

In Hegel's view, this renunciation of the knowledge of God—however well-founded it may give itself out to be—is not problematical in regard, say, to human piety, to the salvation of souls. Nor is it problematical for some such reason as because there would thus no longer be a basis for morality or because of critical consequences for social integration and political life. The problem posed when one renounces the knowledge of God is one for philosophy itself. Without the idea of God, without the idea of the Absolute, to use the terminology employed in German Idealism, philosophy in the strict sense of the term can have neither a beginning nor an end. But philosophy, in the only sense that Hegel is prepared to recognize it, must begin with the Absolute, and must end with it too. Not to begin with it would mean never attaining it. And not to end with it would mean never having been within the Absolute.

It is, however, an inadequate, only one-sided understanding of Hegel's original insight to designate it a diagnosis of the death of God. What characterizes it is rather the simultaneous appearance of diagnosis and therapy, or at least the conviction that therapy is possible. The death of God, attributable to reflective philosophy, is not irrevocable because it is not in fact the death of God but of this philosophy. In order to revoke the knowledge of God, however, it is necessary to elaborate a philosophy that rectifies the false premises that led the Enlightenment to renounce it—not by stepping back behind the Enlightenment, except by directly refuting *in part* the critique which the Enlightenment directed against the former metaphysics. What is in fact required is rather to step beyond the Enlightenment, to a deeper insight into the conditions and possibilities of an improved philosophical knowledge.

In truth, however, this step is not so easy to accomplish. And this is linked to a problem that can also be posed under the rubric "Death of God" even if Hegel does not do so himself. The outcome of Enlightenment philosophy does not after all stand in isolation. Rather it is only one partial aspect of a much more far-reaching process, namely the Western process of rationalization, which does indeed culminate in the Enlightenment but, in point of time as well as in its significance, extends far beyond it. Certainly Hegel did not grasp in their full scope the manifold consequences this process would have at different levels. For this a further century was needed, till Max Weber, or only half a century, till Nietzsche, whose analysis is much more far-reaching than Weber's work, even though it is of earlier date. Let me here pick out only three aspects of this overall process which directly concern religion and of which Hegel was clearly aware—the critique of the inspirational thesis, the critique of tradition and the critique of history.

Hegel did, to be sure, make only an indirect contribution to the elaboration of these three sectors of the critique of religion. Like the other sectors and outcomes of the rationalization process, they do not constitute results but conceptual presuppositions of his philosophy. As can readily be seen, they are also not singled out by chance. The three rubrics inspiration, tradition and history denote the entire range of the traditional methods for establishing the truth of religion. It is not only this goal they have in common, but equally the fact that once the process of rationalization is far advanced they are no longer able to attain this goal. At times when critique in these three fields was in part still undeveloped, in part suppressed by subtle psychological means and also by brute physical force, these pillars of religious truth may have appeared capable of bearing the weight placed on them. On the other hand the process of rationalization gives rise to the demand that such methods of grounding must stand the test before the tribunal of reason. But this they are unable to do.

Hegel himself did not engage, as I have already indicated, in this kind of critique of the foundations of religion. Essentially its formulation occurs wholly outside philosophy, in a process internal to theology which made a decisive contribution to the establishment of a scientific theology. Yet Hegel never entertained any doubt as to whether the critical objections were justified. Once the point has been reached where there is conflict between the traditional pillars supporting religion and the subject's rational insight, "once the need for cognition is awakened and [an awareness of] cognition's split from religion," then "insight has its rights which can no longer be in any way denied" (LPR I E 131 n. 43). However, the task of philosophy also does not consist, say, in joining the chorus of the mainly theological critics of theology and religion. It consists in testing whether the content of religion, under threat from rationalist critique, cannot perhaps be legitimated in another way, and *only* in another way—namely, by philosophy itself. Hegel therefore criticizes the Enlightenment inasmuch as in its final form as reflective philosophy it proceeds to surrender the idea of God or take from it its significance for philosophy, and thereby its significance in general. On the other hand he is a follower of the Enlightenment inasmuch as in it the rationalization process only finds its at that time latest, highest form. And in the absence of any alternatives he undertakes the attempt to use reason itself to reach beyond the results of the critique of reason. If, in good Enlightenment fashion, reason is recognized as the sole basis of legitimation, then the only refuge for the threatened content does not come from any means of escape, any supposed practical necessitude or something similar, nor from a supposedly immediate conviction or the experience of the religious community, but solely from rational knowledge—at all events, from reason. If reason alone counts, then nothing counts but what stands up to reason. But *that* reason alone counts, results from the process of rationalization. To be sure, recognition of that fact can be delayed by atavistic attitudes, but it is irrevocable. Initial attempts, in the spirit of Early Romanticism, to formulate an alternative, for instance by resuscitating myth, were very quickly rejected by Hegel, still in his Jena years, as means that were unsuited to the conditions of the modern world. So the only course that remains is either to abandon the content of religion for reason's sake or, with and through reason, to cast it in a new form.

Hegel was by no means the only one to pose this problem as the new century came in. It can be discerned in a variety of guises in many of his contemporaries, from Lessing and Kant on. Fichte's striking formulation puts it in incisive form:

> For what purpose then is the speculative point of view, and with it the whole of philosophy, if it is not for life? Had humankind never tasted of this forbidden fruit, it could dispense with philosophy in its entirety. But it is implanted in it to seek to discern *that* region that transcends the individual, not merely in reflected light but directly; and the first one who raised a question concerning the existence of God broke through the boundaries, convulsed human beings in their deepest foundations, and engaged them in a conflict with themselves which is not yet settled, and can only be settled by advancing boldly to the highest point, from which the practical and the speculative appear united. We began to philosophize from presumption, and in so doing lost our innocence; we saw that we were naked, and since then must needs philosophize for our salvation. [1]

## Philosophical Theology

In his philosophy Hegel took into account this insight into the precarious relationship between reason and religious content. If philosophy is not to go even beyond Kant's solution of the problem and abandon the idea of God altogether, it must be able to show that the idea of God is not merely threatened by reason but is also legitimated by it—indeed that, properly speaking, reason for the first time provides the means of conceiving it. Philosophy must be able to show that the idea of God is threatened only by a reason that is less than fully understood, namely mere understanding, whereas reason that is rightly understood legitimates it—and necessarily such reason alone, because after all it alone is recognized as legitimizing authority. There is no acceptable alternative to rational subjectivity, to the freedom of self-consciousness: "Thinking is the absolute judge, before which the content must verify and attest its claims" (LPR III E 346).

If the sole content that stands up before reason is one produced out of reason, then fully responsible discourse about God is only possible in the form of philosophical theology. 'Philosophical theology' does not mean the philosophically interested and pretentious form of theological discourse known to us from the better type of academic theology undertaken in church circles. It means that philosophical thought is the *sole* basis and legitimizing authority of discourse about God—not reports concerning actual or supposed historic events, nor theological propositions stemming from one or other tradition, nor by any means the direct inspiration of religious contents, understood as revelation, nor personal experience of some mode of acting of a divine being. The critique of all revelation and the critique of history are chronologically and also in terms of their subject-matter prior to Hegel's philosophy, and for Protestants at any rate tradition is devoid of any binding force. At all events it is common knowledge that no other philosophy has campaigned with greater emphasis or more biting scorn against reliance on immediate knowledge and private experiences of the divine than the Hegelian. Nothing has binding character for thought other than thought itself.

Sadly it is still not superfluous to call to mind that the customary objections to this principle of the autonomy of subjectivity only impinge on it externally, and that they lack all foundation. Lacking foundation, in particular, is the cherished distinction between an idea of God adumbrated by philosophy, in other words by human thought, and the authentic idea of God—as if every idea of God was not a thought, a product of subjectivity, even if it is proclaimed and handed down by tradition as having been revealed. One does not need to spend long refuting such seeming alternatives. They disregard the critique of revelation and suggest that it is possible not only to formulate a concept of revelation that could be brought within the sway of reason but in addition to be able to indicate in what cases it is a matter of genuine revelation and in what a matter of false images and prophets.

Philosophically more respectable but in the final analysis no less erroneous is the proposal that the idealistic principle of subjectivity can only be salvaged by recourse to intersubjectivity. For on the one hand it is a groundless supposition that the concept of intersubjectivity can be contrasted with the idealistic concept of subjectivity—as though the former was not always already subsumed in the latter and the 'subjectivity' of idealism was confined to the singularity of *one* particular subject. The idealistic idea of subjectivity, of freedom of self-consciousness, invariably includes intersubjectivity. Moreover, even such knowledge constituted intersubjectively must, in the last resort, come before the tribunal of reason—by which Idealism understands the tribunal of subjectivity—in the same way as all other knowledge. Nothing else would be compatible with the freedom of self-consciousness. The only question that is philosophically relevant is as follows: does the subject that rejects all heteronomy remain in isolated self-sufficiency and self-containment, a windowless monad from which all content, in Hegel's phrase, has blown away? Or can it reach beyond the mere negation of heteronomy and actualize the autonomy it lays claim to, or in other words develop out of itself a content that can itself lay claim to the possession of binding force? Furthermore, can thought, as it unfurls its contents, think a highest thought of which, following its own rules of evidence, it can say with Aristotle: "touto gar ho theos—for it is this, what God is."[2]

Hegel's whole system is directed to the elaboration of such a thought. This is why he uses this sentence from Aristotle to conclude the presentation of the fundamentals of his system, namely the *Encyclopedia*. On the road that leads from the first category of the *Logic* to this conclusion the development of the concept sometimes comes closer to this highest thought (as in the Absolute Idea at the end of the *Logic*), sometimes remains more remote from it, so that in individual passages it is possible partly to overlook, partly to set methodologically aside the character of philosophical theology that imbues the system as a whole. It is only in the final section of the *Encyclopedia*, concerning Absolute Spirit, that this character once again becomes explicit. But a direct and indispensable prerequisite for this is the development of the concept of spirit at the beginning of the Philosophy of Spirit. To be sure, the few, highly condensed sections (see in particular E §381,

§385) have to be elucidated by the *Lectures on the Philosophy of Spirit*, which have currently not yet been published. But elsewhere, in a paragraph from a little-known fragment relating to the Philosophy of Spirit, Hegel speaks in particularly emphatic fashion about this concept of spirit:

> Whence it comes, is from nature; whither it goes, is to its freedom. What it *is*, is nothing other than the very movement of freeing itself from nature. This is its very substance, so much so that one may not speak of it as a solidly constituted subject that acts in a particular way as if such activity were a matter of chance, a kind of state on which its existence is not conditional; on the contrary, its activity is its substantiality, embodied actuality (*Aktuosität*) is its being.[3]

The highest concept of philosophical theology is the concept of spirit. This hardly sounds surprising, for the fact that God is spirit was also not unknown to tradition. But, as is well known, this can, to say the least, be understood in Biblical as well as Aristotelian terms: spirit (*Geist*) can denote both *pneuma* and *nous*. This in itself makes plain that "spirit" is an empty word unless one says what one means by it. So it is not merely a question of asseverating that God is spirit but of expounding *what* spirit is and *why* the concept of spirit is tantamount to the concept of God.

## Philosophy of Religion

Philosophical theology that seeks to answer these questions necessarily passes over into a philosophy of religion, or vice versa: the philosophy of religion is for Hegel only one part of philosophical theology, that part in which philosophical theology reaches its conclusion and consummation. For to the extent that God is grasped as spirit, "this concept includes the subjective side within it, the side that is introduced into this concept when it is defined as religion;" accordingly "the doctrine of God is to be grasped and  taught only as the doctrine of *religion*" (LPR I E 116). The concept of God necessarily leads to the concept of religion (LPR I E 186). "Spirit" is God not by virtue of his or her being three persons in an essential unity. Philosophical theology leads beyond the sphere of nature to the concept of spirit, and beyond subjective and objective spirit to the concept of spirit's self-relatedness.

As one can easily confirm for oneself, the concept of person is quite devoid of any systematic role in this philosophical theology. God as spirit is *not*, to use the words of the text I have previously cited, a solidly constituted subject that acts in a particular way or allows this or that to happen—we might add, as the religiously minded, and theology too, commonly suppose. But God is also not merely all actuality in the sense of Spinoza's absolute substance; for he is self-relatedness. And not merely self-relatedness but knowing self-relatedness: "the one universal *substance* as spiritual, the primal division (*Urteil*) into *itself* and into a form of *knowing* for which it subsists as spiritual substance" (E §554). This concept Hegel places at the head of the chapter of the *Encyclopedia* devoted to Absolute Spirit, to religion.

But it is not only the *Encyclopedia* that takes this concept of spirit as its point of departure. The same is true of the *Lectures on the Philosophy of Religion*. To be sure, this was not evident from the previous editions, the fault lying partly with Hegel and partly with the former editors. Even by reference to Hegel's manuscript on the philosophy of religion it can be shown that he had already a very precise view as to the link between philosophical theology and philosophy of religion. In his first two lecture series, however, he did not succeed in also expounding this view systematically, that is to say in imparting to the lectures on the philosophy of religion the systematic form they need if they are to live up to the systematic claim made by them. Up to now it might appear as if Hegel wished to give in his lectures as it were an interpretation of religions, and in particular the Christian religion, in the light of his philosophy and using its conceptuality. In the process he would have sought, in a first part based on the way religion is currently represented, to present a provisional explanation of what it signifies. His philosophy of religion would then stand in the same external relationship to religion as is customarily the case in other conceptions of philosophy of religion. Up to now it might also appear as if it was an important task of the philosophy of religion to demonstrate the necessity of the religious standpoint, to justify the concept of religion scientifically. Both points of view are understandable on the basis of Hegel's first two lecture series, and this impression has not been corrected by the editorial presentation of these lectures to date. At the same time these points of view are incorrect. They make of the philosophy of religion a ratiocinative discipline that has its object outside itself and is externally related to it. Admittedly this is how philosophy of religion is understood by other writers, but this is not the sense Hegel gives to it.

What Hegel already affords glimpses of in the first two lecture series and what initially still escapes him, he achieves in the third series (1827), namely the realization of that form which the philosophy of religion must necessarily have for the consummation of philosophical theology. It is not the task of philosophy of religion to extract a concept of religion from the way in which religion is currently represented—as his manuscript still suggests. Such a procedure is permissible for the empirical science of religion. Nor is it the task of the philosophy of religion, as seems to be the case in the first and also the second lecture series, to achieve elevation to the standpoint of religion *a posteriori* and so provide a scientific justification for it. For this justification occurs in the course of the system as a whole, as it is established in its basic outlines in the *Encyclopedia*, and it must be completed by the time the chapter on religion is reached. The task of the philosophy of religion is none other than to expound the concept of spirit as it is attained by the time the chapter of the *Encyclopedia* on religion is arrived at, and as it is presupposed by the *Lectures*. Religion is the knowing of spirit; it is a knowing relationship of the single spirit to spirit as its substance and so a *self*-relationship of spirit—the self-consciousness of spirit, which precisely because it has this self-consciousness, is absolute spirit. Philosophy of religion and philosophical theology cannot therefore be separated. If it wishes to achieve consummation, philosophical theology must necessarily become philosophy of religion. Only when it conceives God as spirit does it conceive the idea of God, and it only conceives him as spirit when it conceives spirit's self-knowledge in religion. Conversely, if it is to do justice to its subject-matter, to religion, the philosophy of religion must be philosophical theology, inasmuch as it views religion not as expressing human consciousness of a God distinct from it but as the form in which the single self-consciousness has cognizance of its essence, with which it forms a unity yet from which it also knows itself to be distinct.

Moreover, it is only this concept of religion that makes intelligible what must otherwise appear as an at best strange mode of expression used by Hegel, namely his assertion that in religion the concept of religion becomes object to itself. If by the concept of religion one understands what is placed under this title in the previous editions, then this expression is plainly unintelligible. A concept of religion extracted from the way in which religion is commonly represented cannot become object to itself, any more than a concept of religion that consists essentially in demonstrating the necessity of the religious standpoint or in expounding the ways in which religion is related to art and to philosophy. The situation is different when philosophy of religion is understood as explication of the knowing self-relationship of spirit that is present in religion. The concept of religion is the self-knowing of spirit, and in religion the single spirit's self-knowledge of its essence becomes its own object. Only the new edition makes it possible to grasp the concept of religion in the manner described as sole content of religion, and only when this is done does it become possible, thanks to the philosophy of religion being firmly embedded in the philosophy of spirit, to see clearly the linkage between the first part of the Lectures, which is in fact entitled "The Concept of Religion," and the two following parts. The concept of religion is the self-relationship of spirit, that is to say the concept of spirit as substantial unity and the primal division (*Urteil*) into this—spirit as substantial unity—and the form of knowing that relates to spirit as to its own essence. The concept of religion becomes object to itself to the extent that in religion these moments are object of knowledge. To this extent all religions are forms of the self-consciousness of spirit, and therefore absolute spirit. This is implicit in them, and it cannot be said that it would be present more in one religion and less in another. They differ, however, in the degree to which what they are implicitly, namely the self-knowledge of spirit, is also explicit, that is to say object of religious representation. This distinction at the same time provides the criterion for the hierarchical structuring of the history of religion. The religions differ from one another in the degree to which the three moments of the concept of spirit that I have mentioned have not only, as Hegel says, sprouted up "fortuitously, like the flowers and creations of nature . . . without [our] knowing where they come from or where they are going to"—in other words, are present only in intuition and in feeling—but have entered into consciousness and "constitute an essential moment of the determination of the absolute object."

This and this alone also determines the absolute character of the Christian religion. In it these determinations are objective; they are "essential moments of the content," they have the "determination of being the truth" (LPR I E 196-197). The consummate religion is not consummate for instance by virtue of the true God having revealed himself in it, sent his Son into the world and redeemed humankind from its sins—whereas this had not previously been the case. It is consummate because in it the three moments of the concept of religion—spirit's substantial unity, and its division into itself and into knowledge—are not only factually present and foreshadowed in the sphere of representation (as they are in the preceding religions) but here, and only here, constitute the central dogmatic content. This also explains the vehemence with which Hegel—contrary to strong currents of theological opinion of his day—holds fast to the idea of the Trinity. In the Trinitarian idea of God the content of religion, namely the concept of spirit, is itself elevated to the level of object of religious representation: "The single self-consciousness finds the consciousness of its essence in it; hence it is free in this object, and it is just this freedom that is spirituality—and this, we say, is religion, i.e., the self-consciousness of freedom" (LPR III E 164). Herein consists the self-consciousness of absolute spirit, so commonly dismissed with a skeptical smile as a richly mystical affair. The reason why the Christian religion is for Hegel the consummate religion is that it sublates the mere relationship-of-consciousness, according to which God stands on the one side while the human worshiper stands on the other. In religions that regard such a relationship-of-consciousness as the religious relationship properly speaking, the single self-consciousness does not know God as what he implicitly is, namely as its essence. In such religions self-consciousness is not at home with itself in the idea of God, it is not free. In Christianity, however, so Hegel implies, inasmuch as in the idea of God the single self-consciousness implicitly has the consciousness of its essence, the mere relationship of consciousness of an object is taken back within self-consciousness. "This freedom of the subject is its rationality- the fact that as subject it is thus liberated and has attained this liberation through religion, that in accord with its religious vocation it is essentially free. This freedom, which has the impulse and determinacy to realize itself, is rationality" (LPR III E 340).

The freedom of self-consciousness is the content of religion, and concerning this content Hegel believes himself capable of showing that in Christianity it is not merely present (as it is in other religions) but is the object of religious representation. It can be criticized as an *interpretatio in bonam partem*, or for that matter as a grievous misinterpretation, that Hegel sought for the idea of the freedom of self-consciousness in the Christian religion, that he proclaimed the principle of subjectivity as that of Christianity. But we should be clear about the fact that such criticism does not yet call in question the appropriateness of the Hegelian concept of religion. And furthermore it may be the case that the majority of those who occupy themselves with religion and the philosophy of religion have, or believe they have, grounds for thinking that philosophy of religion is something quite different from philosophical theology and there is nothing wrong with understanding religion in the sense that Hegel vehemently rejects, namely as a relation-of-consciousness to God. But then—and this too ought to be clear—there is no longer any occasion to have recourse to Hegel's philosophy of religion, unless such recourse were part of an overall, even if not everywhere conscious defensive strategy. For Hegel the only reason why religion is an object of philosophy is that he believes he has grounds for being able to interpret it as a self-relationship of spirit. And the only reason why Christianity is of systematic interest to him, after all the critical utterances of his early writings, is that later, as he elaborates his system, he finds preformed in it what is, according to his philosophy, the highest idea, that of the freedom of self-consciousness. But Hegel categorized this idea of freedom in much more concrete terms than the Enlightenment, from which he inherited it. For "freedom of self-consciousness" means not only the rejection of all heteronomy, but also not solely the autonomy of the subject thrown back on itself, but self-consciousness's being-at-home-with-itself in the concept of spirit from which everything alien is expunged.

It is far from being my intention to maintain that this concept of spirit is wholly above criticism. The more problems one has with the word "spirit," the more reticent one will be vis-à-vis Hegel's conception. But such criticism must be very carefully grounded and developed philosophically. Above all, the significance and value of this idea of freedom are totally independent of whether Hegel was correct in regarding it as prefigured in the Christian religion. Even should it have been Hegel's greatest error to proclaim the principle of subjectivity as that of Christianity, this idea of the freedom of self-consciousness would remain wholly unaffected. If it is to be criticized, the criticism must not be mounted on dogmatic lines, but must show that the idea is conceptually inconsistent.

Not least, the insight into the fact that the philosophy of religion has its starting-point in the philosophy of spirit, and into the systematic consequences that follow from this, necessitates a new approach to interpreting the philosophy of religion. For this new approach I would coin the catch-phrase "transition from theological interpretation to philosophical interpretation." By a theological interpretation I mean one that does not primarily enquire into the systematic consistency of Hegel's philosophy but into its compatibility with Christianity. Within the framework of limited investigations it naturally remains partly justified (even if by no means unproblematic) to enquire into the agreement between Hegel's philosophy and Christianity—whether what he denotes as Christian doctrine and, what is more, whether his philosophy itself is consonant with Christianity. But it is necessary to be clear about the fact that this is not a philosophical question but a question of dogma. For the evidential power of Hegel's philosophy (as of any other philosophy), of its concept of spirit and understanding of religion as a self-relationship of spirit, is totally independent of the assessment of its conformity with dogma. The evidential power of a philosophy is judged by the tribunal of reason, in a philosophical interpretation whose sole criterion is the conceptual rigor of what is said on the subject of philosophy of religion, and not a comparison with texts or tenets derived from religious tradition. The task of the philosophy of religion does not consist in establishing or demonstrating (nor in contesting) the compatibility of religious and philosophical utterances. It consists in comprehending what religion is, and for Hegel this means its task is to make the relationship of the single spirit to spirit as its essence—the relationship implicit in religion—cognizable for spirit too. Inasmuch as it does this, it forms itself a part (and indeed the highest, concluding part) of philosophical theology.

## The End of Religion

Hegel's philosophy of religion accords to religion a much higher status than is otherwise the case. In the last resort, and whatever form of words may be used in the particular case, theology too takes religion to be a relation-of-consciousness to God, that is to say a form of expression of human consciousness. For Hegel on the contrary religion is a self-relationship of spirit, the self-consciousness of absolute spirit, and hence the basic structure of the Absolute. From this standpoint nothing seems less apt than to wish to ascribe to Hegel a statement proclaiming the end of religion.

At the same time this is unavoidable. It follows even from the fact that the philosophy of spirit furnishes the starting-point. To be sure, religion may be, as Hegel says, the single spirit's relationship to spirit as to its essence. It belongs, however, both to its concept and to its reality that what it thus is implicitly it is not explicitly. Religion erroneously understands what it implicitly is, the self-relationship of spirit, as a relationship-of-consciousness of human beings to God. Even for the consummate Religion this disparity still obtains. In it self-consciousness has, to be sure, the consciousness of its essence (LPR III E 164)—but as consciousness of an other essence. It is aware of the identity of universal and single spirit—but it too transposes this unity into a particular divine-human being. It does indeed itself avow that "Once is always" (LPR III E 115)—but it misunderstands this, as if it was only saying, in somewhat banal fashion, "Once is enough." In a word, Christian religion, too, does not elevate the objects of representation to the level of the true self-consciousness of spirit. Once the philosophy of religion has gone beyond what it is implicitly, religion in general, including the Christian religion, is therefore incapable of satisfying the highest concern of spirit, and has thereby reached its end.

As is already indicated by the form of words I have just chosen, talk of the "end of religion" must be understood in analogous fashion to talk of the "end of art." In the same way that the latter does not mean that art will cease or that people will stop going to concerts, theaters and museums, so too talk of the "end of religion" does not mean that churches would close their doors and religion vanish from the face of the earth. It means that within the historical development of absolute spirit religion, as a form of such spirit, is replaced by a new form, viz., philosophy. It is the philosophy of religion and philosophy in general—in the form of philosophical theology—that first elevate the absolute matter to the absolute form, that first confer on the content the form of thought that alone accords with it.

In speaking of the "end of religion," however, this essay has not—in good Hegelian fashion—reverted to its starting-point. For Hegel the "end of religion" means something quite different from the death of God. It means that philosophical theology has now for the first time reached a stage in which it is no longer exposed to the threats which gave rise to talk about the death of God at the close of the Enlightenment. For Hegel's philosophical theology formulates the idea of God in opposition to the critical attitude which by maintaining that God was unknowable provoked his pronouncement of the death of God. It is also not open to question that in turning against the idea of the *ens necessarium* or the *ens realissimum* the Enlightenment's "critique of all speculative theology" does not as it were already refute the Hegelian concept of spirit by anticipation. For in Hegel's philosophy God is precisely no longer the *summum ens* the possibility of thinking and knowing which there were good grounds for doubting. Nor is there any question of the new idea of the self-relationship of spirit being also exposed to the threats which in the late Enlightenment period undermined the traditional pillars of religion, namely inspiration, tradition, and history. Indeed this idea was itself born of the insight that these means of grounding religion were totally invalidated, for two reasons: first, because their probative force is methodologically insufficient; and secondly, because the representations they seek to substantiate are in any event inadequate. If the understanding of religion mediated by scripture and tradition were correct, religion would not only be a mere relationship-of-consciousness; it would also necessarily succumb to the manifold forms of critique leveled against it.

By contrast, the changed, speculative understanding of religion as the self-consciousness of absolute spirit is not exposed to this kind of—in the broadest sense—historical critique. It can, to be sure, only legitimate religion on condition of its being sublated into thought. And this, finally, is the very step that conjures up the end of religion—replacement of the representational substrates by thought—that brings philosophical theology to its consummation and thereby revokes the pronouncement of the death of God. To coin an aphorism, the end of religion is the price paid for revoking the death of God.

It is not unknown that Hegel's solution proved historically short-lived. The first to assail it were the self-appointed spokesmen of a religion understood in very popular terms and a professedly Christian philosophy. It was only considerably later that the onslaught was joined by philosophers who had adopted a radical approach, denying the metaphysical character of philosophy in general and claiming to represent a new philosophical era. It is properly speaking also known, but little taken into account, what this means for the death of God and the end of religion as philosophical themes. By virtue of the idea of the identity of philosophical theology and philosophy of religion Hegel revoked the diagnosis as to the death of God. The rupture of this identity accordingly rehabilitates Hegel's original diagnosis—Friedrich Nietzsche being neither the first nor the only one to exemplify this. Religion at all events derived little profit as a result. Even if beyond the Hegelian School the reasons for which Hegel diagnosed the end of religion are no longer regarded as valid, the general considerations developed in the course of the rationalization process, quite irrespective of Hegelian philosophy, remain as damning as ever. This being so, talk of the end of religion even acquires an added sharpness that goes far beyond the Hegelian attempt at a sublation of religion into philosophy—even where one willingly conceals this from oneself, indeed there specifically.

It would be difficult to find any clearer evidence of this than in the so-called contemporary philosophy of religion—not to speak of certain fashionable or already outmoded currents of theological opinion. The characteristic premises of the contemporary philosophy of religion not only reject, in vehement opposition to everything metaphysical, the philosophical significance which religion has for Hegel. They also abandon completely the prospect of securing a deeper meaning of religion. From the standpoint of linguistic analysis one tends to take the view that what is involved in religious discourse is meaningless sentences; even to the extent that this is not the case, one no longer trusts oneself to thematize the actuality-reference of the religious discourse that has been laboriously analyzed. And from the standpoint of a functional approach to religion one analyses only its function for the individual's way of life or the integration of society, and even for the success of the market economy, possibly under the label "system theory," without entering into the question of that content which religion traditionally regards as its peculiar sphere. On the one hand this may be legitimate, but on the other it is nothing but a readily transparent defensive strategy, not without parallel dating from the late Enlightenment. We are told that there are weighty considerations pertaining to the theory of science why it is not possible to pose precisely those questions (or to have already passed beyond them) an honest answer to which would involve talk of the end of religion—and not only in the moderate Hegelian sense. Yet instead of making the effort to provide such an answer one prefers to indulge in a series of locutions that are best designated as undigested theological fragments in the stomach of analytical philosophy—in talk, for instance, of "ultimate concern," of "what affects us unconditionally," or even of an "other activity," or such downright pretentious terms as "transcendence," "concept of transcendence," or "experience of transcendence," or even "cosmic intimations" ( "*kosmische Erschliessungen* "), about the actuality-status of which it is methodologically impossible to say anything.[4] It is therefore permissible to doubt whether these two approaches we have cited of further approaches characteristic of the present day do justice to religion any better than Hegel's attempt to sublate the truth of religion into an identity of philosophical theology and philosophy of religion.[5]

## Notes

1. Letter from J.G. Fichte to F. H. Jacobi, August 30, 1795, *J. G. Fichte-Gesamtausgabe*, Abt. 3, Bd. 2 (Stuttgart: Fromann), 392f.

2. Aristotle, *Metaphysics* XII, 7.

3. Hegel, Fragment zur Philosophie des Geistes, in *Hegel, Werke in zwanzig Bänden*, Bd. 11, Berliner Schriften 1818-1831 (Frankfurt am Main: Suhrkamp, 1970), 528.

4. See the individual references in Jaeschke, "Feuerbach und die aktuelle religionsphilosophische Diskussion." In *Ludwig Feuerbach und die Philosophie der Zukunft*, eds. Hans-Jürg Braun, Hans-Martin Sass, Werner Schuffenhauer, Francesco Tomasoni (Berlin, 1990), 113-134.

5. I offer my heartfelt gratitude to J. Michael Stewart for translating this essay into English, as he has done in the past for so many of my essays.

# 2

# Philosophical Thinking and the Claims of Religion

*Martin J. De Nys*

I t is most important, for the sake of understanding the aims and achievements of Hegel's philosophy of religion, to appreciate the complexities of Hegel's response to the Enlightenment. Hegel affirms the Enlightenment position regarding the self-determining character of reason. At the same time he criticizes the Enlightenment insofar as it terminates in a philosophy of reflection and a one-sided subjectivity whose consequence is the position that God is unknown and unknowable, a philosophical "death of God." Hegel affirms, by taking up into his own thinking, the Enlightenment critiques of inspiration, tradition, and history as given, extra-philosophical supports for knowledge of God. At the same time he engages the project of developing and legitimizing knowledge of God from the resources of reason as such, a project which one legitimately names philosophical theology. And this opens the possibility of a return to the objects of Enlightenment critique, a return which considers the same not as extra-philosophical presuppositions and grounds of the content of religious knowing, but as matters for autonomous philosophical consideration.

It is this which makes possible the transition, which is for other reasons necessary, from philosophical theology to philosophy of religion. Philosophical theology determines its highest concept to be the concept of spirit, through which it comprehends the concept of God. Philosophical theology must point beyond itself to philosophy of religion, in that it is through appropriating the self-knowing relation of spirit to itself which religion is that philosophical theology thinks the concept of spirit concretely, and thereby the concept of God. In turn, philosophy of religion concludes and completes philosophical

19

theology. It conceptualizes religion as the domain in which individual spirit relates to spirit as its own substance, the domain of the self-consciousness of spirit.

Hegel knows that there can be a tension between philosophy of religion and the matter which it examines, religion as such. He does speak of an antithesis between rational thinking and religion, of an awareness of "cognition's split from religion" which is a situation in which "insight has its rights which can no longer be denied." (LPR I E 131 / G 47). But he also says that, "The more human beings in their rational thinking give the thing itself control within themselves (*im vernünftigen Denken die Sache selbst in sich walten lässt*) and renounce their private concerns . . . the less will reason fall into this antithesis" (LPR I 131 / G 46-47). And he says that "The triumph of cognition is the reconciliation of the antithesis" (LPR I E 131 / G 47). The relation between religion and the philosophy of religion is a delicate one. On the one hand, philosophy of religion comprehends the content of religion through its own autonomous reenactment of that content. At the same time, that reenactment endeavors to comprehend the content of religion itself. It endeavors to "give the thing itself control" within thinking, in the sense of allowing that content to exhibit its intelligibility and necessity in a way that is possible through and only through self-determining philosophical activity.

This can happen, philosophical theology can point beyond itself to philosophy of religion, once the essential constituents of religion are, on the basis of Enlightenment critique, understood not as external, pre-philosophical supports for religious knowledge, but as matters for philosophical comprehension. In one sense philosophy comprehends religion differently and more radically than religion comprehends itself. It comprehends religion through categories unavailable to, and in a radical manner unavailable to, religious self-understanding. In this sense, the legitimacy of philosophical comprehension is determined by rational evidence, and not by its consonance with the pre-philosophical self-understanding of religion. In another sense, the categories through which philosophy of religion thinks religion aim at allowing the content of religion to exhibit itself from its standpoint, and to present its intelligibility with a radicality otherwise unavailable.

In what way does religion, especially that which Hegel calls the consummate religion, exhibit itself in philosophical comprehension? Most immediately, the concern of religion is the divine taken simply and as such; here its focus "is this divine universality, spirit wholly in its indeterminate universality, for which there is positively no distinction" (LPR I 380 / G 277). But, "The second [moment] after this absolute foundation is distinction in general, and only with distinction does religion as such begin" (LPR I E 380-381 / G 277). The reference to distinction as belonging indispensably to religion is in turn a reference to consciousness. "Religion, in accord with its general concept, is the consciousness of God as such, consciousness of absolute essence. Consciousness . . . is a differentiating, a division within itself. Thus we already have two moments: consciousness and its absolute essence" (LPR III 250 / G 178). However, at work in religion in general and expressly at work in the consummate religion is a process that in some manner overcomes this twoness of moments, this duality. For, "when religion grasps itself, its content and object is this whole—*consciousness relating itself to its essence,* knowing itself as its essence and its essence as its own—and that is spiritual religion" (LPR III 251 / G 178-179). One of the essential points these statements make is that religion institutes an essential difference or duality within itself and overcomes that difference or duality within itself, most fully "when religion grasps itself." What, more precisely, is the manner of this overcoming?

Insofar as religion institutes difference, it is a consciousness of the human and of the divine which takes each to be the other of the other. Insofar as religion develops the conception of God beyond its immediate beginning, and especially to the point of completion that for Hegel is attained in the consummate religion, it thinks of God as the principle of a manifold and multiform otherness. "The being of all these things is not of an independent sort, however, but quite simply something upheld and maintained . . . it is only a borrowed being . . . not the absolutely independent being that God is" (LPR I, 369 / G 268). God maintains self-relatedness in God's relation to all else, while "All else that is actual is not actual on its own account, has no subsistence on its own account; the uniquely absolute actuality is God alone" (LPR I 369/ G 269). God brings about what is other from Godself and simultaneously overreaches the otherness of that other by being, in relation to it, self-related. In this self-relation the divine maintains itself in its "absolutely independent being," its "uniquely absolute actuality." What is other from God, in turn, is other only in the context of its relation to the divine principle that surpasses it. Its self-relation is a self-surpassing relation to that which exceeds it and is its most fundamental principle.

Religious consciousness, especially when developed to the point that for Hegel the consummate religion reaches, knows these things. It knows that, as a consciousness of the divine that it distinguishes from itself, it is also "*consciousness relating to its own essence . . .* knowing its essence as its own," and thus knowing itself. But the fact that these statements about the self-understanding of religious consciousness are put in philosophical and not religious terms indicates something important. Religious self-understanding, as such, can not produce a conceptually adequate or sufficiently radical articulation or legitimation of what it knows. It is a form of thinking, but not a form of thinking possessed of the categories or the autonomy that would enable it to meet these aims. Philosophical thinking does possess those categories and that autonomy. It brings about from its own resources the concept of spirit, determines the same as that concept which comprehends the thought of God, realizes this concept through its self-determining appropriation of the content of religion, in a way such that philosophy of religion is both required by and completed by philosophical theology.

Just for these reasons, philosophical thinking can reenact and reinstate the self-understanding of religion as that self-understanding can not enact and institute itself. It can, through its own autonomous appropriation of that self-understanding, allow it to exhibit what I have called the intelligibility and necessity of its standpoint. It can comprehend God as absolute spirit, as that self-relating and self-knowing activity which brings forth what is other from itself, and at the same time relates what is other to itself, knowing what is other in a self-relation and a self-knowing. It can comprehend human selfhood as constituted by, and self-related in virtue of, its self-surpassing relation to what is other, absolute, and its own essence or principle. This is a self-surpassing relation that involves both consciousness and self-consciousness. But if one makes these statements truly, if philosophy of religion in these ways is at once the rational, autonomous appropriation of the content of religion and the process of allowing that content radically to disclose what on its own terms belongs to it, then Hegel's position does not conclude in even a moderate affirmation of the "end of religion." It rather concludes in a radicalized comprehension of the self-related identities and the differences that religion itself affirms.

According to Hegel, "Religion is the self-consciousness of absolute spirit: there are not two kinds of self-consciousness—not both a conceptualizing self-consciousness and a representing self-consciousness, which could be distinguished according to their content. There can only be a diversity in form, and a distinction between *representation* and thought, and we can presuppose a more detailed acquaintance with that" (LPR I 333 / G 235). It is indeed the case that religion, as Hegel understands it, is not merely a human consciousness of a divine other, but "the self-consciousness of absolute spirit." In and through religious understanding, human selfhood knows itself in knowing its self-surpassing relation to what is absolute and divine, and knows what is absolute and divine as it knows itself in its knowledge of its other. To assert that "Religion is the self-consciousness of absolute spirit" is to assert a philosophical statement, one that restates the self consciousness of religion in philosophical terms, and in this way redefines that self-consciousness. But finally "there are not two kinds of self-consciousness" at work here. There is one self-consciousness, achieved and expressed in religion, and comprehended in philosophical conceptualization and in the philosophical appropriation of religion.

These remarks bear on a consideration of the principle of the freedom of self-consciousness. For both the self-consciousness that religion attains through engagement and articulation, and the self-consciousness that philosophy attains through express comprehension, one asserts that,

> Gott ist nur Gott, insofern er sich selber weiss; sein Sichwissen ist ferner sein Selbstbewusstsein im Menschen und das Wissen des Menschen *von* Gott, das fortgeht zum Wissen des Menschen in Gott. (E §564).

God is God insofar as God knows Godself. This knowledge, which God enjoys of Godself, is simultaneously but also "further" the self-consciousness that God enjoys of Godself in human selfhood; it is divine knowledge of the divine in its indwelling in human selfhood. Divine knowledge of the divine indwelling in human selfhood brings about and is in this manner identical with the self's knowledge of God. The self's knowledge of God is, in turn its knowledge of its being as constituted in and through the divine indwelling.

Meister Eckhart could have understood and did understand statements like these. Hegel was capable of giving them philosophical articulation. In both cases, the self-consciousness that religion inaugurates and that philosophy, in critical and ontological terms appreciates, is constitutive of freedom. The freedom of self consciousness resides in the fact that self-consciousness relates to that which is not simply the other of itself but its own essence, is itself this activity of self-relating, and knows itself in this activity of self-relating. The self-consciousness that religion brings about enables the human self to experience the divine simultaneously as other than itself and as its own principle, and to know itself as being constituted through an activity that involves both the surpassing of itself towards the divine and the achievement of knowing self-relatedness in this self-surpassing. This is freedom. But again, on these terms the freedom that philosophical comprehension confirms is the freedom that the self-understanding of religion on its level inaugurates and articulates. Once again, philosophy's autonomous comprehension of the freedom of self-consciousness is its autonomous reenactment and reinstatement of the self-understanding of religion, and not an assertion of the "end of religion."

However warranted these comments might be, for Hegel they convey full sense only if they are, in the last analysis, situated in the context of the project that propels philosophy of religion, the project of philosophically coming to terms with the "death of God." In this connection, however, one might note that Hegel does not allude to the death of God only with the deficiencies of Enlightenment philosophy in mind. He also alludes, in a substantive and central way, to the Christian and Lutheran understanding whose poetic expression he knows:

> O grosse Not
> Gott selbst liegt tot.
> Am Kreuz ist er gestorben;
> hat dadurch das Himmelreich
> uns aus Lieb' erworben.[1]

The last two lines of this verse of a hymn are not unimportant, and the first three lines should be read in conjunction with them. God, these words suggest, enters into the human condition, even into the extremities of the human condition, the extremities of suffering and vulnerability into which the human condition has brought itself. But in submitting to these extreme vulnerabilities and in undergoing these extreme sufferings, God preserves Godself as God.

Hegel does not write hymns. He writes philosophy. The philosophy that he writes, and that conceives of God through the concept of absolute spirit, comprehends spirit as the activity of othering itself in the extremity of the otherness of its other, maintaining itself in this activity and knowing itself therein. For just this reason, finite spirit can know spirit in its absoluticity, and itself in its knowledge of this absoluticity. This suggests that Hegel overcomes the "death of God" that Enlightenment philosophy brings about by philosophically appropriating and maintaining the insight into the death of God that belongs to the consummate religion that precedes philosophy.

If these remarks hold, then for Hegel, philosophical thinking possesses an autonomy and an ultimacy that at the same time, in the words of Paul Ricoeur, "does not abolish, but legitimates, all the shapes that lead to this ultimate stage."[2] It is, again in the felicitous words of Ricoeur, "the ability to recapitulate the inner dynamism of the representation"[3] that determines religious self-understanding. If so, than Hegel's philosophy of religion does not simply call for a move from a theological to a philosophical interpretation of itself. Rather, we are asked to understand Hegel's philosophy of religion as an endeavor at driving religion and theology to the end which each needs to reach for the sake of genuine self-comprehension, the end of becoming genuinely philosophical.

# Notes

1. Cited in LPR III 125.

2. Paul Ricoeur, "The Status of *Vorstellung* in Hegel's Philosophy of Religion," in *Meaning, Truth and God*, edited by Leroy S. Rouner, (Notre Dame: University of Notre Dame Press, 1982), 86.

3. Ricoeur, "The Status of *Vorstellung*," 87.

# 3

# The Integral Relation of Religion and Philosophy in Hegel's Philosophy

*Stephen Rocker*

T here is a danger for many who encounter Hegel's philosophy to categorize too quickly how Hegel as a philosopher treats religion. This danger of hasty categorization (which is moreover a distortion of the subject matter) is present because the student does not realize that in the philosophy of Hegel, religion and philosophy emerge in a new relationship that cannot easily be categorized according to the philosophical tradition preceding Hegel. Philosophy is neither religion's defender nor its antagonist, nor yet is philosophy a border patrol between the kingdoms of religious faith on the one side and all possible knowledge on the other, as for Kant. It is clear that philosophy for Hegel is religion's superior moment. Simply to state this fact of superiority, however, gives little indication of the precise nature, nor the intimate and inseparable character, of their relation. For Hegel religion and philosophy are the progressive developments of one, absolute, universal activity. It is the argument of this paper that philosophy and religion are related to one another by the activity of mutual implication. Philosophy not only has its reality as the higher stage of the history of religions, but it has its recursion and concretion in actual religious life and practice as they bring about the reconciliation of the divine and human, and this reconciliation as a whole is the truth. Religion and philosophy form this relation of mutual implication because they share the same object—God who is truth, though philosophy distinguishes itself from religion by having as its task to demonstrate the rational necessity of its object.[1] Hence for Hegel there can be no thought of religious truth and philosophical truth in opposition with one another. However, religion and philosophy are in principle distinct, and that distinction lies within the unity of the truth as the whole. The purpose of this paper is to clarify the relation of religion and philosophy according to the idea of truth as the concrete whole and to consider the implications of this relation for the present and future status of religion.

For Hegel neither religion nor philosophy can be defined or appraised according to empirical criteria but only according to the concept, that is, according to the inner principle of rationality at work in each. Truth belongs to the inner content of religion and philosophy. We cannot be satisfied with merely studying the various forms of religion and philosophy but must comprehend these forms as a systematic unity as they, with varying degrees of adequacy, express a single truth. This task of systematic comprehension is, of course, properly philosophical—it is explicitly an activity of reason. Its goal, however, is the same as religion's, viz., the fulfillment of the human spirit in the perfect reconciliation of God and humanity. Because this reconciliation is the work of spirit, or simply stated, is spirit, religion cannot accomplish this reconciliation unless it allows the *élan* of spirit to move freely through the subjective, particular, and external forms of religious expression so as to arrive at what is wholly universal and interior to thought itself. This unconstrained activity of spirit that seeks the purely rational expression of truth we call philosophy. In order to understand this single activity of spirit at work in religion and philosophy, let us for a moment consider what Hegel means by philosophy.

Philosophy, Hegel says, is *Erkenntnis durch Vernunft* and as such is common to the cognition of all human beings (LPR II G 42 / E 126). Philosophy cannot rest upon what is subjective or particular, such as feeling or opinion, but must push toward the grasp of what is objectively true for all rational creatures.

As a matter of observable fact, philosophy does not appear to attain this single comprehension of the whole, yet Hegel argues that

> truth is one and one only. As a formula this belongs to our conscious thinking as such, but, in a deeper sense, the starting-point and aim (*Ziel*) of philosophy is to know this one truth as at the same time the source

from which everything else flows, all laws of nature, all phenomena of life and consciousness. . . . Philosophy's aim is to bring back all these laws and phenomena by an apparently reverse way to that single source, but in such a way as to grasp (*begreifen*) them as issuing from it.[2]

When understood in this way philosophy, like religion, is not merely a human endeavor but is the result of divine activity. Philosophy has a history that in complex ways expresses the history of the spiritual maturation of peoples and cultures. Hegel's aim is not to show one philosophical view as false or true against another but to conceive the variety of philosophical systems "as the progressive development of the truth," so that as the succession itself of philosophical systems "their fluid nature makes them at the same time moments of an organic unity."[3] Hegel's frequent use of organic imagery indicates that truth is to be conceived as a process of growth according to an inner teleology. At the end of his *Lectures on the History of Philosophy* Hegel states his aim in the study of the history of philosophy, and (whatever may be our appraisal of Hegel's reading of one or another philosopher) it is this aim that is all important to Hegel's insight on truth.

I wish that you should learn . . . that the history of philosophy is not a blind collection of fanciful ideas, nor a fortuitous progression. . . . The general result of the history of philosophy is this: (1) that throughout all time there has been only one philosophy, the contemporary differences of which constitute the necessary aspects of the one principle; (2) that the succession of philosophic systems is not due to chance but presents the necessary succession of stages of this science.[4]

Truth is not an already existing reality that one or another finite subject discovers—nor can it be constituted *ex nihilo* by any finite subject. The truth must be achieved.

How do religion and philosophy unite and differ in this quest of discovery that is as well the constitution of truth? In relating religion and philosophy Hegel says religion and philosophy are one in content but different in form. Unlike religion which relates human and divine spirit by means of representations which in some measure always remain external to their content, philosophy relates human and divine spirit by thought in which the absolute truth is known in the form of truth. Yet even in making this distinction Hegel is careful to qualify his statement for "religion too has general thoughts," which sometimes are found "in the form of thoughts . . . . Moreover, we encounter within religion philosophies directly expressed, e.g., the philosophy of the Fathers and the Schoolmen."[5] In order to understand how philosophies are directly expressed within religion, we need to be clear that all religious representations are not on one level and that doctrinal expressions of religion's content more closely approach pure thought as they manifest the effort to give rational expression to what is, or should be, believed. Nonetheless doctrine as religiously expressed retains some degree of externality, and the connection of the elements is not completely demonstrated. Yet, even here as Hegel notes, we find "within religion philosophies directly expressed."[6] It is this fact, in conjunction with the rethinking of the relation of religion and philosophy in the light of Hegel's philosophy, that leads me to argue that philosophy as a purely conceptual grasp of the truth turns back upon religion and informs its doctrines and praxis, purifying it of the elements that hamper its development in the truth.

Philosophy's sublation of religion is the preservation of religion, but it is equally the destruction of a self-understanding of religion that sets religion in opposition to its philosophical comprehension. Religion must go through a purgatorial fire so as to cleanse itself for a clear understanding of its own truth. Hegel's philosophy of religion has in part the object of criticizing a religious outlook that opposes itself to reason or that is satisfied with a separate peace which is, for Hegel, no peace.[7] There cannot be a religious satisfaction in separation from philosophical satisfaction because "there can only be one 'most inward', and so the satisfaction of this innermost self by its own means can also be one only."[8] At the level of what is "most inward" religion and philosophy unite, and that in which they unite is the quest of the truth as absolute, eternal, infinite. Religion and philosophy for Hegel differ within the unity of this quest and they do so not only in their respective *modi operandi* but in their achievement, for only pure thought for Hegel can achieve truth in its pure form. Pure thought, however, is not an ethereal realm in separation from the productions and activities of the human spirit.

Thought is the universal substance of the spirit; from it everything else develops. In everything human it is thinking, thought, which is the effective thing (*das Wirksame*). . . . An animal has sensuous feelings, desires etc., but no religion, science, art, imagination; in all these thought is at work (*ist wirksame*).[9]

My argument here is that the achievement of the truth as the goal of the endeavor of philosophy informs religion and brings it to its perfection so that religion may bring about the reconciliation of the divine and human.

If the perfection of religion is its total agreement with the concept of religion by which in the practical order the human self finds its self-conscious unity in God (Cf. LPR I G 330-32 / E 442-43), and if philosophy has the proper task of explicating the truth in wholly rational form, do not religion and philosophy unite in their goal in such a way that philosophy's sublation of religion is the elucidation of religion according to philosophy's proper form? There are some texts in Hegel that may suggest how we are to proceed in clarifying the relation of religion and philosophy.

In the 1827 lectures on the concept of religion Hegel compares one's activity within the religious cultus to one's activity within philosophy. To the extent that the highest form of the cultus is to renounce all that is external to one's inmost self so as to purify one's heart and "raise oneself up to the realm of the purely spiritual," to this extent, Hegel says "philosophy is a continual cultus" (LPR I G 335 / E 446). Philosophy, like religious life, demands the renunciation of external attachments so as to be freely united with God.

> It is part of knowing the true that one should dismiss one's subjectivity, the subjective fancies of personal vanity, and concern oneself with the true purely in thought, conducting oneself solely in accordance with objective thought. (LPR I G 335 / E 447)

Hegel's statement that "philosophy is a continual cultus" is not merely a metaphor but expresses in speculative form what in religious terms is the *unio mystica* which he describes as "the feeling of this enjoyment that I am with God in his grace, . . . the consciousness of my union and reconciliation with God" (LPR I G 333 / E 445). Hence can we not say that the highest goal of religious life is identical with the object of philosophy, viz., the free, spiritual union with God that has transcended all external means so as to achieve a wholly interior relation with God which is recognized as God's activity within the deepest self?

I would add that this "mystical union" is not present *ab initio*, and if it is achieved at all, the human subject must ascend by means of the ladder of intuition, representation, and life within a spiritual community. Hegel asserts that "religion is the truth *for all*" (E §573z) or "religion is that form of the consciousness of truth which is available to all."[10] I would argue that Hegel's assertion is not a concession to the fact that the mass of humanity is incapable of speculative thought but implies that truth in its pure form has its concretion and practical actualization in rational religion wherein the spiritual and mundane realms are brought into harmony according to the truth.[11] In the ontological proof according to the 1831 *Lectures on the Philosophy of Religion* Hegel makes the statement that

> religion must be for all humanity as a whole—for those who have so purified their thinking that they know what is in the pure element of thinking, [i.e., for] those who have attained to speculative cognition of what God is, as well as for those who have not advanced beyond feeling and representation. (LPR III G 275-76 / E 357)

It seems that "those who have attained to the speculative cognition of what God is" are not apart from the less enlightened, but that those who know in pure thinking, like the disciples in their descent from the mount of transfiguration (Mt. 17:1-9), must actualize this knowledge in concrete life and in *Gottesdienst* to the end that humanity may perfect its relationship to God. And simply stated "religion is relationship to God (*ist Beziehung auf Gott*)" (LPR I G 336 / E 448).

In this perspective, namely, the comprehension of religion as relationship to God, philosophy is "higher" than religion as it comprehends religion, but philosophy is equally "within" religion as "the leaven that makes the whole mass rise." In this perspective, religion and philosophy are not separable, at least not ultimately, rather they are united and distinguished as forms of thought.

> Humanity does not exist as pure thinking; instead, thinking itself is manifested as intuiting, as representing. . . . Philosophy thinks what otherwise only is for representation and intuition. In representing, human beings are also thinking, and the content of truth comes to them as thinking beings. Only what thinks can have religion; and thinking is also representation but it is only thinking that is the free form of truth. (LPR III G 276 / E 357)

It may be that in his later years Hegel came to be more at ease with truth as expressed in religious form and that he no longer needed to denigrate (if this term is not too strong) the religious forms of expression in his effort to establish absolute knowledge as the summit of knowledge and the pure form of truth. It must be remembered with regard to his treatment of religion that Hegel is often at pains to demonstrate that religion's content is rational over against those who would place intuition or representation above rational thought and that this polemic is often present in his philosophy of religion. But once it is established that religion is rational, what then is the continuing status of religion so conceived? Hegel's admission that "humanity does not exist as pure thinking" may allow us to interpret Hegel as saying that philosophy is "within" religion, not as subordinate to it but as its higher, animating principle, analogous to the way the soul exists in its body, and that religion is the concrete means by which philosophy actualizes the truth for all humanity. If it is correct to say that philosophy has no subsistence outside concrete human life, then philosophy, as the pure expression of absolute knowledge is, as Paul Ricoeur says in an article on Hegel's philosophy of religion, "the thoughtfulness of all the modes that generate it."[12] Thus philosophy is the guiding principle and the ground of religion.

It is impossible to think of truth as other than self-revealing, hence, it must actualize itself, incarnate itself, in such a way that the infinite overreaches the finite (E §215z). The finite is essential to the actualization of the truth. "That which is in and for itself, and that which is finite and temporal—these are the two fundamental determinations (*Grundbestimmungen*) which must be found in a doctrine of truth."[13] The truth is eternal, but it is not outside time. Time is a characteristic of the natural world in so far as it is finite, "the true, on the other hand, the idea, spirit, is *eternal.* But the concept of eternity must not be grasped negatively as abstraction from time, as existing, as it were, outside of time" (E §258z). Infinite, eternal truth has its concretion, its essential determination in, by, and through what is finite and temporal. Because the eternal nature of truth is to appear, "[t]he absolute truth itself assumes its appearance in temporal shape and in its external conditions, relationships, and circumstances."[14] It is the achievement of philosophy to conceive the relation of truth and its appearance in such a way that the essential, eternal truth is found in its appearance.

> [T]he aspect of the momentary, local, external non-essential element (*Beiwesens*) must be clearly distinguished from the eternal appearance which is inherent in the essence (*Wesen*) of truth so as not to confuse the finite with the infinite, the indifferent with the substantial.[15]

We often characterize the religious, as opposed to the secular, outlook as finding God within the ephemeral and phenomenal. As William Blake wrote,

> To see a World in a Grain of Sand
> And a Heaven in a Wild Flower,
> Hold Infinity in the palm of your hand
> And Eternity in an hour.
> (from "Augeries of Innocence")

This outlook is essentially religious, more specifically, sacramental, even mystical. Spirit appears. It is for the human spirit to see God in and through the phenomenal surface. The understanding focuses upon the empirical and finite elements of the world and possesses only the surface or *Beiwesen* of the appearance. Philosophy, as the activity of reason in systematic form, separates the *Wesen* from the *Beiwesen* of the appearance. By so doing philosophy restores religion's essential content, and religion as the concrete means by which the human community relates itself to God is preserved by philosophy.

A new phase in the history of spirit has been accomplished in Hegel's elucidation of the goal of absolute knowledge, and we cannot turn back from this stage without regressing from the truth, but we need not conclude on Hegelian grounds that religion has come to an end with the rise of speculative philosophy. Philosophy is above religion in the sense that it succeeds revealed religion as its more mature form within the single unifying activity of absolute spirit. Succession, however, is not the same as replacement. I agree with Quentin Lauer's interpretation of Hegel's thought that "religion itself is perfected in philosophy in such a way that the two are no longer distinct; religion is now philosophical religion."[16]

The sublation of religion in philosophy is only the negation of a religion that essentially defines itself in terms of subjective feelings, non-rational commitment, and historical events. But the sublation of religion as defined by its divine content, i.e., its dogmas, is the explicit recognition of the dialectical identity-in-difference of religion (most specifically, of the consummate religion) and speculative philosophy in the inclusive activity of absolute subjectivity or spirit.

There is in Hegel's philosophy a rethinking of the relation of religion and philosophy. Philosophy is not the handmaid of religious faith as for Aquinas, nor is religion simply an incidental object, even an impediment, in philosophy's independent quest for the truth as in Enlightenment philosophy, nor are religion and philosophy in separate compartments, dwelling in an uneasy truce where knowledge belongs to the empirical, finite realm and faith to the supersensible, infinite realm as in Kant's philosophy.[17] For Hegel religion is "the relationship (*Beziehung*) of human consciousness to God" (LPR I G 61 / E 150), in which humanity finds "the thought, the consciousness of God" (LPR I G 61 / E 150). Religion for Hegel has a privileged place within philosophy, for it is religion's content that is God's "infinite appearance as spirit" (LPR I G 37 / E 120). In a way of speaking God "needs" religion. As spirit God cannot remain "shut up in himself" but must manifest himself in ever more adequate modes, the most adequate of which for Hegel is in the form of pure thought as the absolute idea wherein the content, or what appears, is its form, or its appearing. "That God is spirit consists in this: that he is not only the essence that maintains itself in thought but also the essence that appears, the essence that endows itself with revelation and objectivity" (LPR I G 35/ E 119).

Pure thought, however, thought in the form of thought, is the comprehension of all the stages of its realization, that rather than being abstract, is what is most concrete. Thus I would argue that philosophy's relation to religion is not a final achievement of spirit as pure thought separated in its realization from religion but the turning back of thought into the concrete spiritual community.

> God can only be genuinely conceived (*wahrhaft begriffen*) as he is as spirit
> and so makes himself into the counterpart (*Gegenbild*) of a community
> and brings about the activity of a community in relation (*Beziehung*) to
> him, and thus the doctrine of God is to be grasped and taught only as
> the doctrine of religion. (LPR I G 33 / E 116)

In contrast, then, with a common initial reading of Hegel's philosophy
of religion which views religion as superseded in its philosophical
comprehension, we can see that philosophy serves religion, yet not as
in the scholastic era as religion's servant, but as its master "that comes
not to be served but to serve." Philosophy has privileged status as the
elucidation and purification of representative modes of religious
thought, but philosophy only has its meaning and place within a
spiritual community in its relation to God. This community is the faith
community that is "the certainty of the truth of the intrinsic connect-
edness (*an sich seienden Zusammenhangs*) of spirit within itself and in its
community" (LPR I G 242 / E 342), not based upon external authority
but upon the inner witness of the spirit that dwells within it. Here in
the community of faith we find the bringing together of thought and
belief as the concretion (literally, "the growing together") of the
divine spirit in the human spirit.

## Notes

1. Cf. E §1. Except for the *Encyclopaedia*, the *Werke in zwanzig Bänden* will be
abbreviated W with volume number. Throughout the paper I have altered
translations where I thought appropriate.

2. *Introduction to the Lectures on the History of Philosophy*, trans. T. M. Knox and
A. V. Miller (Oxford: Clarendon Press, 1985), 18. Henceforth this work will
be abbreviated ILHP. *Einleitung in die Geschichte der Philosophie*, ed. Johannes
Hoffmeister (Hamburg: Felix Meiner, 1940), 29. Henceforth this work will be
abbreviated H.

3. W3, 12 / *The Phenomenology of Spirit*, trans. A. V. Miller (Oxford: Clarendon
Press, 1977), 2.

4. W20, 461 / *Hegel's Lectures on the History of Philosophy*, vol. III, trans. E. S.
Haldane and Frances Simson (London: Kegan Paul, Trench, Trübner, 1896;
reprint, London: Routledge and Kegan Paul, 1963), 552.

5. H 168-69 / ILHP 125.

6. H 169 / ILHP 125.

7. W2, 288 / *Faith and Knowledge,* trans. Walter Cerf and H. S. Harris (Albany: State University of New York Press, 1977), 55; H 196 / ILHP 145; W11, 42-43 / "Hegel's Forword to Hinrichs' *Die Religion im inneren Verhältnisse zur Wissenschaft,*" trans. A. V. Miller, in *Beyond Epistemology,* ed. Frederick Weiss (The Hague: Nijhoff, 1974), 227-28. This "Foreword" will henceforth be abbreviated F.

8. H 197 / ILHP 145.

9. H 82 / ILHP 55.

10. H 192 / ILHP 142.

11. Cf. H 200 / ILHP 149.

12. Paul Ricoeur, "The Status of *Vorstellung* in Hegel's Philosophy of Religion," in *Meaning, Truth, and God,* ed. Leroy Rouner (Notre Dame: University of Notre Dame Press, 1982), 86.

13. W11, 52 / F 234.

14. W11, 45 / F 230.

15. W11, 46 / F 230.

16. Quentin Lauer, "Hegel on the Identity of Content in Religion and Philosophy," in *Hegel and the Philosophy of Religion,* ed. Darrel Christensen (The Hague: Nijhoff, 1970), 273.

17. Cf. W2, 288 / FK 55.

# 4

# Theology and Tragedy

*Robert R. Williams*

**D**econstruction turns in part on the recognition that philosophy and its fundamental concept of Being are historical. Philosophy does not simply begin *de novo* and create itself in a seemingly unmotivated yet Promethean act of transcendental reflection. Hegel was among the first to assert that philosophical thinking arises within a pre-philosophical historical situation or context, born in a crisis of alienation, estrangement and disunion, and that philosophy is its own time comprehended in thought.[1] With the recognition of the historical shaping and influencing of thought, not only does the history of philosophy assume importance as a philosophical discipline, Being itself is discovered to be historical. Being cannot be reduced to presence, without violating the plurality of modes of time, and without reducing difference to self-sameness. The idea of a history of Being, and the corresponding idea of a deconstruction of metaphysics, acknowledge the historical nature of thought and reflection, as well as the need to move beyond the one-sided exclusiveness of traditional thought and recover the primordial historical insights that have been concealed.[2]

To be sure, the "yield" of such hermeneutical reflections is a matter of dispute. One view is that 'deconstruction' strips away obscuring overlays and allows a retrieval/recovery of the original meaning of Being. This meaning is a priori, eternally true and immutable. All that is needed is a contemporary retrieval of the original sense, which, since it is accorded a priori status, need not be changed, only restated. This view represents an a-historical view of Being masquerading in the dress of hermeneutics.

But is there such a thing as a privileged, much less absolute beginning? The history of being may be a history of the forgetting of

Being. To strip away the accumulated sedimented meanings is to undermine the metaphysical tradition which is predicated upon a concealment of, and flight from, finitude and historicity. Being may turn out to be nothing but vapor and smoke. If so, there would be nothing to retrieve or be corrected. Hence there is talk about the end of philosophy or the end of metaphysics that suggests 'philosophy' and 'metaphysics' are errors from which deconstruction has liberated us.

Since theology in the metaphysical-cognitive sense arose in and along with the philosophical tradition and its understanding of Being, theology is necessarily caught up in debates whether Being is a-historical self-sameness, or merely historical difference. Is theology necessarily bound up with pre-critical metaphysics, or can it be part of the modern, or post-modern situation? Although Hegel is not a theologian but a philosopher of religion, he thinks that the philosophy of religion is more than philosophical anthropology. Hegel's development of the philosophy of religion shows that he rejects the view that the tradition is immutable and cannot be changed. He believes that theological deconstruction is necessary (owing to the self-subversion of the tradition) and that theological reconstruction is possible. But he also rejects the claim that the tradition is an error that cannot be retrieved or corrected because there is nothing salvageable. The tradition can and must be corrected, for it has been influenced by metaphysics and has become oblivious to its own insights. Hegel is after a post-metaphysical and post-modern alternative.

In what follows I shall sketch briefly Hegel's history of Being in his discussion, "Three Attitudes of Thought Towards Objectivity" (E §§19-78, *Drei Stellungen des Gedankens zur Objektivität*) and explore its implications for philosophical theology. I shall suggest briefly some theological implications of this *Seinsgeschichte,* drawing upon Paul Ricoeur's analysis that the theological tradition tends to suppress the tragic dimension of evil and suffering. My thesis is that Hegel recovers the suppressed tragic elements and incorporates them in his treatment of the death of God. This incorporation of the tragic involves a reconstruction and critical corrective to the tradition.

## The Natural Attitude and Metaphysics

Hegel identifies three attitudes of thought towards objectivity, three construals of genuine being or the real. Deconstruction is evident in that what the precritical tradition regarded as an a priori given, is now regarded as in part a subjective accomplishment, a transcendental attitude (*Stellung*) towards objectivity. These three attitudes are (1) the natural attitude and the world of everyday life (Husserl) that gives rise to metaphysics and onto-theology, (2) its inversion in the modern transcendental attitude that reduces theology to foundationalist anthropology, and (3) Hegel's post-modern, holistic alternative in which every category of the logic is a determination of the absolute, or a metaphysical definition of God (E §85). The first attitude construes Being as substance, the second construes Being as subject. Both of these are foundational, but differ sharply as to whether the foundation is a transcendent highest being (onto-theology) or immanent as anthropology. The latter is the modern inversion of traditional metaphysics. The third attitude builds on the collapse of the first two owing to their one-sidedness, and construes Being as process. Being is neither a foundational substance nor a foundational subject, but rather is a social process in which opposites coincide while remaining distinct. However, although the first two attitudes can be correlated with epochs in the history of philosophy, they are not simply identifiable as particular philosophical systems. As underlying attitudes and/or construals, they pervade epistemologies and ontologies, influencing the way in which the ontological and epistemological task is construed and understood.

The first attitude is naively realistic. It lives immersed in the surrounding world and so has a mundanizing orientation. It lives in the unquestioning belief that thought presents things as they are in themselves. Without entertaining any doubts on this point, thought proceeds straightforwardly to the things themselves. Hegel observes that philosophy in its early stages, all the sciences, as well as everyday action and ordinary consciousness, live in this belief.[3]

While this attitude is naive, it is by no means philosophically neutral. It may generate what Hegel calls the epoch of metaphysics. The direct presencing of things serves as the model for construing all being, including Being itself. Being is construed as a mundane object, that is what it is apart from and independent of thought. Since mundane entities are involved in flux, evanescence and perishing, they are not ideally stable and fixed. They need a ground or foundation. There is a passage beyond the realm of becoming towards Ideas, universals or essences, which are eternal, pure presence.[4] There occurs an inversion of the real that is a flight from and concealment of primordial temporality and historicity. Everything, including the self, world, and God, is interpreted as if it were a thing, a mundane entity already complete, i.e., something that already is what it is, and present as a given (E §30). This conception of Being is naive in that the highest being is *a* being, and it is also a-historical.

## Theological Implications of the First Attitude

Hegel's critique of the tradition identifies issues which have by now become standard in process philosophy. However it is important to note that Hegel's critique is directed chiefly at the categories of the understanding, not at the theological substance coming to expression in such categories. Hegel believes the metaphysical tradition conceived self, world and God as super or large entities, that exist in separation or isolation from everything else.[5] In other words, Hegel thinks that traditional theology is formulated in terms that are an expression of the block universe (William James). The tradition tended to draw a sharp distinction between God and world, and conceived God as the Beyond. Hegel observes that to push this distinction hard is to end by subverting the very point that is supposed to be made, for an infinite being that is opposed to the finite is restricted by that very opposition and is itself finite (E §28). Moreover, to attribute existence to God is to embrace onto-theology, i.e., it is to conceive God as *a* being, albeit the highest being. Onto-theology demands an ontic foundation for ontology, and is part and parcel of the so-called metaphysics of presence.[6] Hegel believes that, after Kant, theology is no longer possible as a special metaphysics of a supersensible large entity. Rather it becomes a philosophical theology of spirit that culminates in the philosophy of religion.[7]

The onto-theological conception underlies the royal or monarchical metaphor of classical theism. According to this metaphor, God creates and rules the world as an absolute monarch. God is the absolute master, and the religious is the slave. Although the slave can rebel, such rebellion is not capable of threatening, much less thwarting divine rule. In this view there is a final teleology or salvation history which is anchored in the immutability of divine being. Thus the classical view issues in a divine comedy: whatever powers may try to oppose God are simply dispersed as impotent. Conflict is without seriousness or substance.[8] There is no recognition of the tragic depth of evil; rather the tragic is excluded.

## Modernity: the Primacy of the Subject

The construal of Being as a ready-made entity ignores and passes over the contribution of the mind to knowledge and truth. This is the primacy of subjectivity thesis of modernity. Hegel accepts this with qualifications, and contends that in classical philosophy there is insufficient acknowledgement of freedom and subjectivity. The recognition of freedom signals a break from the past, which was dominated by the given. Instead things must correspond to thought and its conditions (Kant). This requirement signifies a tearing loose from traditions, foundations and moorings. If there is no exemplary past to appeal to, if there are no ready-made norms and criteria which can be accepted as givens, then these must be created.[9]

The second attitude of thought towards objectivity is an inversion of the first. If in the first attitude thought is dominated by its object (or the past), the second attitude asserts the primacy of subjectivity and freedom. Being, formerly construed as already complete and given to subjectivity, is now grasped as relative to and shaped by subjectivity itself. Objectivity is an accomplishment of transcendental subjectivity. The reflective-transcendental turn creates the philosophical situation of modernity, which Hegel describes as follows:

> the philosophies [of Kant, Jacobi, Fichte] we have considered have... recast the dogmatism of being into the dogmatism of thinking, the metaphysic of objectivity into the metaphysic of subjectivity. Thus, through this whole philosophical revolution the old dogmatism and the metaphysic of reflection have... merely taken on the hue of inwardness.... The soul as thing is transformed into the Ego, the soul as practical reason into the absoluteness of personality and singularity of the subject. The world as thing is transformed into the system of

phenomena or affections of the subject, whereas the Absolute as the [proper] matter and absolute object of reason is transformed into something that is absolutely beyond rational cognition.[10]

Modernity inverts metaphysics, but remains on its soil: it shifts the foundation from the world to subjectivity, from metaphysical theology to anthropocentric transcendentalism, but despite such a shift, Modernity retains a mundanizing, foundationalist orientation.[11]

To absolutize subjectivity is to elevate non-identity into a first principle.[12] When subjectivity is thus absolutized, it is sharply distinguished and separated from the world; conversely the world is denied intrinsic meaning and value and is reduced to a mere object of utility or natural resource. For Hegel the Enlightenment culminates in a utilitarian outlook that has an instrumental conception of knowledge as power and mastery over nature, and whose fundamental criterion is relevance to subjectivity as determined by utility.

## Theological Implications

This second attitude of thought towards objectivity may be hostile to theology. The traditional absolute is interpreted as an empty beyond, transcendent to reason and experience. Hegel observes that modernity creates a terrible dilemma for theology: either God (*ens realissimum*) is not an object at all and cannot be known, or God becomes a 'mere object', a block of wood or stone. Ontic transcendence is reduced to mundane presence, or, in Hegel's more poetic phrase, the sacred grove is reduced to mere timber.[13] The skeptical side of the Enlightenment culminates in anthropocentrism that finds expression in utilitarianism, positivism and technism. But "if the Ideas [of pure reason: God, freedom world] cannot be reduced to the block and stones of a wholly mundane reality, they are made into fictions."[14] Thus theology becomes a non-cognitive moral postulate (Kant) or yearning (Jacobi, Fichte). But as a postulate, God has no being independent of the postulating moral consciousness.[15]

Hegel does not accept the Enlightenment's elevation of subjectivity to the status of a first principle. He observes that "It is the great advance of our time that subjectivity is now recognized as an absolute moment; this is an essential determination. However, everything depends on how subjectivity is interpreted."[16] Modernity, or the Enlightenment, errs in identifying subjectivity as foundation: the Enlightenment, in its positive aspect, was a hubbub of vanity without a firm core.[17] In other words, the Enlightenment's principle of finite human subjectivity is insufficient to regenerate the unifying power, the normative content of philosophy, religion and politics.[18] The Enlightenment's formal individualistic rationalism is itself a source of alienation, and is unable to overcome it.

## Towards a Sketch of Hegel's Alternative

Hegel's logic replaces and reformulates classical objectivist metaphysics as well as the subjective metaphysics of modernity. Every category of the logic, he tells us, may be taken as a definition of the absolute. The *Logic* therefore provides one aspect of Hegel's triadic holism. But the *Logic* is by no means the whole story. It is an abstract formal ontology, a realm of shadows.[19] The logical absolute is not a theology, because it does not yet apprehend God as spirit. The latter is the concern of the Philosophy of Spirit, which is completed in the Philosophy of Religion. I shall follow this order and comment first briefly on the third attitude of thought towards objectivity, and then consider the Realphilosophical topic of God and tragedy.

The first attitude of thought towards objectivity grasped thought and being together in an immediate unity and identity. Thereby it absolutized substance and failed to give difference, i.e., subjective freedom, its due. It conceives Being as substance, an abstract identity that excludes difference. The second attitude asserts the rights of subjectivity and freedom against the first. Against abstract identity it asserts difference. In Hegel's view, it replaces abstract identity with an equally abstract absolute difference. Moreover, finite subjectivity and self-identity are insufficient to ground and unify culture.

It is necessary to move beyond mundanizing foundationalism, whether onto-theology or transcendental anthropology. The other, the difference, must be given its due, and allowed to be. But this does not mean that it must be absolutized or taken in abstract separation. Neither a monism of abstract undifferentiated universal being, nor a dualism between being and nothingness are acceptable. These are two sides of the same coin of abstract identity:

The claims of separation must be admitted just as much as those of identity. When identity and separation are placed in opposition to each other, both are absolute, and if one aims to maintain identity through nullification of the dichotomy, they [identity and difference] remain opposed to each other. Philosophy must give the separation into subject and object its due.[20]

Hegel's proposal is to mediate the quarrel between the ancients and the moderns, or the first and second attitudes towards objectivity. Substance must become subject[21] while remaining different from it.[22]

To be sure, it is disputed whether Hegel succeeds. Critics charge that when difference is incorporated into identity, even dialectically, it ceases to be difference.[23] It becomes subordinate to identity and self-sameness; thus all mediation turns out to be dialectical self-media-tion.[24] Not surprisingly these critics identify Hegel as the culmination of metaphysics and onto-theology. If true, this would imply that Hegel remains bound to the first attitude towards objectivity, and lapses into abstract identity. While a full reply is not possible here, it should be noted that it is the critics, and not Hegel, who confuse concrete mediated identity with abstract immediate identity (*Verstand*). Hegel writes concerning this confusion:

We must be careful when we say that the ground is the unity of identity and difference, not to understand by this unity an abstract identity. Otherwise we only change the name, while we still think this identity (of the understanding) already seen to be false. To avoid this misconception, we may say that the ground, besides being the *unity*, is also the *difference* of identity and difference. (E §121z, my italics)

This unity that not merely preserves, but *requires* difference, involves a conception of being as social, a unity that is constituted by difference.

However, such a concrete identity is not a given, but a result, emerging through a process of conflict and opposition. Practically considered, this implies the possibility of struggle and suffering. Hegel sees that subjectivity involves ontological separation (distance) between subjects, and lives in an ontological or constitutive anxiety concerning its freedom. Such anxiety and ontological separation of subjects are not evil in themselves, but to acknowledge them is to acknowledge something like a tragic aspect, if not flaw, that is constitutive of subjectivity. Ontological anxiety and separation of subjects are conditions of evil and violence, as well as conditions of freedom and reconciliation.[25] Intersubjective community is not a given, but must be brought about. As Master and Slave make clear, conflict, if not violence, cannot be excluded.

## Theological Implications: Rethinking the Tragic

I am going to shift the focus from general logical considerations to topics in Realphilosophy, namely, Hegel's treatment of theology and tragedy. This is relevant to the question of his alternative to the ancients and the moderns. I shall begin from the former perspective. The classical theological tradition rejected and suppressed the tragic dimension of evil and suffering. Instead it propounds an anthropological theory of the origin of evil, which separates the origin of evil from the origin of being by tracing evil to the disobedience of the primal ancestors of the human race.[26] Evil is identified with the Fall, that occurs within a creation already complete and good. In this scheme, evil inexplicably occurs in a paradise, in which there is no cognitive distance between subjects or between the human pair and God. In concentrating the origin of evil into anthropology, the tradition tends to suppress the tragic aspect of evil that Ricoeur identifies as the evil already there, to which the human being yields.[27] In the classical account, evil does not have tragic conditions; rather it appears as rebellion.[28] The suppression of the tragic also finds expression in the traditional claims concerning divine immutability. Absolute immutability stands behind the tradition's denial that God suffered in the death of Christ, or Patripassianism. The classical view requires deconstruction because it sides with one side of a dichotomy and suppresses the other. When this suppression is overcome, and dichotomy is restored, conflict and tragedy become possible.

Hegel has a peculiar view of tragedy, in that it does not exclude mediation or reconciliation.[29] Tragedy is marked by conflict, comedy by the dissolution of conflict. Comedy can take two forms, ancient or modern. One ancient form is found in classical Christian theism. Hegel characterizes the classical Christianity of Dante's *Divine Comedy* as "without fate and without a genuine struggle, because absolute confidence and assurance of the reality of the absolute exist in it without opposition, and whatever opposition brings movement into this perfect security and calm is merely opposition without seriousness or inner truth." The *Divine Comedy* expresses the dissolution of opposition and conflict in an undifferentiated absolute. The modern form of comedy presents the absolute itself as an illusion.[30]

Comedy points either to classical theism (Dante), of which monism is perhaps the ultimate metaphysical expression, or to atheism, in which human subjectivity is the fate of the gods.[31] Hegel thinks tragedy is superior to the comedy of classical theism because it exhibits the absolute relation, namely conflict and suffering: "the true and absolute relation is that the one [nature] really does illumine the other; each [nature] has a living bearing on the other, and each is the other's serious fate. The absolute relation, then,  is set forth in tragedy."[32]

Hegel conceives the absolute tragically; he speaks of "the tragedy which the absolute eternally enacts with itself, by eternally bringing itself forth into objectivity, submitting in this objective form to suffering and death, and rising from its ashes into glory."[33] Although this text is from the early *Natural Law* essay, Hegel returns to the tragic theme in his late *Lectures on the Philosophy of Religion.*

He cites a Lutheran hymn in which the phrase "God himself lies dead" occurs. Debate about this hymn revisited classical theological discussions about the suffering and death of Jesus.[34] The orthodox conception of the person of Christ maintained that only the human nature suffers and dies. The divine nature, as eternal, simple and thus immutable, is incapable of suffering and death. Against this background, the phrase "God himself lies dead" is an evident departure from classical metaphysical theism, for it signifies that suffering and death pertain to the divine nature as well. In other words, God, and not merely the human Jesus, suffers. A condition of this suffering is that God must become other, i.e., undergo change. Consequently, divine immutability must be qualified.

Hegel's concept of the death of God gathers up the ancient tragic experience, including the deaths of Socrates and Jesus, and the modern experience of the desacralization of nature, the Enlightenment reduction of the sacred grove to mere timber.[35] Post-classical and post-modern theological thinking must incorporate the theme of desacralization or divine absence. The death of Jesus is God's highest self-divestment (*Entäusserung*): in it God has died, God himself is dead. This fearful picture brings before the imagination the deepest abyss of alienation (LPR III G 60).

Hegel formulates the divine self-divestment as a deconstructive critique of metaphysical theology or substance metaphysics. The death of God signifies a theological criticism of abstract eternity and transcendence. What dies is not the divine being *per se*, but its abstraction, i.e., abstract transcendence, the infinite that, since it is opposed to the finite, is itself finite. Hegel expands this theme to a critique of substance metaphysics and classical metaphysical theology.

> The death of this representation contains at the same time the death of the abstraction of the divine being, that is not posited as self. It is the painful feeling of the unhappy consciousness, that God himself is dead. This hard word is the expression of the innermost simple self-knowledge, the return of consciousness into the depths of the night of the I=I, which distinguishes and knows nothing besides itself.... This knowing therefore is the inspiration through which substance has become subject, its abstraction and lifelessness perishes, and it becomes actual, simple and universal self-consciousness.[36]

In this passage the death of God signifies a theological and not an atheistic critique of traditional theology. Hegel speaks here of the death, the nullity of abstract substance. He criticizes classical metaphysics for conceiving God as actual apart from relation, and when in relation, as absolute non-reciprocal Master, i.e., the monarchial metaphor. Such abstract immediacy must be qualified if God is to enter into relation, as the central Christian doctrine of incarnation presupposes and requires. That is, substance must undergo a process of mediation with other, i.e., become subject. This entry into mediation implies that conflict and tragedy are now theological possibilities as well.[37]

Hegel breaks with the tradition and asserts that there is tragic suffering in God. He observes that Dante's divine comedy is without fate or a genuine struggle, because the absolute exists in it as sheer presence without opposition. This view of comedy belongs to the metaphysics of pure light and transparency. However, Werner Marx charges that Hegel holds the same view. Marx acknowledges that from the time of his youth Hegel was convinced that "reality in itself is in the deepest sense rent, sundered, estranged, full of contradiction.... that there is... darkness in the form of untruth, error, evil and death."[38] Nevertheless, says Marx, Hegel subordinates this conviction to the optimistic rationalism of Aristotle that reason can heal and reconcile all oppositions, and overcome all estrangement. Hence for Hegel, light prevails over darkness. Although the absolute may contain the harshest internal opposition, it nevertheless overcomes it. Hegel's teleological thinking thus "guarantees conclusive victory to the light, to the truth undisguised by the untruth."[39] Marx's talk of "conclusive victory for the light" makes it appear as if opposition is finally nonserious, excluded in principle from the absolute. If that were so, then Hegel would be serving up another version of the *Divine Comedy*.

To be sure, Hegel agrees with the tradition that the death of God, or divine suffering, is not the only word that theology has to say. In the 1831 lectures we find: "However, the process does not come to an end at this point [viz., the death of God, the loss of everything eternal and true]; rather a reversal [*Umkehrung*] takes place: God, that is to say, maintains himself in this process, and the latter is only the death of death. God rises again to life and thus things are reversed." (LPR III 323n) This suggests that the death of God is finally transformed into a death of death. The question is, what does this reversal mean? Does it signal a return to the metaphysics of light as Marx suggests? Does it imply a vindication of onto-theology and metaphysics that suppresses the tragic and suffering, or makes them instrumental to divine goodness and reconciliation?[40]

Such a judgment cannot stand. Although some passages appear to favor a teleological triumphalism over conflict, such a reading overlooks the weight of the tragic in Hegel's thought, particularly in his *Lectures on the Philosophy of Religion*. By introducing and emphasizing the death of God as a theological theme, Hegel criticizes the tradition and recovers the tragic aspect of evil and suffering that it suppressed. The death of God means that there is suffering, pain and negation in God, there is suffering and tragedy in the divine itself. This point is made explicitly in several texts from Hegel's earliest writings to his latest. In *Faith and Knowledge*, Hegel insists that infinite grief must be incorporated as an *essential moment* in the absolute or divine Idea. Philosophy must establish the speculative Good Friday in place of the historical Good Friday. Good Friday, he says, "must be speculatively re-

established in the whole truth and harshness of its God-forsakenness. "[41]
In the 1827 *Lectures on Philosophy of Religion* Hegel writes:

> "God himself is dead," it says in a Lutheran hymn, expressing an
> awareness that the human, the finite, the weak, the negative, are
> themselves a moment of the divine, that they are within God himself,
> that finitude, negativity, otherness are not outside of God and do not,
> as otherness, hinder unity with God. Otherness, the negative, is known
> to be a moment of the divine nature itself. This involves *the highest idea
> of spirit.* (LPR III 326)

The theme of tragic suffering and negation in God is clear and
consistent. Stephen Crites observes that "The horrendous notion that
God himself has died on the cross, which has been obscured by
harmless conventional renderings of the story, is here restored not
merely as an historical event but as a supreme speculative insight
restored in all its original force and pitiless severity. "[42]

At the speculative ontological level, the death of God signifies that
otherness is not a mere contingent feature that vanishes into self-
sameness, but a constitutive feature of Spirit. On such constitutive
otherness or negativity rests the *possibility* of divine suffering. But
constitutive *otherness* or negativity does not mean that *suffering* is necessary, i.e., a requirement of God's nature. At the level of the logical
Idea, there is *otherness* but not *suffering.* The suffering God is found not
in the logic, but in history. The logic does not involve any distinction
between concept and its realization in history, but the philosophy of
religion is structured fundamentally by this distinction. For this reason
it completes the concept of religion and transforms the concept of the
absolute into the concept of absolute spirit.[43] Suffering is not ontological, but gratuitous, i.e., for the sake of an other.

Hegel's view, while Christian, diverges significantly from classical
orthodoxy by emphasizing divine suffering. This departure from
orthodoxy is a retrieval of the tragic dimension of evil that the
traditional metaphysical doctrines suppressed. Hegel speaks of the
need to incorporate infinite grief into the divine Idea. This has as its
condition the triadic conception that incorporates a *constitutive* otherness and negativity that belies any reduction of the divine triad to a
sheer undifferentiated unity or light, or to sheer self-sameness. Further, any divine sweetness and light is broken and darkened by

historical conflict between the divine and human and the accompanying infinite grief: in its development this process is the going forth of the divine idea into the uttermost cleavage [*Entzweiung*] even to the opposite pole of the anguish of death, which is itself the absolute reversal, the highest love, containing the negation of the negative within itself [and being in this way] the absolute reconciliation (LPR III 132).

Reconciling love arises out of anguish at separation and death: love as originating in infinite anguish is precisely the concept of spirit itself (LPR III 140). Reconciling love cannot be conceived apart from infinite anguish. For this reason such love has a tragic aspect. For Hegel any divine comedy is found in and therefore is *inseparable* from the infinite anguish of Good Friday. The metaphysical tradition, under the domination of abstract impassible identity, separated the divine from the human, the comic from the tragic. Classical Christology not only failed to express adequately its deepest intentions, it condemned these as Patripassianism.

Hegel rejects the classical concept of abstract supersensible transcendence, or onto-theology. However, this not a repudiation of theology as such, but merely a repudiation of one possible conception. But this raises a puzzle. The rejection of theology as special metaphysics is part of Hegel's—and much of post-modernity's—critique of foundationalism. Isn't theology essentially in the foundationalist business? An affirmative answer would take us back to the claim that in repudiating metaphysical onto-theology we repudiate theology as such. That is the way things appear at the level of the first attitude of thought towards objectivity.[44] However, if foundationalism is rejected, the implications for theology are far from clear. What would non-foundationalist discourse about God be like?

The question can be formulated more sharply: can there be non-foundational discourse about God that does not lapse into foundationalist anthropology, i.e., into Feuerbach's inversion of Hegel? Here the interpretation of God as a projection implies that the concrete bearer of divine predicates is the human being. Such progress merely takes us from the  first to the second attitude of thought towards objectivity. The fundamental values of Christian anthropology—namely freedom and liberation—can be realized only by abandoning Christian *theology*.[45] There is nothing left to salvage, except foundationalist anthropology.

I wonder if Hegel has not provided us with an example of what non-foundationalist theological discourse might be with his treatment of the death of God and tragic suffering in God. His claim that God gratuitously suffers, and undergoes self-divestment even to the point of death, is unfoundational. Hegel's God is not a monopolar absolute that excludes relations or reduces the other to the same, but is supremely related even to the point of dying for the sake of the other. This is Hegel's version of Eckhart's *Gelassenheit*, releasement, letting the other be.[46] God releases the other and allows it to be such that it can oppose God even to the point of death. This suffering God signals the abandonment of onto-theology and the death of the representation of the highest being, conceived in terms of abstract identity and omnipotence. Such a God is not prisoner to onto-theological absoluteness, but is free to love and suffer. Both God and the human are united in a community of forgiveness that has broken the grip of mastery, domination, and servile rebellion.

At the logical level Hegel's alternative to foundationalist onto-theology and anthropo-ontology is a holistic triadic conception of God. For only such a concept articulates the constitutive otherness that underlies the possibility of freedom and suffering. Abstract identity has a dyadic structure (I=I) that collapses the other into egology, or the self-same. It is merely comic because it excludes otherness and suffering. According to Hegel, if there is divine comedy, it results from a reconciling love arising out of infinite anguish, the anguish of the infinite. Reconciliation does not exclude, but presupposes negativity and opposition while preserving otherness: in love the separate does still remain, but as something united and no longer as something separate.[47]

## Notes

1. "Differenz zwischen des Fichteschen und Schellingschen System der Philosophie," in *Werke, Theorie Werkausgabe* (Frankfurt: Suhrkamp Verlag, 1970), 2:9-116; English translation, *The Difference between the Fichte's and Schelling's System of Philosophy*, trans. H. S. Harris and Walter Cerf (Albany: SUNY Press,

1977), hereafter cited as *Difference.* "Every individual is a child of his time; so philosophy too is its own time comprehended in thoughts" (*Rechtsphilosophie,* Werke 7, preface; English translation, *Philosophy of Right,* trans. T. M. Knox, [Oxford: Oxford University Press, 1952]).

2. Heidegger introduced the concept of a destruction (*Destruktion*) of ontology in *Sein und Zeit* (Tübingen: Niemayer Verlag, 1979), §6; cf. also *Die Grundprobleme der Phänomenologie, Gesamtausgabe,* Bd 24 (Frankfurt: Vittorio Klostermann, 1975), 31f, where Heidegger identifies the three steps of phenomenological method in relation to ontology as reduction, construction and destruction (*Abbau*). In philosophy construction is necessarily destruction.

3. E §26. This is Hegel's version of what Husserl later was to call the natural attitude of everyday life and consciousness. It is natural in that it does not have to be sustained by any deliberate abstraction or narrowed focus of attention. It would be a serious mistake to think of the 'natural attitude' in simply historical terms as something primitive, or something left behind. For, as Hegel observes, the spontaneous natural attitude towards objectivity is by no means a merely historical phenomenon limited to a past historical age. It is only in reference to the discussion in the history of philosophy that the natural attitude is to be regarded as past. The thing itself, namely the naivete towards objectivity, is reborn in every age, and is not to be dismissed simply as error. See also E §§26-27.

4. Otto Pöggeler, "Being as Appropriation," in *Heidegger and Modern Philosophy,* ed. Michael Murray (New Haven: Yale University Press, 1978), 94.

5. The primary target Hegel has in mind is Wolffian metaphysics. However, since his critique is categorial, it is general, and thus deals with typifications rather than with actual historical figures.

6. Otto Pöggeler, "Being as Appropriation," 94ff. However, it should be pointed out that Hegel, like Tillich, denies that the category of existence applies to God. The point is not a denial of God's existence, rather that existence is too poor a category to do justice to its object.

7. On this shift, cf. Walter Jaeschke, *Reason in Religion: The Foundations of Hegel's Philosophy of Religion,* trans. Peter C. Hodgson and Michael Stewart (Berkeley: University of California Press, 1990), 230ff.

8. *Natural Law,* trans. T. M. Knox (Philadelphia: University of Pennsylvania Press, 1975), 105-6. Hereafter cited as NL.

9. Cf. Jürgen Habermas, *The Philosophical Discourse of Modernity,* trans. F. Lawrence, (Cambridge, Mass.: MIT Press, 1987), 20. Habermas is correct in noting that Hegel's critique of the Enlightenment and subjective idealism is in effect his critique of modernity. See also David Kolb, *The Critique of Pure Modernity: Hegel, Heidegger and After* (Chicago: University of Chicago Press, 1986).

10. *Glauben und Wissen, Werke: Theorie Werkausgabe,* Bd 2 (Frankfurt: Suhrkamp, 1970); English Translation: *Faith and Knowledge* trans. Cerf and Harris (Albany: SUNY Press, 1977), 189-190. Hereafter cited as FK.

11. For example, Edmund Husserl describes mundanzing as a naturalistic misconstruction, that grasps consciousness itself as a mundane entity, and passes over its freedom and transcendence. Mundanization of consciousness leads to psychologism and positivism. Husserl also characterizes Kant's attempt to provide transcendental justification for Newtonian science as a mundane transcendental philosophy. Cf. *The Crisis of European Sciences and Transcendental Phenomenology,* trans. D. Carr (Evanston: Northwestern University Press, 1970).

12. FK, Introduction.

13. FK 58; cf. Walter Jaeschke, *Reason in Religion,* 163.

14. FK 58.

15. For a non-cognitive, purely anthropological reading of the content of Kant's Postulates of Practical Reason, see Yirmiahu Yovel, *Kant and the Philosophy of History* (Princeton: Princeton University Press, 1980), 81-121.

16. *Vorlesungen über die Philosophie der Religion, Werke, Theorie Werkausgabe,* 17:290. Hereafter cited as TWA.

17. FK 56.

18. Cf. Habermas, *Philosophical Discourse of Modernity* (1985).

19. The Logic differs from Kant's formal transcendental ontology in that Kant isolated the structures of subjectivity and considered them in abstraction from nature. Thus his transcendental analysis considers the categories in abstraction from the world, as if they were merely empty and idling. But Kant held that they have actual meaning and significance only in nature, i.e., admit of merely empirical and not transcendent employment. For Hegel the universe does not have to wait upon transcendental human subjectivity in order to have categorical structure. The categories studied by the Logic are already at work in the world. Consequently the categories are not merely empty thought forms; they have an internal meaning and connection of their own. Nevertheless, considered in themselves they are abstract, or underdetermined, a realm of shadows. Thus in addition to the *Logic* a *Realphilosophie* is a necessary part of the Hegelian system. To *Realphilosophie* belong the Philosophy of Nature, and Philosophy of Spirit, including the Philosophy of Religion. This creates one of the central interpretive difficulties: for the Logic is the *Grundwissenschaft,* the whole of the system in an abstract structural sense, and at the same time it is but a part of the system in the larger empirical sense, and as such dependent on and mediated by the other parts.

20. *Difference* 156.

21. "In my view, which can be justified only through the development of the entire system, everything depends on conceiving and expressing the True not [simply] as substance, but equally as subject" (*Phänomenologie des Geistes*, ed. Hoffmeister [Hamburg: Meiner, 1952], 19.

22. This point is made in Hegel's discussion of the first category of the logic, namely *Werden. Werden* is a transformation of *Sein* and *Nichts*, which are revealed to be abstractions. Hegel's concrete identity is the event of coincidence of opposites that remain distinct, rather than a substantial or entitative identity.

23. See Emmanuel Levinas, *Totality and Infinity*, translated by A. Lingis (Pittsburgh: Duquesne University Press, 1969), 43ff. Levinas claims that ontology reduces the other to the same, and is essentially egology. See also Werner Marx, who maintains that Hegel conceives difference so much a part of identity that he treats both of these categories as one, the category of non-identical identity (*Heidegger and the Tradition*, trans. T. Kisiel, [Evanston: Northwestern University Press, 1971], 61, 129). Jacques Taminiaux puts the criticism in this way, Hegel buries difference in the category of the different. ("Dialectic and Difference," in *Dialectic and Difference: Finitude in Modern Thought*, trans. R. Crease and J. Decker (Atlantic Highlands: Humanities Press, 1985) 79-90. See also Irene E. Harvey, *Derrida and the Economy of Differance* (Bloomington: Indiana University Press 1986), 93-124. Harvey portrays Hegel as the culmination of metaphysical logocentrism: "the system is closed, finitude is essentially united with infinity, and all differences are essentially subsumed within one unity" (106).

24. This caricature is close enough to Hegel to mislead even some Hegelians. Cf. William Desmond, *Desire Dialectic and Otherness* (New Haven: Yale University Press 1987), 118ff. For a critique of Desmond's interpretation of the *Phenomenology*, cf. my *Recognition: Fichte and Hegel on Otherness*, forthcoming from SUNY Press.

25. Hegel, like most theology that acknowledges historical-critical thought, rejects the traditional theological account of creation and fall as two separate events, by means of which the tradition sought to distinguish finitude from sin and evil. Hegel thus confronts the problem facing most contemporary theological reconstructions that reject the temporal distinction between creation and fall, namely, *how to maintain the non-coincidence of sin with finitude.* Instead of locating evil in the fall, Hegel finds its condition in the restlessness of spirit, or the ontological anxiety that accompanies the self-consciousness of freedom. Such restlessness and anxiety are not evil, but are conditions of evil. On this crucial distinction, cf. Hegel, *The Philosophy of Right*, §139. Hegel's account of evil finds expression in his account of the life and death struggle that culminates in Master and Slave, and his tragic view of life.

26. Paul Ricoeur, *The Symbolism of Evil*, trans. Emerson Buchanan (Boston: Beacon Press, 1967), 232ff. For an analysis of the traditional concepts of creation and fall, and the problems that arise when the classical framework is abandoned by historical-critical theology, cf. my "Sin and Evil," in *Christian Theology: An Introduction to its Traditions and Tasks*, ed. Peter C. Hodgson and Robert King (Philadelphia: Fortress Press, 1982).

27. Ricoeur, *Symbolism of Evil*, 257f.

28. For a discussion of the influence of the royal-monarchial metaphor on this account of evil as rebellion, see Edward Farley, *Good and Evil* (Minneapolis: Fortress Press, 1990), 124ff.

29. That is, Hegel, while acknowledging a tragic dimension in life, stops short of embracing entirely the classical tragic view. For a discussion, cf. Otto Pöggeler, "Hegel und die griechische Tragödie," in *Hegel's Idee einer Phänomenologie des Geistes*, (Freiburg/München: Alber Verlag, 1973). Goethe criticized Hegel's conception of tragedy because it allows for the possibility of a reconciliation and mediation that seems to be excluded by classical Greek tragedy. But this establishes only that Hegel has a different conception of tragedy than the purely classical one. What is peculiar to Hegel is a dialectical mediation between tragedy and comedy. His criticism of the metaphysical tradition is that it separates the comic from the tragic and conceives these as pure forms that exclude each other.

30. NL 105-6.

31. Feuerbach's reduction of theology to anthropology is a modern expression of comedy.

32. NL 108.

33. NL 104.

34. Cited in LPR III 125 n163: "O grosse Not, Gott selbst liegt tot. Am Kreuz ist er gestorben; hat dadurch das Himmelreich uns aus Lieb' erworben." The hymn was written by Johannes Rist. For a discussion of the Lutheran debate, cf. Eberhard Jüngel, *God as the Mystery of the World*, translated by Darrell L. Guder (Grand Rapids, Michigan: Eerdmans Publishing Company, 1983), 64. The theological dispute in Lutheran circles revived the ancient debate over divine impassibility and suffering, i.e., whether God suffers and dies, or only the human nature of the second person of the trinity.

35. FK 57-8.

36. PhG 546.

37. Although finitude is a moment of the absolute logical Idea, it is not to be equated with sin. Hence in God there is otherness, but not evil. Evil occurs at the level of history, occasioned but not caused by the ontological restlessness and anxiety constitutive of human freedom.

38. Werner Marx, *Heidegger and the Tradition*, 55.

39. Werner Marx, *Heidegger and the Tradition*, 57. Marx cites the Logic (TWA 6:467-8) for the claim that the absolute "eternally overcomes" opposition. However his quoting is highly selective, and makes it appear as if Hegel holds the same position as Dante, namely that the absolute exists above and/or without opposition, that opposition is excluded in principle from the absolute. Marx overlooks the fact that Hegel criticizes and rejects Dante's *Divine Comedy* on the grounds that it excludes opposition and the tragic.

40. It should be noted that Otto Pöggeler also maintains that Hegel abandoned his early preference for tragedy over comedy, and subordinated tragedy to Aristotelian teleology (see his "Hegel und die griechische Tragödie," in *Hegel's Idee einer Phänomenologie des Geistes*). This corresponds to a shift from pantragedism to panlogism. In the latter view, conflict and suffering are instrumental to the unity of spirit, and evil is instrumental to good. However Pöggeler overlooks the fact that Hegel retains the tragic interpretation in his *Lectures on the Philosophy of Religion*, and qualifies the Aristotelian teleology. For a critique of Pöggeler, see chapter 19 of my *Recognition: Fichte and Hegel on Otherness*, forthcoming from SUNY Press.

41. FK 190f.

42. Stephen Crites, "The Golgatha of Absolute Spirit," *Method and Speculation in Hegel's Phenomenology*, ed. M. Westphal (Atlantic Highlands: Humanities Press, 1982), 51.

43. Cf. Walter Jaeschke, *Reason in Religion*, 212, 216f. Hegel's *Philosophy of Religion* belongs to the theory of *Sittlichkeit* and completes the *Philosophy of Spirit*. It is not simply an instantiation of the logic, but a determinate modification of the logical categories.

44. It is worth noting that Hegel, after criticizing classical theology, nevertheless appears to continue its theodicy scheme when he makes such assertions as reason governs the world, or that history is the growth and development of the consciousness of freedom. Those assertions sound foundationalist, although they need not be so interpreted.

45. Alexandre Kojève, *Introduction to the Reading of Hegel*, trans. J. Nichols (New York: Basic Books, 1969), 67.

46. See Reiner Schürmann, *Meister Eckhart: Mystic and Philosopher* (Bloomington: Indiana University Press, 1978), 113.

47. *Early Theological Writings*, trans. T. M. Knox (New York: Harper, 1961), 305. See above, note 30: reconciliation presupposes rather then eliminates the ontological separation of subjects, and the way this separation is overcome is not through a loss of individuality in an ocean of infinity, but in the formation of a community. The problem to which reconciliation is addressed is alienation, not ontological separation.

# 5

# Hegel and Creuzer:
# or, Did Hegel Believe in Myth?

*Martin Donougho*

Philosophy rules *Vorstellungen* and these rule the world.
—*Hegel, "Wastebook"*[1]

It strikes me, in fact, that any philosophical work must be in some sense allegorical (or symbolical).
—*Friedrich Creuzer, writing to his lover, the poet Karoline von Günderode.*[2]

> I made my song a coat
> Covered with embroideries
> Out of old mythologies
> From heel to throat;
> But the fools caught it,
> Wore it in the world's eyes
> As though they'd wrought it.
> Song, let them take it,
> For there's more enterprise
> In walking naked.
> —*W. B. Yeats, "A Coat."*[3]

I n a recent book Paul Veyne poses the question "Did the Greeks believe in their myths?"[4] His answer is both yes and no—just as with children, who believe in Santa Claus while knowing full well it's their parents who deliver the goods. Like Feyerabend[5] he would avoid imputing to the Greeks too rigid a separation between truth and fiction, a separation that is a fiction of modern science. Following Nietzsche he thinks that Greek religion lived under a "dispensation to lie" (*Berechtigung zur Lüge*)—a regime of creative falsehoods.[6] Now, Veyne's question ushers in another: are the Greek gods indeed God(s)? (Do they deserve a capital letter?!) In other words, should their mythology have any authority for us (whoever "we" are)? Or is it all "just" myth? Veyne's provocation serves to raise an issue for Hegel and his philosophy of religion: whether and in what way myth retains any legitimacy, with respect either to "consummate religion" or to philosophical reflexion. Is Hegel's speculative enterprise like Yeats's "walking naked"? Or does the mythological embroidery have any value, *an sich*, or as through a glass, darkly, an occluded representation/distortion of the logos?

Hegel's express attitude to mythology varies. Early on he could speak of realizing a "mythology of reason" as the goal of philosophy in the modern world, an "idea" that echoes through the entire Jena period.[7] But in the (arguably authoritative) Berlin lectures on the philosophy of religion, myth appears to be demoted to the rank of "image" (*Bild*), below "representation" (*Vorstellung*) and "thought" or the "concept"; compared to religion proper it belongs to art, as mere "sensuous intuition" or story-telling (LPR I, e.g. 238-39, 498-99). The *Encyclopaedia* similarly contrasts a mythic mode of presentation—sc. the myth of the Fall—with a properly speculative presentation.[8] The *Phenomenology* more ambiguously—perhaps because its very element is that of *Vorstellung* rather than thought—does allow that religious representation does not have to travel second-class. Representation both shapes the divine into the terms of human apprehension and reveals its own structure as consciousness: a mode of worship and cult on the one hand is a mode of self-cognition (and partial mis-cognition) on the other. Moreover, in Chapter VI Hegel presents in the "dialectic of enlightenment" a critique of the rationalist critique of religion (*a fortiori* of mythic consciousness as well).[9]

I intend to come back to Hegel's attitude towards myth in conclusion, following a detour via another approach, that of Friedrich Creuzer (1771-1858), Hegel's friend and Heidelberg colleague. Creuzer is a figure of more than historical interest, it seems to me: his career epitomizes many of the problems faced by any proposed study of—or at least coming to terms with—myth. As one of the first to welcome Neoplatonic thought back into the mainstream of philosophy, he not only produced valuable editions of Proclus and Olympiadorus (Frankfurt, 1820-22) and of Plotinus (Oxford, 1835), but also sought to apply Neoplatonic hermeneutics to ancient mythology and imagery. His main work was the monumental *Symbolik und Mythologie der alten Völker, besonders der Griechen* (1810-12 (1); 1819 (2); 1837-43 (3)). Recall the opening quote from Creuzer—"It strikes me . . . that any philosophical work must be in some sense allegorical (or symbolical)." Motivated by such a detective spirit, the *Symbolik* attempted to provide an encyclopaedic basis for an scientific understanding of myth—"a key to all mythologies," we might say. Creuzer sent his friend a copy of the second edition, and Hegel made use of it not merely to model his notion of "symbolic" art (in the *Aesthetics*) but also as source material for the lectures on religion. Although (as Creuzer complained) Hegel turned out to be as much anti-symbolic as pro-, the theory of myth-as-symbol is worth examining both as an attempt at grasping a cultural phenomenon which eludes us still, and as an alternative approach that throws light on Hegel's own.[10]

I shall first provide some general background to the notion of "mythology," then summarize Creuzer's approach, and finally compare it with Hegel's.

## Mythology

A grip on such terms as "myth" and "mythology," notorious for their slipperiness, would obviously be desirable. Just what do they mean? How would we recognize a myth if we came across one? Mythology bids fair to be what has been alleged of aesthetics: a subject without an object. Yet after all that is to say a good deal, in that it serves to direct attention more towards the *pragmatics* of the term, the way it gets *used*. Following the lead of Marcel Detienne, Jean-Pierre Vernant, and G. S. Kirk, we may summarize the early usage and educe several main characteristics.[11] In the first place, "mythology" operates in a double semantic register, as Detienne points out[12]; it is a discourse *about* discourse, whether as a retelling of myth (the ancient sense of *mythologia* found in Plato), as a written and relatively unified corpus (like Hesiod's *Works and Days*), or as a scientific study (in nineteenth-century practice). Turning to "myth," the term first appears with Xenophanes and his accusation of anthropomorphism. "To speak of myth is a way of crying scandal, of pointing the finger," as Detienne puts it[13]—a critical tinge that has infused Christian and Enlightenment iconoclasm and works its way into Feuerbach, Marx, Barthes, and many others.[14] Myth is defined primarily by exclusion. It is (i) non-real, or fictional, (ii) non-rational, or absurd, and (iii) not ours but barbarous—*we* speak good sense, *logos* not *muthos*. Its rejection seemed legitimized for good in the twin discourses of history (Thucydides, rather than Herodotus[15]) and philosophy (e.g. Plato), both of them written under the aegis of "truth." We must (as Plutarch has it) "purify myth by reason."[16] At the same time—and this is a second pragmatic feature—myth has *meaning*, which is another way of saying that it can be both tamed and granted a certain status through interpretation: a mythological corpus is not just any old set of tales. Myth is scandalous and alien, but luckily can be made respectable and fit for domestic consumption.

These two features—*scandal* and *significance*—give rise to a paradox. Myth is defined, within the unified orbit of mythology, by that which it is *not*. In the beginning was the *logos*, i.e. precisely *not* the *muthos*. Truth, reason, goodness, justice, beauty, etc. come along to replace myth, which is thereby marginalized and alienated. Yet oddly enough reason is in turn defined by the *mythos* it constitutionally rejects—a version of the "logic of the supplement" or "the proper" with which Derrida has made us all too familiar.[17] While Plato anathematizes the oral, the visible, the emotive, and would banish the poets from the city, he allows at the same time that demonstrative reason cannot be applied unconditionally to such phenomena as justice or beauty, in contrast to geometrical entities. In other words, a mythic presentation has its uses. The *Republic* is a myth (501c), *The Laws* too (752a)—a beautiful lie, Rousseau might say. More to the point, Plato's account of our passage from the cave of myth to the sun of reason is itself a mythic one, the *muthos* of *logos*. If (as Herodotus said) Homer and Hesiod gave the Greeks their gods, we can equally pay a compliment to Plato and Aristotle and say that they gave the West its own divine values of truth and knowledge, etc. And this evolutionary tale of myth giving way to scientific knowledge—"from *mythos* to *logos*"[18]—is repeated over and again. In the Enlightenment account, an age of reason supersedes the age of superstition, yet does so by a fetishizing of reason, in what Adorno and Horkheimer (following Hegel's *Phe-*

*nomenology*) call "the dialectic of enlightenment": the sleep of (instrumental) reason brings forth (mythic) monsters (*Ungetümen*). The dialectic is repeated in those accounts of myth that see it as a pre-scientific stage, animistic or pseudo-explanatory, to be succeeded by reason proper, whether of the Cantabrian or Parisian variety (Cornford/Lévi-Bruhl).

There is a further dialectical twist to the story, however. For although the authority of science might now seem no better than that of myth or magic (and no worse, as Feyerabend indeed argues), that does not quite catch the peculiar quality of its claim to legitimacy. Against Karl Löwith's thesis that the legitimacy of modernity's self-account as secularization devolves upon the very transcendence it rejects, Hans Blumenberg rightly pointed to the claim that marks out modernity, the claim that is to self-preservation, self-reflexion, autonomy. Yet Blumenberg later went on to suggest, in his magisterial *Work on Myth* (1979),[19] that the "myth of modernity" should be understood functionally, as with any fundamental myth-making: it amounts to a coping with chaos, a strategy of cultural survival. It should be added that such a naturalistic "explanation" seems to leave little room for the notion of legitimacy or value, even though Blumenberg himself values myth's position midway between human fear and control of nature.

My point in rehearsing this bit of dialectics is to put the Romantic confrontation with myth in a more comprehensive frame. The *Frühromantiker* adopted a dual vision, that is, of myth-making and of mythology-making (a second-order reflection on myth), with the aim of avoiding both Enlightenment reductiveness and reliance on the transcendent authority of tradition. This dual vision was entirely in character: for the early Romantics were the first to reflect on their *own* historicity. They saw a division between antique and modern deeper than the old "Quérelle des Anciens et des Modernes," dubbing it (with Friedrich Schlegel) "classical" versus "romantic," where the latter includes the whole Roman-Christian world. More to the point, they uncovered (or invented) a third "world-view," the *oriental*.[20] The *discovery* of traditions, world-views or "values" is also their *loss*, however, since they can be articulated and wished for only *after* the fall. Habermas rightly says that Hegel was the first to thematize this loss of authority following on the friability of local traditions.[21]

It was in reaction to this threat that figures like Herder sought to "orient" the relativism of cultures in "History" (the singular form of which was also a discovery/invention of the time). Cultures are seen as relative to an origin, that is, a pure *Ur-Monotheismus*. The question remains whether such a retrospective on History is anything more than an empathetic projection upon the past. Is the distinction between oriental, classical, and romantic itself just a dream of those early Romantics? Many of them were fascinated by the legend of the statue raised to goddess Isis, whose veil concealed—a mirror image of the beholder.[22] Was the Romantics' orient simply their own self-image, mere *"Morgendländerei"* (a term used by K. O. Müller of Creuzer)?

## Creuzer's Approach to Mythology

That at any rate is the general background to the attempt at deciphering symbolic meaning in myth. As Arnaldo Momigliano writes,[23] Creuzer sought to generalize the Neoplatonist interpretation of Greek mythology, extending it beyond "literary" to visual imagery, or what Christian Heyne termed *"die Bildersprache"* of the ancient world, oriental as well as classical. Heyne (1729-1812, Professor at Göttingen) had even pointed the way by suggesting that everything could be interpreted as *symbol*,[24] at once signifying a universal "philosopheme," and symptomatic of popular culture and climatic context. "Creuzer subjected the ancient world as a whole to a religious treatment; in this lies his significance."[25] Did ancient peoples trade only in elephant tusks and gold? he asks: didn't they also exchange religious customs and gods? Creuzer simply took Heyne's idea further, while also transforming it; for in his view symbolic interpretation was *not* reductive—that is, reducing either to rational or to natural terms. It preserved the religious integrity of the symbols themselves.

Yet how does the claim that myth is essentially symbolic elucidate mythology? And what does Creuzer understand by "symbol"? Very roughly his theory of symbolism goes as follows: In the first place, it is a version of what Edward Beach calls the "primordial revelation" hypothesis.[26] An original and monistic truth is subsequently dispersed, diffused, and even becomes subject to degeneration into anthropomorphism (rather than the authentic theomorphism). This primordial One is refracted by the "mythic prism" into its polytheistic component rays, only to be refocused into the mystical unity of Christian monotheism (it is typical of Creuzer to use the same light imagery that he sees as central to the mythic traditions, or that he derives from interpretations of myth—the rainbow-like refraction of myth is Plutarch's image). Primitive humanity, confronted by an astonishing, divinely charged yet seemingly measureless universe, attempts to articulate its meaning in image and symbol. More exactly, one class of society—a priestly caste of exegetes—explicates nature to the rest, the uncultured masses. In historical terms, they bring their esoteric wisdom from the east and pass it on to the Greeks. Priests give names to the nameless, translate it into discrete formulae, and interpret the various signs of nature (entrails, dreams, bird formations, etc). Whether in image or word, in architecture or writing, the priests uncover and reveal something of the transcendent meaning of nature—symbols, in other words, harbor a divine meaning. This is a Romantic (or proto-Romantic) commonplace:

> Nature! great parent! whose unceasing hand
> Rolls round the Seasons of the changeful year.
> How mighty, how majestic are thy works!
> With what a pleasing dread they swell the soul,
> That sees astonish'd and, astonish'd, sings!

as James Thomson puts it in *The Seasons*. Romantic too is the claim that "explicating symbols and making symbols are . . . one and the same."[27] On this view, then, naming the gods or giving them their characteristic shapes serves to legitimate rather than fictionalize them—Creuzer is here not on Xenophanes' side. The symbol inhabits a liminal realm between ideal (soul or spirit) and sensuous (body or earthly form). It joins divine and human, but also expresses a mutual tension. Creuzer detected such an ambivalent relation in animism and personification of natural forces—along with the danger that such forms would reduce the original revelation to naturalistic terms—as well as in the gradual refinement thorough Greek and Christian cult.

The symbol manifests the following chief traits: (1) a state of *suspension* (*Schweben*), stemming from an "incongruence" or "indeterminacy" as between essence and form (§30), and from an "excess" (*Überfulle*) of content as compared with its expression. The symbol displays a certain instability of presence/absence: we glimpse something that at the same moment escapes our grasp. (2) A process of *concision* (*der Kürze*) (§31):

> It is like a suddenly appearing spirit, or like a lightning flash which all at once lights up the dark night. It is a moment which lays claim to our whole being, a look into a limitless distance, from which our spirit returns enriched. For this momentariness bears fruit in the feeling sensibility, and the intellect, in resolving into its parts and appropriating the multiplicity locked up in the image's pregnant moment, experiences a lively delight and becomes satisfied by the abundance of this yield which it takes in piecemeal.

Such "fearsome" and "pregnant" concision combines blinding revelation with obscure utterance, sheer light with shadowy darkness. (3) In its restless striving to express the inexpressible, to display the infinite in finite shape, the symbol can tend in two divergent directions (we could call them the sublime and the beautiful, though Creuzer does not use such terms). Either (a) it seeks to say everything at once, in human form especially, and in its necessary failure points towards the *mystic* content it can only gesture at in allegorical mode (§32). Christianity too shares a mystic side. Or (b) it selects the mean between divine and human, and in its "swelling exuberance" shows how the god in some measure appears in human form. This "most beautiful fruit" of the symbolic realm is the "*plastic*" symbol epitomized in Greek sculpture. And so, we might note, Creuzer manages to integrate both Christian and classical norms within the symbolist paradigm. (He notes incidentally that the symbol tends to be absent from the German tradition, with the notable exception of *emblematics*—a suggestion Walter Benjamin was much later to take up.)

How then does myth fit in the picture? Creuzer argues that it is derivative of the original symbol, a verbal interpretation of its mysterious nature. If we describe the symbol (figuratively!) as the pupa which still conceals the colored wings under its hard casing, myth is the butterfly lightly flitting in and out of the sunlight (§40). It blends in colorful confusion a legendary account of a nation's adventures with religious tradition (*Überlieferung*) and belief, treating of a people's gods; myth is an admixture of historical "Faktum" and doctrinal truth. Where symbol proper consists of a "momentary totality," allegory is a

progression through a series of moments, and myth even more so—
its essence being expressed most fully as an unfolding epic narrative.
In other words, symbol and allegory (and hence myth) are at bottom
the same, the latter merely a making explicit what is in the former—
namely both divine presence *and* a tension between sense and idea.
(As is well known, Creuzer's rehabilitation of allegory was rehabili-
tated in turn by Walter Benjamin in his polemic against realism. It is
incidentally false to suppose "symbol" was uniformly opposed to
"allegory" as organic to mechanical, Romantic to pre-Romantic; that
was typical only of Weimar classicism, and was perceived as such by the
Romantics themselves.[28]) Homeric, and to an extent Hesiodic, myth
amounts to "perfected anthropism," depicting the divine-made-human;
it oscillates between freedom and fatalism with regard to the gods, and
thus demonstrates mankind's peculiar status, both natural and spiritual. Other myths, such as those about Heracles, mix anthropism with
apotheosis, showing how humans by their own labors attain to divine
status. Both are distinguished from "exanthropism" or euhemerism,
that is, the *reduction* of myth to human projection, fiction or lies.
Creuzer accuses Roman religion of a similar worship of human ends
and projects as if they were divine. In contrast, the ancient Greeks, in
Creuzer's view, found a poetic mode in which to express the true
nature of both men and gods, a truth which remained mysterious even
in its telling. They presented their mythic narratives not as the literal
but rather as the allegorical truth. Accordingly, Plato's complaint that
young men were unable to distinguish between the literal and the
figurative (*Republic* 378a-d) does not attack the status of allegory itself,
only its misuse. For, properly understood, myth captures the gulf as
well as the link between human actions and a transcendent nature—
it acknowledges its own falsity in other words.

Now, the *Symbolik* had an immediate influence, not least on
Schelling.[29] Yet in the end it was more famous as an object of ferocious
attack, and from two quite different directions, the *philological* and the
*mythological.* On the one hand, classical philologists marked their
coming of age as a discipline by a frontal assault on Creuzer's
methodological failings, which were considerable and an easy victim
of Voß's positivism.[30] With Lobeck's *Aglaophamus*[31] of 1827 Creuzer
appeared to be decisively refuted, with the result that the study of myth
went underground as a rather suspect academic line (from Welcker,

K. O. Müller and Bachofen, down to Warburg, Cassirer, Kerenyi, Otto and others in our own day). Paradoxically, the *Symbolik*'s "refutation" by Lobeck and the establishment became, for this alternative line, part of its prestige.[32]

Of course, the philologists and neoclassicists ignored their *own* marmorealizing myth of Hellas—an interesting tale in itself, but one for another day.[33] What they felt they had to resist at all costs was any suggestion that the Greeks had borrowed their myths and deities from barbarians, or indeed, that myth was as such a derivative form. Creuzer's suggestion that there was a "Dionysian" irrationality underlying the transparent simplicity of Apollonian Greece was sacrilege.[34] As far as they were concerned, one simply could *not* compare the Greek Ideal with the childish and illegitimate ravings of the primitive mind! Creuzer's attempt to legitimize myth by placing it under the aegis of symbol, so granting a universal color of right to particular cultural traditions, struck them as scandalous, for its effect was rather to render Greek myth *il*legitimate. True, Creuzer had tried at the same time to dignify the classical worldview by the term "plastic symbol," thus making it with Christian mysticism one of the peaks of cultural achievement. But classical philologists remained unpersuaded by Creuzer's allegorical explanations. For all that, as Vernant notes, the failure of his project left the discipline powerless to rebut the scandalous comparison of civilization with the nonsensical language of primitive tribal myth.[35] Only in recent years have anthropologists been granted access to the classical sanctum (e.g. E. R. Dodds or Walter Burkert).

Now if the philologists took umbrage, equally Creuzer's explanations of the mythic imagination and his vast "Iconism" of types offended those promoting a proper "philosophy of mythology." Schelling for one became leery of the word "symbol," tainted as it had become by the controversy. He preferred a term borrowed from Coleridge, "tautegory," or that which means only itself, form and content entirely fused.[36] To suggest that symbolism was the sensuous clothing put on by "philosophemes" (as Creuzer, following Heyne, at first called them) was to impose a false dualism.

Such varied tactics left poor Creuzer bewildered. Nevertheless they serve to point up an ambiguity in Creuzer's whole project. Like his own "symbol," he has a foot in both camps, the rationalist and the Romantic. On the one hand, while decrying any reduction of myth to poetic fiction, he imputes to the *Bildersprache* a pedagogic function, namely, its use by a priestly caste consciously to dress up religious truths in imagery suitable for popular understanding: priestly exegesis rather than deceit. His other, Romantic side, allied with the Görres circle in Heidelberg and with his lover, Karoline von Günderode, led him to downplay any discursivity lying somehow *behind* the sensible form.[37] A numinous mystery, through which divine presence comes as a sudden all-illumining flash of lightning in the depth of the night, was the essence of symbol. It is momentary, inexpressible, intuitive in mode, infinitely pregnant, and laconic all at once. But the two aspects of unconscious inspiration and conscious image-making sit ill together. No wonder then that Hegel raided Creuzer's vast compendium for whatever booty he could carry off.

## Hegel and Creuzer

Hegel's appropriation of Creuzer caused the latter some discomfort. The association of the "philosopheme" with Hegelian speculation was another point in Creuzer's disfavor as far as the classicists were concerned—so much so that Creuzer was forced in the third edition to distance himself from any philosophical interpretation put upon his findings.[38]

To summarize Hegel's main borrowings:

First, the term and concept of "*Symbolik*" allowed him to organize his lecture material on art; a tripartite division symbolic/classical/romantic seems to stem from his reading of Creuzer in 1821 or thereabouts.[39] As Hegel defines "symbol" it (i) comprises an intuitional element which at the same time points to a universal meaning, (ii) links meaning and expression not abstractly but concretely, by a motivated or (as Peirce would say) iconic resemblance: "The lion and the fox do in fact possess for themselves the very properties whose meaning they are meant to express."[40] Yet there remains a certain vagueness as to *which* properties are salient for signification (as Hegel had argued in the sections on *Vorstellung* from the *Encyclopaedia*), a vagueness that renders the symbol "essentially *ambiguous*" (A 397 / 306). Like Creuzer, then, Hegel sees the symbol as characterized by a state of "suspension" between meaning and expression, an incommensurability between inner meaning and outer figuration.

Second, Hegel sees the various forms of symbolic "art" (he also terms it "pre-art") as attempted interpretations of nature. Creuzer surely helped shape Hegel's account of symbolism as above all an "exegetical" and pedagogic culture. But Creuzer saw exegesis as typifying ancient Greece as well, and Hegel follows suit in part, as witness the *Lectures on Philosophy of History*, where the Greeks are said to look for the meaning of nature everywhere.[41] The only difference is that they *succeeded*, in Hegel's view, where the Egyptians et al still struggled to find the answer to the riddle which nature presents. The answer of course (as Oedipus said) is "man." (As we shall see, that is for Hegel not the whole answer, for it remains "human, all too human.") In sum, where for Creuzer symbolism was "particularly of the Greeks," as his title has it, for Hegel it was particularly pre-Hellenic.

Third, Hegel agreed with Creuzer that Greece took many of its gods and myths from oriental cultures, in this siding with his friend against Müller's objections to deriving Apollo from a sun-god (LPR 1827 648). Similarly the *Aesthetics* and the *Philosophy of History* borrow Creuzer's interpretation of the Hercules myth (the twelve labours represent the months of the year, etc., as well as a rapprochement between god and man), and of Ceres et al as nature-deities. But again for Hegel the deeper meaning is that such symbolic significance is a mere survival, and nature is *transfigured* rather than simply preserved in Greek culture, just as Greek art frees itself from natural constraints.

Fourth, Hegel agrees that the "mystic" symbol constitutes "die eigentliche Symbolik"—Creuzer's phrase—even while he holds that the "plastic" Ideal escapes symbolism altogether (Hegel's appropriation of the label "die eigentliche Symbolik" may well have prompted Creuzer to drop it from the third edition). Egyptian religion really *is* a mystery, at least for us—we cannot decipher it.

Hegel's differences run deeper, however, and it is no surprise that Creuzer declared his friend as much anti-symbolic as pro-.[42] For Hegel, symbolism comprehends at least three distinct things:

- a phenomenon or practice—one that Hegel examines under the name of "Unconscious Symbolism";
- a *method* of interpreting phenomena—which he thinks is properly applied only to that phenomenon;
- a *normative stance* towards the world as a whole—a stance Hegel declares he does not share. In sum, Hegel puts the symbolic in its

place—*within* his scheme of artistic periods and cultural formations. The twin crises to which Creuzer responded, namely, the loss of authority for Christian and for classical norms, are answered by Hegel in a different way. With respect to art, Hegel remains a (neo) classicist[43]; with respect to religion, he supposes that both myth and art reduce in part to sensuous intuition. Moreover, he objects to Creuzer's project on methodological and historiographic grounds: in place of Creuzer's "degenerative" model he supplies a dialectical account of what I would call retrospective significance.

Summarizing the resultant differences:

First, Hegel distinguished sharply between Greek and oriental signifying practices.

> The Greek gods are not symbolic: they have no meaning other than what they show; they are what they portray, in the same way as the concept of a work of art is to express what is meant, not that what lies within should differ from the exterior.[44]

Hercules, as we have noted, is for him a hold-over from the past. We may link this support for the classical Ideal with another difference.

Second, inasmuch as Hegel makes art a seamless unity of *Bedeutung* and *Gestalt*—and that is what the work of art *is*—he opposes the view that in every artistic representation there is an allegory trying to escape (a view he associates with Friedrich Schlegel—never a good sign with him), as if all we had to do was peek behind the mirror, in Goethe's phrase.[45]

Third, Creuzer's historiography seemed suspect to Hegel—to that extent he was definitely on Lobeck's side. In particular, he saw the origin not as the richest but as the poorest determination: "The beginning is, in its meaning, always something abstract and indeterminate" (A 411 / 317). It is "the proper, unconscious, original symbolism, whose shapes are not yet *posited* as symbol" (A 412 / 318). Far from containing wisdom," [t]he mysteries were rather a serving of old gods, and it is as unhistorical as it is foolish to wish to find profound philosophemes there."[46]

Fourth, hence Creuzer's theory of a priestly formulation of myth risks importing conscious activity where none could have existed at the time. Hegel even seeks to defend Creuzer against himself:

> Now, Creuzer has often been taxed with the reproof that he, following the example of the Neoplatonists, first *reads* these broader meanings *into* the myths and looks in them for thoughts there is no reason historically to say they actually reside there, and where it is possible to prove historically that in order to find these thoughts one must first have imported them. For the peoples, poets and priests ... have no inkling of such thoughts, which would have been incompatible with the degree of culture of their time. The latter point is of course entirely correct. The people, poets and priests did not in fact have the universal thoughts—those lying at the root of their mythological representations—before them in this universal form, so that they would then have veiled these deliberately in a symbolic shape. But that is not claimed even by Creuzer. (A 403-04 / 311)

For Hegel, the rational *reflection* on nature comes later than the symbolic worldview proper, namely, in ancient Greece and post-classical culture.

Fifth, Hegel similarly would limit symbolic interpretations to symbolism alone. And here the meaning—while there—is explicit only "for us," retrospective hermeneutes:

> [I]f we speak here of meaning, this is *our* reflexion, which proceeds from our need to regard the form that encapsulates the spiritual and inner in an intuitional mode as generally something external, through which we, in order to be able to understand it, wish to peer inside, into the soul, the meaning. Consequently we must draw an essential distinction in respect of such universal intuitions as to whether those peoples who first apprehended these intuitions themselves had the inner, the meaning in mind, or whether it is only *we* who cognize there a meaning receiving its external expression in the intuition. (A 419 / 324)

*We* may see it as symbol; the symbol-maker/interpreter presumably does not.

Yet matters are never as simple as they seem, and Hegel's delimitation from "Symbolik," his apparent sublation of the ruins of Creuzer's system into his own system, is hardly clear-cut. Setting up a rigid dichotomy between intrinsic versus imputed significance is both ingenuous and preemptive. A  significance that is only for us, in hermeneutical retrospect, runs the risk of being imposed from without, of reductive immediacy. The question therefore is how there can be meaning *to* a phenomenon—*an ihm*—when it is there only *for us*, not for itself.

Let me in closing, rehearse the general options facing Hegel with respect to myth/symbol. Myth is usually identified as a scandal, then tamed by interpretation. Either one "sees through" myth (as Marx suggested we see through ideology) to its naturalistic or euhemerist foundation; or one gives its true, higher, allegorical meaning, thus in a sense explaining it away. In any event, normative authority is preserved, whether in the guise of neo-classicism, of Christian revelation, or of the logos of reason. Creuzer attempted a middle path between these strategies, so as to legitimate an ecumenism of the symbolic imagination.

Hegel too wished to avoid the reductivist extremes we have seen to be self-defeating—the dialectic of enlightenment, or the myth that reason supersedes myth *tout court.* How to avoid the Scylla and Charybdis of rationalism vs romanticism, or again, Creuzer's unstable *Schweben* between the two?

On the one hand, he has to allow a measure of continuity between the "alien wisdom"[47] found in polytheism, and "our" own monotheism or philosophy, perhaps via some new "mythology of reason." On the other hand, such a mythology would still seem to require some rational authority or validity. The danger then is that Hegel becomes—as he was perceived by both Schelling and Creuzer—a cognitivist, if not allegorist, presupposing and seeking to decipher the infinite content behind every form. The tenor of the Berlin lectures often supports such a view, with its assurance of truth without remainder, whether in the classical Greek Ideal, in Christian religion, or in speculative thought.

Yet other considerations tell against such an impression. For instance, it is of more than anecdotal interest that in the *Aesthetics* Hegel remained fascinated by the symbolic, much more than by the "classical" and the "romantic" (sc. Roman-Christian) worldviews. Similarly, despite Hegel's rather exclusive attitude to extra-Christian religions, at his death the history of religions was at "the cutting edge of Hegel's interest," the English-language editors write (LPR I 13).

Moreover, the symbolic moment of *dis*parity between sensuous and "spiritual" condemns both the Greek gods and the plastic Ideal they (in a dual sense) represent to a death that cannot be thematized in "the religion of beauty." To rephrase, the sublime (second moment of the symbolic) returns to haunt the beautiful, and it remains in the guise of Christian mysticism. To that extent Paul de Man was entirely justified in maintaining (against the objections of Raymond Geuss and Rodolphe Gasché) that for Hegel art is essentially symbolic (*un*-aesthetic, if you will).[48] What they miss is the way in which the dialectic undermines or renders fluid any positive determination, in this case, that of the beautiful semblance constitutive of the (classical) Ideal.

Again, Hegel's historiography, while critical of orientation by origin à la Creuzer and preferring an account of progressive self-transformation, must run the risk of falling back into a species of "reflective" narrative, imprinting the observer's interest upon the past.

For all these reasons I suggest that the symbolic might be more than a piece in the jigsaw puzzle of Hegel's system, and more than a scandalous item that must (repeatedly) be expelled from the polis or the academy. I suggest further that the "symbolic world-view" operates as a kind of test of the Hegelian system itself, for it poses the central question as to whether there *is* indeed reason in the world of appearances, images and representations. Hegel had already thematized the question as being characteristic of the symbolic: we are unsure (a) what the meaning is, and (b) whether there *is* meaning there to begin with. We might even see Hegel's project as recapitulating the movement from unconscious to conscious symbolism (in the *Aesthetics*), where the latter is the deliberate and artificial imposition of tropes and figures upon the material. In that sense philosophical dialectic might not after all be so far removed from allegory (in a dynamic sense rather than the cold and rational allegory Hegel and others condemn). Hegel too had to construct as well as explicate the significant forms of the history of religion; he had to make philosophy speak not just in German, but also in myth and symbol as it were.[49] He too confronted the myth of the goddess at Saïs, and with it the risk that the meaning one deciphers—or even the wish to *find* coherent meaning—is just the reflection of a questing, mantic subjectivity.

# Notes

1. *Werke in zwanzig Bänden* (Frankfurt: Suhrkamp, 1971), Bd 2, *Jenaer Schriften*, 560.

2. Letter of February 6, 1806: in *Die Liebe der Günderode: Friedrich Creuzers Briefe an Karoline von Günderode*, ed. Preisendanz (München: Piper, 1912), 225. The letter goes on to praise Schelling as the first to see that such philosophical symbolism must be "necessary" rather than mere convention.

3. 1912: published in the collection *Responsibilities* (1914). The phrase "old mythologies" refers to the Celtic myths the poet had made use of in the 1890s, and which he (or his persona) wished now to renounce. Of course, we should beware of taking the words at their face value: Yeats continued to use various personae and other mythological imagery.

4. *Did the Greeks Believe in their Myths? An Essay on the Constitutive Imagination* ([1983] Chicago: University of Chicago Press, 1988).

5. See *Against Method: Outline of an Anarchistic Theory of Knowledge* (London: NLB, 1975), chaps. 17-18.

6. Veyne cites (on p. 141) an 1873 remark of Nietzsche's: "With what poetic liberty did the Greeks treat their gods! . . . We have the greatest difficulty in reviving the mythical feeling of the freedom of thought to lie; the great Greek philosophers still lived entirely within this right to lie."

7. See the "Earliest System-Programme of German Idealism," translated by H. S. Harris in his *Hegel's Development: Toward the Sunlight 1770-1801* (Oxford: Clarendon Press, 1972), 511-12. Hegel's authorship of the fragment remains moot, and the question seems intractable; for the current state of play, see the magisterial survey in Frank-Peter Hansen, *Das älteste Systemprogram des deutschen Idealismus: Rezeptionsgeschichte und Interpretation* (Berlin: de Gruyter, 1989). Harris shows the continued influence of the idea of a "new mythology" in his "Religion as the Mythology of Reason," *Thought* 56 (1981): 301-15, as well as in his *Hegel's Development: Night Thoughts (Jena 1801-1806)* (Oxford: Clarendon Press, 1983), *passim*—it is a major theme of Harris's interpretation. In his essay "Die neue Mythologie. Grenzen der Brauchbarkeit des deutschen Romantik-Begriffs" in *Romantik in Deutschland* ed. Brinckmann (Stuttgart: Metzler, 1979), 341-54, Otto Pöggeler shows himself skeptical of any attempted renewal of myth, and argues that Hegel passed beyond such tendencies by the middle of the Jena period. For a general treatment of the topic, see e.g. Manfred Frank, *Der kommende Gott: Vorlesungen über die Neue Mythologie* (Frankfurt: Suhrkamp, 1982), esp. Lectures 6, 7, and 9 (Frank's title alludes to Hölderlin's "Brod und Wein").

8. E §24a. Cf. Hegel's treatment of the myth in LPR III 101-08 (1821), 207-11 (1824), and 300-04 (1827).

9. That is not to claim that the *Phenomenology*—*science* of experience, after all—is itself mythic in mode. Equally it is not to claim that its approach *excludes* myth. In his *Hegel's Recollection: A Study of the Images in the Phenomenology of Spirit* (Albany: SUNY Press, 1985), 31-32, Donald Verene renews Cassirer's complaint that Hegel's "ladder" does not begin low enough, and that there is a mythic stratum below the level of "Sense Certainty." In fact, however, Cassirer's "original" mythic consciousness is already quite sophisticated: it seeks to *name* the primordial "force" at work in nature. Hegel does, of course, exclude the possibility of a supposedly "pre-rational" consciousness.

10. Although Hegel's relation to Creuzer has been little studied, mention should be made of Johannes Hoffmeister, "Hegel und Creuzer," in *Deutsche Vierteljahrsschrift für Literaturwissenschaft und Geistesgeschichte* 8 (1930): 260-82; H.-G. Gadamer, "Hegel und die Heidelberger Romantic" (1961) in his *Hegels Dialektik: Fünf hermeneutische Studien* (Tübingen: Mohr, 1971), 71-81 (an essay omitted from the English version); and Otto Pöggeler, "Hegel und Heidelberg" in *Hegel-Studien* 6 (1971): 65-133.

11. See especially Marcel Detienne, "Rethinking Mythology" in *Between Belief and Transgression: Structuralist Essays in Religion, History, and Myth* (in French, 1979; Chicago: University of Chicago Press, 1981), 43-52, and *The Creation of Mythology* (in French, 1981; Chicago: University of Chicago Press, 1986), chapters 3-5; Jean-Paul Vernant, "The Reason of Myth" in his *Myth and Society in Ancient Greece* (Brighton: Harvester, 1980), 186-242; G. S. Kirk, *The Nature of Greek Myths* (Harmondsworth: Penguin, 1974), 1-29.

12. Detienne, "Rethinking Mythology," 43. Detienne also points out that the primary sense of mythology is a *written* discourse, not oral as the nineteenth century thought.

13. Detienne, "Rethinking Mythology," 49.

14. I remember hearing of an academic who once attended a conference in Yugoslavia on the myth of the state, only to find that all the participants from Eastern Europe treated myth as something one *believed* in. Presumably no longer—*Entmythisierung* is all over.

15. See "The Herodotean and the Thucydidean Tradition" in Arnaldo Momigliano, *The Classical Foundations of Modern Historiography* (Berkeley: University of California Press, 1990), 29-53. Thucydides wrote political history, and from the Greek standpoint; Herodotus ranged over many cultures, in a critical spirit while open to alien traditions.

16. *Life of Theseus* 1.5; cited by Veyne, *Did the Greeks...?*, 1.

17. An apt example would be the essay called "White Mythology." In the same vein, Jean-Luc Nancy takes Detienne's idea of the "untraceability" of myth to an extreme in claiming that "le mythe est un mythe" in "Le mythe interrompu," second part of his *La Communauté désoeuvrée* (Paris: Bourgeois, 1986), e.g. 132ff.

18. See e.g. W. Nestle, *Vom Mythos zum Logos* (Stuttgart: Metzler, 1940), for one instance of the cliché.

19. In English translation, Cambridge: MIT Press, 1985; see also *The Legitimacy of the Modern Age* (in German, 1966, English translation from MIT Press, 1983). A similarly instrumental view of myth, which sees its source in cultural exigencies, a source shared with science, is Leszek Kolakowski's *The Presence of Myth* (written in 1966, published in German 1973, and in English by the University of Chicago Press in 1989). Kolakowski argues that myth is a way of making the relativity and chaos of experience more permanent, continuous, and intelligible. But again, to *explain* a need is not to *justify* the thing needed. Both Blumenberg and Kolakowski are surveyed in Frank, *Der kommende Gott*, 59-66 and 66-72.

20. This is of course a complex story. For a good survey, see René Gérard, *L'Orient et la pensée romantique allemande* (Paris: Didier, 1963). On the role of the Higher Criticism in these excursions way down east, see E. S. Shaffer's *"Kubla Khan" and "The Fall of Jerusalem": The Mythological School in Biblical Criticism and Secular Literature 1770-1880* (Cambridge: Cambridge University Press, 1975).

21. *The Philosophical Discourse of Modernity* ([1985] Cambridge: Harvard University Press, 1988).

22. Kant opined in the *Critique of Judgement* (Indianapolis: Hackett, 1987), §49, 185, that nothing was more sublime than the inscription over the temple to Isis, "I am all that is, was, and will be, no mortal has yet lifted my veil." For Hegel's comments see LPR 1827 II 638-39; according to the editors, he relies on Proclus, and draws on Schiller's poem "Das verschleierte Bild zu Saïs." In *Die Lehrlinge zu Saïs*—that centerpiece of Romanticism—Novalis wrote: "Einem gelang es—er hof den Schleier der Göttin zu Saïs/ Aber was sah er? er sah— Wunder des Wunders—Sich Selbst" (1798), *Werke* ed. H.-J. Mähl & R. Samuel (München: Hanser, 1978) ii, 234. A great deal lies behind this topos of the veil, of course, including the theme of the "unveiling" of truth that philosophy is supposed to perform. Some of the Romantics were aware of the ironies here, as is shown in Philippe Lacoue-Labarthe and Jean-Luc Nancy, *The Literary Absolute: The Theory of Literature in German Romanticism* ([1978] Albany: SUNY Press, 1988), 71-78; though in this connection I think the authors wrong to pit philosophy (e.g. Hegel's) *against* aesthetics (i.e. the "veil" of imagery or representations).

23. "Friedrich Creuzer and Greek Historiography" (1946) in his *Studies in Greek Historiography* (London: Weidenfeld & Nicholson, 1966), 75-90. Ernst Gombrich claims that the attempt was highly original: see "The Use of Art for the Study of Symbols," *American Psychologist* 20 (1965): 34-50, at 48—a suggestion that has not (so far as I know) been taken up in writing the pre-history of "art history."

24. See e.g. his *Quaestio de causis fabularum seu mythorum veterum physicis* (1764) or *Sermonis mythici seu symbolici interpretatio ad causas et rationes ductasque inde regulas revocata* (1807), brief excerpts from which appear in *The Rise of Modern Mythology: 1680-1860* (Bloomington: Indiana University Press, 1972), 215-23.

Heyne's views on an original *Bildersprache* developed in cooperation with those of his close friend Herder, though Heyne thought that mythic meaning was accessible only through philological excavation, and not by empathetic analogy with folksong.

25. Alfred Baeumler, *Das mythischer Weltalter: Bachofens romantische Deutung des Altertums* (München: Beck, 1965)—the introduction to a 1926 reissue of Bachofen's *Der Mythus von Orient und Occident.*

26. In his unpublished work entitled *Schelling's Philosophy of Mythology,* chapter 1: "The Origins of Pagan Religion," which he kindly let me consult.

27. *Symbolik,* 1st ed. I, 1 §9. In the third edition this introduction appears in volume 4; in what follows I cite the section number only.

28. See on this Bengt A. Sorensen, *Symbol und Symbolismus in der Ästhetischen Theorien des 18: Jahrhunderts und der deutschen Romantik* (Copenhagen: Münksgrad, 1963). Writers such as H.-G. Gadamer and Tzvetan Todorov persist in supposing symbol and allegory were mutually exclusive for the Romantics.

29. Apart from *The Deities of Samothrace* of 1815, the late *Philosophy of Mythology* shows this influence in a host of places; see Edward Beach, *Schelling's Philosophy of Mythology,* chap. 1, p. 6, and footnote #23. Another person Creuzer influenced was Richard Wagner.

30. See *Der Kampf um Creuzers Symbolik: Eine Auswahl von Dokumenten,* introduced and edited by Ernst Howald (Tübingen: Mohr, 1926). I should add that it was not just a fight for academic status: Weimar neo-classicists like Goethe took exception to what they perceived as Creuzer's muddying of the pure Attic waters.

31. So titled after one of Pythagoras' Orphic teachers.

32. Momigliano, *The Classical Foundations of Modern Historiography,* 80.

33. See Martin Bernal, *Black Athena: The Afroasiatic Roots of Classical Civilization,* vol 1, The Fabrication of Ancient Greece 1785-1985 (London: Free Association Press, 1987), especially chapters 6 and 7.

34. Nietzsche was ostracized for the same offense. Creuzer had in 1808 published a study entitled *Dionysus,* anticipating his later systematic claims; see Frank, *Der kommende Gott,* 89ff.

35. Vernant, "The Reason of Myth," 207.

36. *Sämtliche Werke* (Stuttgart/Augsburg: Cotta, 1856-61), XI, 195-6: "Mythology is not *allegorical,* it is tautegorical.* The gods are for it actually existing beings, which *are* not something different, *mean* something different, but mean

*only* what they are. [*I borrow this expression from the well-known Coleridge, the first of his countrymen to understand and have significant use for German poetry and science, in particular philosophy." The first to use the term "tautegorical" was apparently Karl Philip Moritz in his *Götterlehre* of 1795.

37. On Creuzer's Romanticism, see especially Ugo M. Ugazio, "Friedrich Creuzer e l'infinito romantico," *Filosofia* 33/4 (1982): 405-62, for a very rich treatment.

38. See the Preface to the 3rd ed. (Leipzig/Darmstadt 1836) p. xv: "I am indeed member of a philosophical faculty—but no philosopher; I did not wish, nor was able, to write a philosophy of myths, symbols and systems of belief, but a philological-mythological ethnography."

39. See Gadamer "Hegel und die Heidelberger Romantic," cited above; Otto Pöggeler, "Die neue Mythologie," esp. 348-49; and Helmut Schneider, "Neue Quellen zu Hegels Ästhetik" in *Hegel-Studien* 19 (1984): 9ff, esp. 13-21.

40. *Vorlesungen über die Ästhetik, Werke* 13, 395 / *Aesthetics: Lectures on Fine Art,* trans. Malcolm Knox (Oxford: Clarendon Press, 1975), 304. Citations in the text to "A" are to these editions.

41. *Werke* 12,290: "Everywhere the Greeks looked for an explication [*Auslegung*] and interpretation [*Deutung*] of the natural"; *manteia* supplied a key to the immanent meaning.

42. "Sie sind wenigstens gegen die Symbol als nachsinnig gewesen": *Briefe von und an Hegel,* ed. Johannes Hoffmeister and Friedhelm Nicolin (Hamburg: Meiner, 1961) ii, 288 (8/9/21). Their correspondence, once so warm, petered out during the 1820s.

43. At least up to and including the Nuremberg period, Hegel remained a neo-humanist in his pedagogical views, close to the views of his friend Niethammer. On this see John H. Smith, *The Spirit and its Letter: Traces of Rhetoric in Hegel's Philosophy of Bildung* (Ithaca: Cornell University Press, 1988). Of course it does not follow that Hegel was a neo-humanist beyond this sphere or this period.

44. LPR 1824 492. Many passages in the *Aesthetics* or the *Philosophy of History* say the same.

45. For the ritual Schlegel jibe, see *Werke* 13:513-14;400, and 404;312. Cf. Friedrich Schlegel, "Gespräche über Poesie die Poesie" (1800) in *Kritische Friedrich-Schlegel-Ausgabe* (München: Schöningh, 1958-), ii, 324: "Alle Schönheit ist Allegorie. Das Höchste kann man, eben weil es unausprechlich ist, nur allegorisch sagen." (In the 1832 edition Schlegel often substituted "symbol" for "allegory," thanks to his friendship with Creuzer.) For Goethe, see *Conversations with Eckermann,* trans. John Oxenford (London: Dent, 1930) 18/2/29. Sorenson refers also to *Faust* ll. 5531f, where the Knaben Lenker challenges the herald to decipher the various allegorical shapes: "Denn wir

sind Allegorien. Und so solltest du uns kennen. . . . Bin die Verschwendung, bin der Poesie" (if not the boy's joke, it is certainly Goethe's).

46. *Philosophie der Weltgeschichte, Werke* 12, 303; for the separation of the "poetic" gods from these, see p. 304.

47. On which see Arnaldo Momigliano, *Alien Wisdom: The Limits of Hellenization* (Cambridge: Cambridge University Press, 1975).

48. See "Sign and Symbol in Hegel's *Aesthetics*" in *Critical Inquiry* 8 (1982): 761-75; cf. Raymond Geuss's criticism in the following issue, and de Man's reply *Critical Inquiry* 10 (1983); also Rodolphe Gasché, "In-Difference to Philosophy: de Man on Kant, Hegel, and Nietzsche" in *Reading de Man Reading* (Minneapolis: University of Minnesota Press, 1989), 259-94, esp. 268f.

49. See the draft of a letter of April 1805 to J. H. Voß (*Briefe* I 99), where Hegel writes of trying "to make philosophy speak German" as Voß had in his role as translator done for Homer. (There is some irony therefore in Hegel's later defence of Creuzer *against* Voß.) H. S. Harris uses the phrase "to teach philosophy to speak German" as the title of Chapter IX of *Hegel's Development: Night Thoughts.*

# 6

# Transitions and Tensions in Hegel's Treatment of Determinate Religion

*Louis Dupré*

## I.

The transition from the concept of religion to its phenomenal appearance poses problems directly connected with the spiritual nature of religion. In the Introduction to the Lectures of 1824 Hegel states: "Spirit, insofar as it is called divine spirit, is not a spirit beyond the stars or beyond the world; for God is present, is omnipresent, and strictly *as spirit* is God present in spirit... Religion is a begetting of the divine spirit, not an invention of human beings but an effect of the divine at work" (LPR I G 46 / E 130).[1] Any religion, however primitive, preserves this intrinsically spiritual significance. Its finite appearance expresses the infinite concept far more directly than, say, nature expresses Spirit. Nevertheless, taken singularly particular religions display differences that separate them from each other. The concept, though present in each, appears fully in none.

The Christian faith, however, escapes this limiting one-sidedness, according to Hegel. Being all-inclusive, even its phenomenal appearance must count as fully spiritual. As such, it determines the meaning and spiritual rank of all others. Hence we might expect Hegel to rank all other religions in an order of increasing spirituality. We even might anticipate this order to be one of historical succession, leading up to the consummate religion at the end. Such an account would seem all the more plausible since the historical emergence of religions was, certainly in Hegel's time, broadly assumed to ascend from the primitive toward the more spiritual and to attain its historical completion in Christianity. In fact, however, Hegel rightly regarded

81

such an historical account as philosophically inadequate. All historical religions had originated within a short span of some eight centuries. Karl Jaspers would later describe this remarkable outburst as the religious *axis* period of the human race. Most of those religions have continued to coexist since that creative epoch and to preserve their own identity. This fact would change the order from one of historical succession to one of spiritual proximity to the alleged perfection of revealed faith.

What we find, however, is neither an order of historical succession nor a hierarchy of increasing perfection from a Christian perspective—as is evident in the place—immediately before Christianity—of the by Hegel's account spiritually low-ranking religion of the Romans. With some hesitation I would describe it as a *typology* of religions arranged in an order that unfolds the logical conditions required for the very possibility of the consummately spiritual religion in which the *idea* becomes fully *manifest.*[2]

Hegel himself presents his attempt as "educing the concept of religion" (*den Begriff der Religion auszuführen*).[3] Both the idea and the metaphor evoke a comparison with Lessing's development of religion as a gradual "education of the human race," except that for Hegel the Christian faith functions as the final goal of that process rather than, as for Lessing, being a part of it. Christianity surpasses other religions in the same way in which the infinite surpasses the finite. But that also implies that, as a *spiritual* infinite, it must include them. The same 1832 introduction describes this all-inclusiveness of the Christian faith:

> The determinate religions are not our religion, yet as essential, albeit subordinate, moments that cannot be devoid of truth they are included in ours. In them, then, we are dealing not with an alien faith, but with our own, and the knowledge of this fact reconciles the true religion with the false ones" (Lasson II, 6).

Not only do non-Christian religions display a partial truth: they are "historically extant" (*geschichtlich vorhanden*) stages of a development toward that perfect religion (Lasson II, 8).

Such an arrangement, however consistent in its own right, creates nevertheless new difficulties when viewed in the total context of Hegel's philosophy. For how can the various religions both follow an *ideal* order and be stepping stones to another, *empirically concrete* and hence phenomenally limited, religion? Hegel perceived the problem but never succeeded in satisfactorily solving it. Until the final series of lectures delivered in the year of his death (1831) he kept changing the order and, more significantly, the principle of classification. One early attempt to satisfy the demand to follow an "ideal" order while at the same time preparing the historically concrete conditions of the Christian faith was the one he adopted in the 1824 lectures. The so-called religions of nature corresponded to *Being*, the religions of spiritual individuality to *Essence*, while Christianity represented the *Concept*. To remain consistent, however, such a scheme would have to assign to the religion of the concept, as the synthetic moment, a place among the determinate (i.e., particular) religions. Since Hegel refused to place Christianity on a par with those "particular" religions, he was forced to separate the conceptual moment from the moments of being and essence. In his later lectures Hegel abandoned this arrangement which excluded a third, synthetic moment from the phenomenal appearance. But the essential ambiguity in his conception of the Christian religion remained. As a phenomenally concrete religion, essentially different from others, Christianity could not be claimed to coincide with the concept. Nonetheless, as the concept's moment of individuality it had to function as the *conceptual* synthesis of all particular religions. We may be inclined to regard this problem as created by Hegel's formal structures. But this is by no means the case. It already emerged in eighteenth century reflection on Christianity's relation to other faiths, specifically in Reimarus and Lessing. It still continues to frustrate the attempts made by Christian believers to define their position with respect to other faiths as both unique and all-inclusive. How can a faith that advances claims of absolute truth be one that conflicts with others as much as they conflict with each other?

In his later series Hegel compromised between the demand for a purely ideal order and that for a hierarchy oriented toward the Christian faith by structuring his presentation loosely around a vague but comprehensive dialectic of immediacy, differentiation, and reconciliation. But even that simplified scheme could not be consistently maintained as long as the principal reconciler (Christianity) remained outside the sphere of differentiation and conflict. The religion of "expediency" (Roman) was no more fit to function as a reconciling synthesis—as it had to do—than the great religions of the East—

Buddhism, Hinduism, Zoroastrianism—could aptly be referred to as religions of "nature" where nature meant the "immediate." Only in the final series (1831) did Hegel succeed in fully recognizing the specific nature of the determinate religions while at the same time conferring to them a more or less consistently ideal order. The notes left of that series present the following arrangement:

1. Natural religions: primitive religion and the religion of magic.
2. The internal rupture of the religious consciousness: Daoism, Hinduism, Buddhism.
3. Religions of freedom: Persian, Jewish, Egyptian, Greek, and Roman.

Even here, however, the final place of Roman religion, as preparing the conditions for the concrete appearance of the Christian faith, failed to conform to an ideal order of succession.

## II.

Having been unable to establish a fully satisfactory account of the order of succession based on an analysis of spiritual content, we ought to investigate whether we may not learn more about the rationale underlying Hegel's treatment of determinate religions by considering the structure of the dialectic itself. I propose to do so by focusing on two critical transitions in Hegel's conceptual scheme: the one leading from particular religions to the "consummate religion," and the other linking the universal concept of religion to those particular religions. With respect to the former we note that the final position of Roman religion remained constant throughout the four series of lectures, even though in 1827 it provided the transition from Jewish religion and in the other series from Greek religion to Christianity. Hegel's criticism of Roman religion had been severe from the beginning— never more so than in the 1821 when he gave it, in his own manuscript, its most extensive development. We may then be assured that the category of *purpose* which the religion of "expediency" presents must play a crucial role in creating the conditions for the consummate religion. That role consists, of course, in detaching the idea of *freedom* from all higher necessity. In the manuscript for his 1821 lectures Hegel defines purpose as "the identity of different actualities, . . . a unity determined in and for itself, that maintains its own determinateness as opposed to other forms of determinateness" (LPR II G 99 / E 193). Essential herein is the dynamic unification, achieved by purpose, of ideal and reality.

Both the Jewish and the Greek religion constitute earlier stages in the development of purposiveness. In the religion of sublimity (Israel) the idea of purpose had, especially in the 1827 lectures, played a religiously significant part. Israel's existence as a people is entirely determined by a divine purpose. Yet as Hegel presents it, that purpose lay entirely *outside* God's own nature. "The wisdom and self-determining of God does not yet include God's [own] development" (LPR II G 574 / E 683). The therefrom resulting abstract quality somewhat arbitrarily narrowed God's purpose to the well-being of one people, of which in an equally non-ideal way, it submitted even the most natural aspects of life to detailed divine regulation (see the 1831 lectures passage excerpted in LPR II E 684-685). In such a vision the ethical life, even at the level of the nation, remains "natural" according to the sense Hegel had given to that term in his description of the family in the *Philosophy of Right*, namely, as falling short of the more spiritual, detached freedom of the State, even of the Roman State.

Greek religion expressed a very different idea of purpose. Less reflective and more immediately intuitive it possessed an internal teleology, the kind of aesthetic harmony which Kant had described as "purposiveness without purpose". Yet such inner purposiveness implied an aesthetic necessity that lacked the reflective distance required for genuine freedom. Which one was religiously superior? The free form but internal necessity of the Greeks, or God's sovereign freedom, subject to no formal necessity yet dominating life with divine commands? Hegel continued to hesitate and, despite polytheism and fatalism, replaced the Greek religion after Judaism in the 1831 lectures.

Roman religion clearly differs from either one and what constitutes its major religious weakness also accounts for its unique significance in Hegel's categorization. It pulls the aesthetic unity of the ideal and the real apart: the real "resists" the realization of the ideal. Nor was there an overall divine purpose at work in the Roman conception of the world as Hegel understood it. Romans set themselves strictly finite purposes for the attainment of which they used the gods as means. Only by helping to accomplish goals that remain external to them do the gods attain an ideal status. Unlike for the Greeks and the Jews, the worldly end, even when conceived as a universal end (the greatness of Rome), did not "fall within God himself" (LPR II G 581 / E 689). The State, though divinized, is not conceived as an intrinsically spiritual organism but merely as a dominion over others to be realized by brute conquest.

> The State is the principal goal of this religion, but it is not a political religion in the sense that . . . . the people had its highest consciousness of the State and its ethical life in religion so that veneration was due to the gods as free universal powers. (LPR II G 117 / E 212).

The universality of the Roman purposiveness, then, is not a spiritual one, but consists in an abstract consenting to particular, finite purposes. It logically resulted in the arbitrary, unmediated power of the emperor and the legal concept of "person"—the empty subject of formal rights.

Hegel's description, of course, falls short of rendering an adequate picture of Roman religion by modern standards. Nevertheless, his insight far surpasses that of his main source K. Ph. Moritz (*ANTHOUSA oder Roms Alterthümer* (Berlin, 1791)), who still interpreted it as a decanted version of Greek mythology. Hegel's report points the way toward such modern students of Roman religion as George Dumézil, K. Latte, or Karl Kerenyi who detached its origins from Greek mythology altogether. Yet of greater interest to us than historical accuracy are the elements in that religion which Hegel emphasizes: the self-conscious freedom and, negatively, the breach with *nature*.

This latter aspect had gradually increased its significance in Hegel's view of non-Christian religions from one lecture series to the next. While the 1821 manuscript had restricted the clear affirmation of freedom to the religion of expediency and the lectures of 1824 had included Roman with Jewish and Greek religion under the comprehensive, but vague, heading "Religions of Spiritual Individuality," the 1827 series revealingly combines the religions preceding the Roman, i.e., the Greek and the Jewish, under the title "The Elevation of the Spiritual Above the Natural." In 1831 the entire third division, now entitled "The Religion of Freedom," is expanded to include, next to the Jewish, Greek, and Roman, the Persian and Egyptian religions.

Here it clearly appears in what the signal contribution of Roman religion and, indeed, of all non-Oriental religions above the "primitive" level, consisted, namely in the detachment of freedom from *nature.* The term *nature* in this context refers to the low degree of transcendence characteristic of the way in which some religions (in ever decreasing number, as Hegel's thought developed!) differentiated the divine from finite being, while for Hegel the opposition to nature distinguished Christian faith as well as Hegelian philosophy from any kind of pantheism.

The full religious significance of the concept of nature appears in the *Philosophy of Nature.* There we learn that nature holds an essential revelation of God and that one of the tasks of religion consists in recognizing Spirit in nature.

> God has two revelations, as nature and as spirit, and both manifestations are temples which He fills, and in which He is present. God as an abstraction is not the true God; His truth is the positing of his other, the living process, the world which is his Son when it is comprehended in its divine form.[4]

Yet nature is Spirit only in its otherness—self-alienated Spirit: "A bacchantic god innocent of restraint and reflection has merely been *let loose* into it" (E §247z). Nature is *implicitly* divine insofar as it is immanent in the idea, "but in reality its being does not correspond to the notion [concept]" (E §248z). Now, in a *religion* of nature the mind stands already in a self-conscious relation to God, without which there would be no religion at all. But in this "immediate religion" the two sides still remain undividedly united in an "intuition of God in all things without distinction" (LPR II G 5 / E 99). In the religion of nature the mind succeeds in seeing Being, the first pure category of thought, as itself "sublime" without regard for the specific nature of the finite and determinate (LPR II G 6 / E 100).

That undivided natural unity is broken long before we arrive at the Roman religion or, in the 1831 lectures, to any of the religions of freedom to which the Roman belongs. In 1827 Hegel classified the two preceding religions as "The Elevation of the Spiritual Above the Natural." In 1831 he reserved the predicate "natural" exclusively for primitive religion and the religion of magic, while ranking all others that precede the religion of freedom under "The Internal Rupture of Religious Consciousness." Nevertheless, a *full* detachment from the natural does not occur until a thoroughly venal Roman religion with total disregard of the *given* quality of the divine presence, so prominent in the religions of nature, subjects the gods to the pursuit of strictly human ends. Precisely its negative, disruptive quality renders Roman religion effective in preparing that spiritual faith which totally detaches the freedom of Spirit from any unreflective linkage to nature. Purposiveness, especially purposiveness without necessity, random and arbitrary, definitively severs the last tie of natural necessity that obstructed the coming of the realm of freedom.

## III.

Now let us consider the earlier transition, the section on *cultus* that links the concept of religion to its phenomenal appearance in the determinate religions. The term "cultus" does not accurately describe what this transitional moment achieves, namely to establish a clear *self*-awareness next to the objective *God*-awareness constituted in religious representation and thought. Religious feeling, whether through cultural participation or private devotion, unites all objective forms of religious cognition with an intense subjective consciousness. Hegel links this subjectification, in a somewhat unconvincing argument, exclusively to the *cultus.* Yet the main point concerns the process of interiorization itself. In theoretical knowledge, he claims, "I am immersed in my object and know nothing of myself" (LPR II G 330 / E 442). Any "spiritual" relationship to God, however, must include an intense consciousness of oneself. This, Hegel surprisingly concludes, is attained in *acting* whereby I assimilate the sacred object to myself. Only sacred action conveys that simultaneous awareness of otherness and selfhood characteristic of the religious consciousness. "God is on one side, I am on the other, and the determination is the *including, within my own self, of myself* within God and of God within me" (LPR II G 331 / E 443).

Several points strike the reader as peculiar in the argument. First, the alleged lack of self-awareness in theoretical knowledge contrasts strongly with Kant's account of the constitution of the object through the unity of apperception, perhaps even with Hegel's own interpretation of the emergence of the *religious* object in Chapter VII of the *Phenomenology*. Nor does it appear obvious why a practical attitude ought to be more *self*-conscious than a theoretical. More importantly, the "mystical" consciousness described under this heading by no means coincides with the "practical" one. To be sure, Hegel's discussion also includes the more active and external aspects of worship such as sacrifice and sacrament. But they appear as the external expression of an internal attitude that begins with "devotion" and ends with "repentance." He introduces the section with a defense of the treatise *de unione mystica* in traditional theology which an ill-inspired aversion for the mystical has induced contemporary theology to abandon altogether. Still, the fact remains: the first form of the cultus consists in devotion "when the subject prays and is occupied with this content not merely in objective fashion but becomes immersed therein" (LPR I G 333 / E 445). Already in the *Phenomenology*, *Andacht* (devotion) had appeared as the first moment of Greek religion. Even before the religious consciousness distinguishes itself from its divine object *Andacht* "raises the self into being this pure element" (*Phenomenology*, Lasson 499 / Baillie 720). From this primary, undifferentiated mental attitude concrete cultural activities receive their internal meaning and spiritual substance. That internal quality of the cultus is reemphasized in its final state (the third moment of the section) when the devout mind interiorizes the external act of sacrifice and "offers one's heart or inmost self to God" (LPR I G 334 / E 446).

In the second edition of the *Werke* (1840) the transitional function of the cultus between the concept and the determinate religions appears even more clearly. Worship, the text states, realizes "the substantial unity of Spirit with itself which is essential and infinite form, knowledge in itself" (*Werke* (1840), Lasson I, 151). Precisely in mystical devotion the soul knows its essence united with the divine essence. Witnessing to the divine Spirit within itself it raises its singularity to spiritual universality. Yet, Hegel insists, this transition occurs via *particular, historical* forms. The one Spirit appears as "the spirit of a people in the way it is determined within the individual periods of world history—the national spirit" (*Werke* (1840), Lasson I, 260; trans. in LPR I E 447 footnote). Most individuals concretely encounter the universal Spirit in the particular faith in which they are born. Originally the acceptance of such an ancestral religion requires no personal decision. Nor does the *particular* quality of such a "natural" faith appear until it comes into collision with another religion. A confrontation of this nature forces believers to reflect on their religion and eventually breaks up the religious homogeneity. In the end it may even lead to an abstract universal religion that submerges all particularity as it did in eighteenth century European Deism. (It is hard not to suspect some polemical irony in Hegel's decision during the 1831 series of lectures to range this rationalist universalism, together with primitive religion and magic, at the beginning as a *particular*, spiritually undeveloped form of "natural religion").

But before the particular is thus broken up, individual believers attain a consciousness of universality through their *particular* faith. The more a religion approaches spiritual individuality (the final, highest stage), the more the particular expression of an intrinsically universal truth creates tensions. In Greek religion this tension remained mostly internal. The gods present "the essential spiritual powers, the universal powers of ethical life" (LPR II G 536 / E 644) on which State, family, agriculture, commerce, etc., rest. Yet those powers were symbolized in distinct, occasionally conflicting forms. Their conflicts provided the content of Greek tragedy. Thus in *Antigone* the gods of the netherworld, protectors of the family, collide with the gods of the city. "Each of these two sides [Antigone and Creon] actualizes only one of the two, has only one side as its content. That is the one-sidedness, and the meaning of eternal justice is that both are in the wrong because they are one-sided, but both are also in the right" (LPR II G 558 / E 665). Hints of the need for their reconciliation are dramatically suggested in the divinization of Oedipus at Colonos and in the acquittal of the matricidal Orestes by the Areopagus. But the emerging ethical concept of religion cannot be fully accommodated in a polytheistic religion.

The Hebrew concept of one God embraces the various ethical powers within its spiritual unity. Being infinitely powerful and wise, Yahweh is not subject to the blind necessity of a higher Fate (as the Greek gods were). At least in the 1827 lectures Hegel had come to appreciate the full spiritual significance of the Jewish faith. He ranked it after the Greek and before the Roman religion. More revealing than the position itself are the words with which he justified it:

The necessity of the *elevation* of the religion of beauty into the religion of sublimity lies in what we have discussed already, i.e., in the need that the particular spiritual powers, the ethical powers, should be embraced within a spiritual unity. (LPR II G 561 / E 669)

The key term "elevation" (underlined by me) refers to a higher spiritual order, thus clearly reflecting a spiritual significance, in contrast to the position of other religions (most notoriously the Roman one at the end). It had taken Hegel a long time to reach this high evalution of the spiritual power of Judaism. In his early Frankfurt writing on "The Spirit of Christianity and Its Fate" he had depicted Abraham's faith as the alienation of a man who had been forced to leave his land and wander homeless from one place to another.[5] In the *Phenomenology* Judaism does not appear among those religious mentalities that lead reason to full spirituality: the lengthy treatment of classical religion results, without transition, into the Christian one. Even in the 1821 and 1824 lectures—and, surprisingly, but for different reasons in 1831—he placed Judaism before Greek religion despite Greek polytheism, aestheticism, and remaining naturalism.

At the end of his most sympathetic 1827 treatment Hegel critically refers to an intrinsic limitation inherent in Israel's faith—"a limitation understood partly in terms of the fact that the Jewish God is only a national God, has restricted himself to this nation" (LPR II G 575 / E 684). Yet, he claims, a similar restriction affects even Christianity which, though universal in its recruitment, remains exclusive in its salvific power. In 1831 he criticizes the exclusiveness of God's Lordship over Israel more severely: "This exclusiveness rightly astonishes us more in the case of the Jewish people, for the binding of religion to nationality completely contradicts the view that God is grasped only in universal thought and not in a partial definition" (LPR II G 575 / E 683 footnote).

This second transition suggests that the succession of particular religions follows a pattern of increasing internalization and universalization. Those two principles do not always follow an identical development, however, as Hegel's continuing hesitation about the place of the Jewish religion—internal but not universal—indicates. Moreover, as appeared in the transition between the final determinate religion and the Christian, they remain ultimately subordinate to the historical appearance of a faith that constituted the immediate condition for the emergence of the "manifest religion," namely, the Roman religion which was neither internal nor universal.

The preceding reflections seem to lead to the conclusion that no single coherent pattern rules Hegel's "typology" but rather an irreducible multiplicity of ordering principles which in the end all play a role in preparing the event of the Christian to a revelation. Some of them do so by "universalizing" the particular; others by interiorizing it and yet others by detaching religion, however particular, from its "natural" state and elevating it to a level of pure (albeit wholly abstract) freedom. In Hegel's shifting classification over the years the removal from the "natural" remained the single permanent element. The more general categories used as classifying principles needed to be supplemented by more specific ones, concerning which Hegel never reached a definitive position.

This negative conclusion actually turns to Hegel's credit. It shows his concern for an empirical investigation of the content of each religion. In his discussion of Roman religion he was well in advance of his contemporaries. His analysis of the Greek religion of the classical period, however restricted in scope, has remained deservedly famous. But even his treatments of Hinduism and Buddhism are surprisingly perceptive, considering the scarcity of sources at his disposal. Precisely a mature awareness of the complexity of those faiths caused Hegel constantly to rearrange their order.

## Notes

1. References are to the new German edition (LPR G) ed. by Walter Jaeschke (Hamburg: Felix Meiner Verlag, 1983) and the English edition (LPR E) by Peter C. Hodgson (Berkeley, L.A.: University of California Press, 1984). A few references are to the edition by Georg Lasson, 2 vols. in 4 parts (1925-1929) (Hamburg: Felix Meiner Verlag, 1966).

2. I borrow the term "typology" together with some of the critical analysis that led to it from Walter Jaeschke: "Zur Logik der bestimmten Religion" in *Hegels Logik der Philosophie*, ed. Dieter Henrich and Rolf-Peter Horstmann (Stuttgart: Klett-Cotta, 1984), 172-188.

3. In the introduction to "Determinate Religion" as it appears in the first edition of the *Werke* (1832). In Lasson: Vol. I, part II, p. 5.

4. E §246z; *Philosophy of Nature* I, trans. M. J. Petrie (London: George Allen and Unwin, 1969), 204.

5. *Hegels theologische Jugendschriften*, ed. by Hermann Nohl (Tübingen, 1907), 243-48.

# 7

# Is Hegel a Christian?

*John Burbidge*

I n his detective story, "The Man in the Passage," G. K. Chesterton sets the final scene in court. A number of witnesses had seen a figure in the passage that led to a murdered actress. Sir William Seymour saw a tall man, or at least "there was something about the thing that was not exactly a woman and yet was not quite a man; somehow the curves were different. And it had something that looked like long hair." Captain Cutler said it looked more like a beast, for "the brute has huge humped shoulders like a chimpanzee, and bristles sticking out of his head like a pig." Father Brown said, "the shape was short and thick, but had two sharp, black projections curved upwards on each side of the head or top, rather like horns."

The court was in confusion, but Father Brown calmly restored order. A panel had been slid across the passage, he suggested, and it had a looking glass on its face. Each witness, in describing what he thought was the murderer, had only been talking about himself.[1]

That is rather like what happens when people turn to Hegel. What is his ultimate religious commitment? Findlay calls him "the philosopher of liberal humanism."[2] Kaufmann represents him as saying: "In God I do not believe; spirit suffices for me."[3] And Roger Garaudy says: "Son Dieu est le Dieu-programme des humanistes et non le Dieu-personne des théologiens."[4]

Yet in contrast Lauer reports: "It is not strange that Hegel should see in the Christian revelation of the God-man a revelation just as much of what man is as of what God is."[5] And Claude Bruaire writes of the *Science of Logic*, "Non seulement cette *Logique* constitue l'assise conceptuelle du discours sur le Dieu révélé, non seulement elle lui fournit son organisation spéculative, mais elle prétend transcrire le Verbe éternel divin."[6]

We are as confused as those sitting in Chesterton's court room. And we rather suspect that the explanation is the same. Each writer sees in Hegel a version of his own image. To be sure, there are those who contrast their own position with Hegel's so that they can then offer a trenchant criticism. Merold Westphal accepts the humanist reading of a withering away of religion so that he can then offer a Christian response.[7] And Karl Marx rejects Hegel's Christianity so that he can establish his "new materialism."[8]

Nonetheless the situation is confusing. And we crave for a Father Brown who will not only remind us that we have been using the mirrors of speculation and reflection all along, but will also help us to get at the real Hegel. It is, perhaps, presumptuous, but let me try to fill that rôle.

Our first question is one of criteria. How can we decide? For, as Hegel himself realized, our preconceptions of what makes sense and what is reasonable mould and constrain our interpretations of philosophy. If something is nonsense to us, then (we shall confidently assume) it must be nonsense to this obviously intelligent person we are studying. And if something has been profound and challenging in our intellectual history, we anticipate that any philosopher we respect will find it profound and challenging as well. It is because we bring our own presuppositions to the hermeneutical task that we discover in our author judgements and conclusions that are reasonably similar to our own. When we do not, we almost invariably caricature her or him in precisely those areas where we disagree.

Let us approach the question cautiously, then, and start from Hegel himself. He does not define religion in terms of doctrines or beliefs alone: not simply ideas are important. Religion incorporates much more: it includes religious practice–the immediate sentiment of feeling and the public practice of cult. Feeling, cult and doctrine make up the reality of religion.[9] Assessed against these three standards, where does Hegel stand with respect to Christianity?

I start with feeling. And I start at the very point from which the humanistic and atheistic interpretation draws its evidence: the feeling of the death of God. Let me cite, in my own translation, the passage from the *Phenomenology* in full:

> The death of the mediator is the death not only of his *natural* side, that is, of his particular being-for-self. It is not only the dead shell from which the essence has already departed that dies, but the *abstraction* of the divine

essence as well. For, in so far as his death has not yet completed the reconciliation, it is one-sided, knowing the simplicity of thought as the *essence* in contrast to reality. The extreme of the self has not yet achieved equal value with the essence; the self has this only in the spirit. The death of this representation contains, therefore, at the same time the death of the *abstraction of the divine being* which has not yet been posited as self. This is the agonizing feeling of the unhappy consciousness, that *God himself* has *died*. This hard expression is the expression of the most inner self-knowing in its simplicity, the return of consciousness into the depth of the night of I=I, which neither distinguishes nor knows anything outside of itself any longer. Hence this feeling is in fact the loss of *substance*—of its taking a position over against consciousness.[10]

The death of God as an abstract being. The return into isolation for the self. The self left alone to create its own world. These are the claims of humanism. And it is to this passage that Garaudy and others appeal when justifying their stance.

But we need to pause. For Hegel is not here talking about an intellectual liberation, a recognition that we are no longer slaves to an alien master, now free and independent in our own house.

He is talking about feeling—the feeling of an unhappy consciousness. And he describes it as agonizing: *schmerzliche*. This is not a description of doctrine, but of lived experience.

As lived it is a moment in a process of becoming. And we should follow it through to its completion:

At the same time, however, this feeling is the pure *subjectivity* of substance—the pure certainty of itself—which is lacking in substance as object, as immediate or as pure essence. This knowing, therefore, is an enspiriting through which—its abstraction and lifelessness having died—substance has become subject; hence substance has become *actual*, a simple and universal self-consciousness.[11]

Here, it would seem, we have arrived at humanism. But humanists seldom report the range of experience here described. They do not talk of the agonizing feeling of the death of God, nor of the deep night of the lonely soul. They describe this movement in terms of exhilaration, of self-discovery. And if they do talk about the loss of faith in traumatic terms, they soon forget the trauma, and put it away as a part of their childish past.

But Hegel does not seem to do so. For he goes on in the next paragraph to stress the importance of movement—this movement through agonizing feeling to pure self-certainty. It is not simply as finished product, but as process and transition that spirit is present. The movement retains all its moments, including the agonizing night of God's death. Only by dwelling within that total dynamic is spirit and community constituted.

The recurrent movement through dark night to simple self-certainty is not what I find in humanist religion, I must confess; nor do I find it in much Christianity. Evangelicals talk about the deep night of self-condemnation and the light of redemption. Liberals talk about finding oneself in love. Neither talk about the experience of the death of God.

Yet there are some who refer to an experience more profound and recognize that such an experience is not to be forgotten, but to be woven into the fabric of one's religious life. Indeed they talk about "the dark night of the soul." It is those wise in Christian mysticism who describe it.

Listen to Augustine Barker: "If the soul would elevate her spirit, she sees nothing but clouds and darkness. She seeks God, and cannot find the least marks or footsteps of His Presence; something there is that hinders her from executing the sinful suggestions within her, but what that is she knows not, for to her thinking she has no spirit at all, and, indeed, she is now in a region of all other most distant from spirit and spiritual operations—I mean, such as are perceptible."[12]

Or consider St. John of the Cross: "Under the stress of this oppression and weight, a man feels so much a stranger to being favoured that he thinks, and so it is, that even that which previously upheld him *has ended* along with everything else, and that there is no one who will take pity on him."[13]

But that is not the end. For that moment of utter darkness is the transition to what Underhill calls the Unitive Life. "And later, when God judged that it was time, He rewarded the poor martyr for all his suffering. And he enjoyed peace of heart, and received in tranquillity and quietness many precious graces," writes Suso.[14]

St. John of the Cross adds: "It remains to be said, then, that even though this happy night darkens the spirit, it does so only to impart light concerning all things; and even though it humbles a person and reveals his miseries, it does so only to exalt him; and even though it impoverishes and empties him of all possessions and natural affection, it does so only that he may reach out divinely to the enjoyment of all earthly and heavenly things, with a general freedom of spirit in them all."[15]

Here in the confessions of great Christian mystics we discover the movement of feeling that Hegel has described–through the deep night of a lonely soul into a simple and universal self-consciousness. The lonely soul cannot find the least sign of God's presence; that which has previously upheld the proficient in religious faith has ended. But for Hegel this is not something transcendent, beyond time. Within the Lutheran tradition this experience of profound loss has been closely tied to the crucifixion. And Hegel's words echo those of Johann Rist's hymn: "O grosse Not! Gott selbst liegt tot. Am Kreuz ist er gestorben." God himself has died. Yet that loss is not dismissed into the irrelevant past in the manner of the humanists; it is retained and incorporated into a more profound experience of the spirit of God: "hat dadurch das Himmelreich uns aus Lieb erworben."[16]

The parallel is striking. Indeed the very language Hegel uses suggests the comparison: "The agonizing feeling that God himself has died . . . the return of consciousness into the depth of the night of I=I . . . . This knowing is an enspiriting through which, its abstraction and lifelessness having died, substance has become subject."

Does it tell us anything about Hegel? I think it does. For the fact that he can describe the whole experience, and that he can recognize its importance as a complete movement, suggests that he is not talking about something alien. All too often, those who have not plumbed the depths dismiss and ignore this experience. Even if it is part of their past, they do not recognise its significance. They abandon themselves to the exhilarating freedom of the humanist or the confident assurance of the saved. The fact that Hegel places it only three pages before he starts talking about absolute knowing, however, suggests it is not something to be forgotten, relegated to the early obscurity of unhappy consciousness or the transient irrelevance of faith. And the fact that he describes it so accurately suggests that it is not simply something heard about, but something he himself has felt.

I conclude, then, that within Hegel's experience is to be found the profound religious feeling that only a few of the mystics talk about: the movement through the dark night of the soul into the unitive life. Such an experience, for all that it has found its echo in other traditions, can only be called Christian, for it is intimately tied up with the "one-sided representation of the death of the mediator" as its counter-part and completion.

Let me turn to our second criterion: the question of cult.

The chapter on Absolute Knowing in the *Phenomenology* integrates two moments out of the preceding discussion: the inherence of truth (*an sich*) expressed in revealed religion, and truth on its own account (*für sich*) as captured in the dynamic of the beautiful soul. Experience has picked up the first of these; I now turn to the beautiful soul.

The important point here, once again, is the movement—the total picture. It starts with a moment of purity. "All life, and everything spiritually essential has returned into this self and has lost its distinctness from the I. Hence the moments of consciousness are these extreme abstractions, none of which stand firm, but rather each loses itself in an other, and produces it."[17] Once again Hegel reminds us of the unhappy consciousness.

But the beautiful soul cannot stay in this purity of self-knowing; it must act and make itself actual. Any such action is singular—the product of whim. What was intended as a way of actualizing the good turns out to be evil. And the soul, no longer beautiful, comes under severe judgement. For the other half of the beautiful soul—that which in its self-knowing knows the good—contemptuously condemns the hypocrisy which intends the good and does the evil. Once the acting and the judging have both found firm and independent expression, a new moment appears. The one who acts confesses: "I am evil"; the one who judges becomes more fixed in condemning and repelling, driving the evil one to the point of madness. At the moment where no hope seems possible the one who judges recognizes in the agent his or her own action—that judging is also an act involving singularity and whim. The result is reconciliation.

Fear and trembling of a soul fully conscious of itself; action that inevitably converts into evil; harsh and severe condemnation; confession, forgiveness and reconciliation: these are the moments of the beautiful soul. The claim to certainty at this stage involves the whole pattern starting with pure intention, not just the final moment of reconciliation; this total movement is taken up into absolute knowing.

It is tempting to think of this as the culmination of secular humanity; today we might think of how the self-knowledge provided by psychology and psycho-analysis leads to wisdom. Many have looked for the prototype of this figure in the writings of Novalis, or in the hero of romantic sensibilities. But there is something missing. For the modern approaches to therapy and the romantic ideal both dissolve the moment of condemnation. They encourage action, to be sure. But they accept whatever is done without judgement; and so there is no genuine forgiveness—no real reconciliation. Hegel seems to require more. For the dynamic of the beautiful soul is a movement that must continue to be repeated for the result to be reconfirmed. And the pure self-knowledge of modern secularism in which "tout comprendre c'est tout pardonner" forgets the process while exploiting the product.

This movement, as I said, must continue to be reenacted; and repeated reenactment requires communal institutions—a community in which rituals maintain action, judgement and reconciliation as distinct moments. Hegel makes this clear at the point where, introducing the discussion of the beautiful soul, he differentiates it from conscience.

Conscience "is that character of moral genius which knows the inner voice of its immediate knowledge to be the divine voice, and since in this knowing it knows determinate being in an equally immediate way, it is the divine creative power which has living force in its concept. It is, thereby, divine worship in itself, for its acting is the intuiting of its own divinity."[18]

That would seem to be enough; it talks about pure self-knowledge. One wonders why Hegel has to go on to the beautiful soul, since the romantic ideal intuits its own divinity in its action. The next sentence, however, provides an answer. "This solitary worship is, at the same time, essentially the worship of a *community*, and the pure inner self-*knowing* and self-perceiving goes on to become a moment of *consciousness.*" And the paragraph ends: "As intuited knowing or knowing that has a being, religion is the speaking of the community concerning its spirit."[19] The process must become objective within a community so that it can be perceived and understood; and this communal process involving speech is the work of religion.

By placing this paragraph at the point of transition, Hegel distinguishes the dynamic of the beautiful soul from that of conscience as the divine service of a community in contrast to the worship of a singular soul. He is stressing the importance of cult.

Once we investigate, we find the pattern of action, condemnation, confession and forgiveness captured in the practice of Lutheran confession. Listen to Luther's Small Catechism:

> What is confession? Confession consists of two parts. One is that we confess our sins. The other is that we receive absolution or forgiveness from the confessor as from God himself. . . . What sins should we confess? . . . Before the confessor we should confess only those sins of which we have knowledge and which trouble us. What are such sins? Reflect on your condition in the light of the Ten Commandments.[20]

The reference to the Ten Commandments recalls an earlier part of the Catechism which ends thus:

> God threatens to punish all who transgress these commandments. We should therefore fear his wrath and not disobey these commandments. On the other hand, he promises grace and every blessing to all who keep them. We should therefore love him, trust in him, and cheerfully do what he has commanded.[21]

Luther then offers a brief form for confession that ends:

> Then the confessor shall say: "God be merciful to you and strengthen your faith. Amen." Again he shall say: "Do you believe that the forgiveness I declare is the forgiveness of God?" Answer: "Yes I do." Then he shall say: "Be it done for you as you have believed. According to the command of our Lord Jesus Christ, I forgive you your sins in the name of the Father and of the Son and of the Holy Spirit. Amen. Go in peace."[22]

Lutheranism, unlike the other reforming churches, did not abolish personal confession. As the Augsburg Confession says: "The custom has been retained among us of not administering the sacrament to those who have not previously been examined and absolved."[23] This is a central part of its cultic practice. And it is this act of divine worship on the part of the community that Hegel has analyzed and described in the beautiful soul. For it is this act which continually reenacts the movement from purity through action and judgement to forgiveness as a single movement to be maintained.

Absolute knowing presupposes not only the profound Christian feeling of the dark night of the soul, but also the cultic practice retained in the Lutheran churches of individual confession. By enshrining both as movements to be continually rehearsed, Hegel established himself securely within the Christian, indeed the Lutheran Christian, tradition.

But what about the third moment, the area of doctrine? Could Hegel be called orthodox? Did he believe the elements of Christian doctrine?

Although we could turn once again to the *Phenomenology* to answer this question, I shall refer instead to the chapter on revealed religion in the *Encyclopaedia*.[24] Here Hegel describes Christian doctrine: an eternal creator who begets a son yet is spirit; the creation of heaven and earth, and the independence of evil, or fallen finite, beings; God and man immediately identified in a singular being who dies and thereby becomes universally present; fallen individuals who, in recognizing their own wickedness discover that they then share the life of God; and the continued mediation of this process within the community. Here are the basic ingredients of Christian doctrine. If Hegel has collapsed Easter and Pentecost into one event, talking not about a risen body, but a universal spiritual presence, he has good warrant. For the Gospel of John unites the two in a single incident. In Jesus' first appearance to his disciples, on the evening of Easter, he not only showed his hands and sides, but also "breathed on them, and said to them, 'Receive the Holy Spirit.'"[25]

Is this, however, simply an account of what is reported in the tradition, a recognition that Hegel comes at the end of the Christian era, and so must take account of it, even though he has already moved beyond? I do not think so. For by the second edition of the *Encyclopaedia* he makes explicit what previously was only implicit: the whole doctrinal statement has a logical structure. God before creation is self-determining universality; the created and fallen world is particularity; reconciliation is singularity. But the pattern extends even further. The eternal trinity itself involves the pattern of conceiving: universal, particular and singular relation. Creation and fall reproduce the structures of judging: quality, quantity, relation and modality. And, as I have shown elsewhere, reconciliation embodies the network of three syllogisms.[26]

To be sure, Christian doctrine is not expressed in such logical terms. It needs to be conceived philosophically before the inherent pattern is visible. But the relation is not one-sided. For philosophy also benefits from this encounter. Were it not for the fact that Christian doctrine represents as true of the cosmic order the same pattern that emerged in the processes of pure thought, Hegel could not have assumed that what is rational is actual, and that what is actual is rational.

Certainly the rational pattern is instantiated elsewhere. It is inherent in the whole experiential development described in the *Phenomenology*; it serves to explicate and organize the discoveries of the natural and human sciences into a coherent whole. But all of this could be, as Nietzsche puts it, "that kind of error without which a certain species of living being cannot exist."[27] Only with the affirmation that ultimate reality involves the pattern of creator and creation, fall and reconciliation can Hegel establish his claim that reason and actuality are one. He must believe Christian doctrine; else his philosophy becomes illusion—nothing but a Kantian categorial framework which says nothing about the world in itself.

Let us take stock of where we are: Hegel gives evidence of having himself lived through traumatic feelings, described in similar terms by Christian mystics; he makes the cultic practice of individual confession constitutive of absolute knowing; his belief in Christian doctrine is a necessary condition for the truth of philosophy. In each area he betrays the distinctive traits that define the mainstream of the Christian tradition. We can therefore conclude that Hegel *was* a Christian.

For many, that would be enough to answer our initial question. For they claim that Hegel did not simply describe a process of absolute knowing, but also a state of absolute knowledge. If it is the latter he intended, then nothing that has happened since could affect his conclusion. The basic grammar of thought has been fixed; and Hegel would perforce continue to be Christian to the present day.

For some of us, however, that is not possible. As I argued at the last meeting of the Hegel Society, there is strong evidence to suggest that Hegel saw even his own system as a culminating act of understanding, one that marked the beginning of a new dialectical transition into something other.[28] If Hegel is genuinely open to the novelties and contingencies of history, then he cannot simply rest on his laurels and bask in his achievement. He must take account of *die Sache selbst*: what has actually occurred in the century and a half since his death. When we ask: "*Is* Hegel a Christian?" we have to confront the events of that hundred and fifty years to see whether Hegel's reponse would be the same now.

I must confess that I do not see anything really damaging in the atheism and humanism of Hegel's left-wing followers. When one has followed Hegel's exploration of the depths of religious experience, the traumas of confession and the subtle articulations of doctrine, the criticisms and challenges made by Feuerbach, Bauer and Strauss seem banal and trivial. The real novelties are more significant.

I shall only suggest some; and they reflect my limited perspective. Nonetheless, it seems to me that they are worth taking seriously.

I have talked about the superficiality of humanism. But now even the dark night of the soul described by the mystics is in danger of becoming banal. For when we read the accounts of the gas chambers of Auschwitz, we see a faithful people who experienced the death of God, not as something confined to subjectivity, but as political events in an objective world. The diaries of the survivors and the trenchant stories of Elie Wiezel confront us with an experience of traumatic loss so radical that, even afterwards with the triumphant reestablishment of the state of Israel, it is hard to see the hand of God in those events.

Here is a dark night that surpasses all previous dark nights. And it has been built into the religious experience not of Christians, but of Jews.

In the fall of 1988, the war between Iran and Iraq stumbled to a close. Here, at least on the Iranian side, there had been the action of convinced beautiful souls: radical condemnation and the judgement of evil. Yet even in the midst of the war that condemnation was converted to reconciliation. "The 'conversion' of Iraqi POWs during the war normally began from the moment of their capture," reports Vahe Petrossian in the *Guardian Weekly* of August 26, 1990. "Revolutionary Guards and the Bassij volunteers would rush up to the cowering prisoners, embrace them, kiss them on the cheeks and welcome them as their Muslim brothers." Within a month of the end of the war Iran and Kuwait had reestablished diplomatic relations; and two years later, Iran eagerly accepted Iraq's offer under constraint to make peace. In addition, throughout the darkest days of the conflict, Muslims from both sides put on the pilgrim white to pray side by side around the Kaaba in Mecca.

Here, too, is a process of action, judgement and reconciliation. Once again it is not simply a ritual within a religious congregation. It is a movement of social and political entities; the structure of confession has acquired actuality in the realm of objective spirit. And once again it is not a Christian movement. Christianity has fallen apart into judgement without reconciliation, as in Ireland, or reconciliation without judgement, as in the ecumenical movement. It is Islam that has radicalized the movement of the beautiful soul, not Christianity.

It is not so easy to suggest where doctrine has gone. Certainly Christianity, confronted by the advances of modern science and the integrity of other religions, has been wont to surrender its claims to doctrinal truth and appeal to metaphor or non-rational insight. At the same time we have become aware of the sophisticated logics that the Indian tradition called Hinduism developed to articulate the nature of the world—a reliance on negation and the negation of negation that seems, to the uninitiated, to be far more subtle than that of Hegel. And we are only beginning to discover the rational discipline that found expression in the contradictions of Tao and the paradoxes of Zen. Here is religious doctrine that is not afraid to stretch what we mean by reason when articulating insight into truth. Once again it is not Christian, and once again, as we recall the non-violence of Ghandi and watch the economic success of Japan, we find it embodied in a political and economic order.

Since 1830, then, the world has changed. It is passing through a process of becoming other and has dialectically converted into its opposite. But there is no single opposite. There are many. Jews, Muslims, Hindus and Buddhists have all resurrected their religious faith and traditions from the limbo to which Hegel's philosophical history assigned them. But they are not only different from his Christianity. They are radically different from each other. Otherness seems to reign supreme.

According to Hegel, however, the dialectical production of otherness converts into speculation, the reflective unity of opposites. If we believe in his method, we should expect that out of the radical pluralism of the present there may yet develop a world community—one in which differences are maintained and deepened, even as people live together in mutual recognition. Once such a comprehensive community has become fully actualized, then philosophers will emerge to understand its structure and articulate its truth.

That truth will not be Christian, at least not the kind of Christianity that Hegel espoused. If it is Christianity, it will be Christianity sublated: preserved, but canceled and transformed. However the same thing will also be said about the many other traditions that in their own way have developed self-respect and presence. All will have an equal claim in the comprehensive picture that results.

I have no powers of prophecy. However, Hegel himself admits that only the method his system follows is true; and these predictions have simply applied that method to some facets of our contemporary world: Hegel's philosophical understanding has passed over into its other; reflection will integrate that other with the reality out of which it sprang, producing a comprehensive totality; understanding will re-emerge in that totality to understand its internal structure. In developing my prophecy in this way I am endeavouring to be faithful to Hegel. In other words, if Hegel could not easily be a Christian in our present day, he would at least believe in Providence: that the method will work its inevitable way through history; that the actual will turn out to be rational.

There is, however, one final worry that calls this conclusion into question. Recall that the truth of the method–the pattern of dialectic, speculation and understanding, of conceiving, judging and inference— is finally established by the coherence between the content of Christian doctrine and the logic of rational thought. But we have suggested that Christian doctrine may no longer be the last and only word. And we have no idea what kind of doctrine will emerge in the distant future. Hegel's method itself, despite his confident assertion, may turn out to be partial and incomplete. If that were to happen, the foundations of his belief in Providence itself would be shaken. And the last remnant of his Christianity would crumble. So our prophecy itself may be deception.

Is Hegel a Christian? The answer to that question we can now know only in part. For our knowledge is imperfect and our prophecy is imperfect. Once we become adults we shall put away such childish things. Nonetheless, as long as history continues there will abide some manner of doctrine, some kind of expectant experience and some sort of cultic community, however they find expression.[29]

# Notes

1. The story can be found in *The Wisdom of Father Brown* (Harmondsworth: Penguin, 1970), 58-75.

2. *Hegel: a Re-examination*, (London: Allen and Unwin; New York: Humanities, 1958), 354.

3. *Hegel: a Reinterpretation* (Garden City: Doubleday, 1966), 274.

4. *Pour connaître la pensée de Hegel* (Paris: Bordas, 1966), 188.

5. *A Reading of Hegel's Phenomenology of Spirit* (New York: Fordham, 1978), 245.

6. *Logique et religion chrétienne dans la philosophie de Hegel* (Paris: du Seuil, 1964), 181.

7. *History and Truth in Hegel's Phenomenology* (Atlantic Highlands: Humanities, 1979), 212.

8. See, for example, the tenth of the "Theses on Feuerbach," and the Introduction to his "Contribution to the Critique of Hegel's Philosophy of Right."

9. See in particular the various introductions to his *Lectures on the Philosophy of Religion* in which he discusses the concept of religion: LPR I G 95-108, 227-264 and 265-338. Compare LPR 151-197.

10. All references to the *Phenomenology* will be from the critical edition: *Gesammelte Werke*, (Hamburg: Meiner, 1968ff), Volume 9 (identified as HGW, 9) and to A. V. Miller's translation: *Phenomenology of Spirit*, (Oxford: Clarendon, 1977), identified as Phen. This citation comes from HGW 9:419 / Phen. 476.

In discussion a number of people suggested that the expression "I=I" was a reference to Fichte's use of that phrase in "First, absolutely unconditioned Principle" in the *Foundations of the entire Science of Knowledge*. (*Fichtes Werke*, ed. I. H. Fichte [Berlin: de Gruyter, 1971], I, 91-101 / *Fichte: Science of Knowledge*, ed. and trans. P. Heath and J. Lachs [New York: Appleton Century Crofts, 1970], 93-102.)

This strikes me as a misreading. Fichte's "I=I" identifies an act of absolute self-positing, of confident self-affirmation; here, in contrast, Hegel is talking about the depth of the night. Fichte takes the assertion of self-identity as a beginning; Hegel talks of it as a despairing consequence. Fichte is exploring the rational, conceptual foundation of knowing; Hegel is talking about the feeling of the lack of substance. The difference in context indicates that the expression is being used in quite a different sense. If it is a reference to Fichte, it is used more ironically than directly.

11. HGW 9:419 / Phen. 476.

12. "Holy Wisdom," cited by E. Underhill, *Mysticism* (New York: Meridian, 1957), 387. It was the discussion in this work that first directed me to the mystical significance of the dark night.

13. *The Dark Night*, Book 2, Chapter 5, Paragraph 7; cited from *The Collected Works of St. John of the Cross*, trans. K. Kavanaugh and O. Rodriguez (Washington: ICS Publications, 1979), 337. My italics. It was in response to a challenge from the editor of this volume that I went to this text of St. John of the Cross to see if my thesis could be maintained. A second aspect of his challenge, however, I concede. Meister Eckhart's mysticism, as far as I am aware, does not incorprate this moment of despairing trauma.

14. "Leben," in Underhill, *Mysticism*, 412.

15. *The Dark Night*, Book 2, Chapter 9, Paragraph 1 (*Collected Works*, 346).

16. I cite this from the *Evangelisches Kirchengesangbuch* (Karlsruhe, 1961), #73, although this version has amended the second line to read: "Gotts Sohn liegt todt." The original is cited in G. Lasson's edition of the *Vorlesungen über die Philosophie der Religion* (Hamburg: Meiner, 1966) II (*Die absolute Religion*), 158n1.

This hymn suggests that the death of God is the death on the cross. But that explanation is not sufficient. For Hegel, the death of God is not something reported in the tradition but personal feeling. The wording of the hymn ambiguously allows this interpretation when it talks of "grosse Not."

17. HGW 9:354 / Phen. 399.

18. HGW 9:352f / Phen. 397.

19. HGW 9:353 / Phen. 397f.

20. Cited from *Creeds of the Church*, ed. Leith (Richmond, Virginia: John Knox Press, 1973), 121-2.

21. *Creeds*, 115.

22. *Creeds*, 122.

23. *Creeds*, 88. A number of people brought up as Lutherans mentioned to me that they were not aware that personal confession was a part of Lutheran ritual. Current practice has replaced it with communal confession. I have not had the opportunity to investigate what was the practice in Hegel's time. The fact that Hegel introduces this section by talking about the divine worship of a community suggests that personal confession was the norm.

24. E §§564-571. A translation of this section that offers all three editions in parallel can be found in the article cited in note 26.

25. John 20:22.

26. "The Syllogisms of Revealed Religion, or the Reasonableness of Christianity," *The Owl of Minerva*, XVIII, 1 (1986): 29-42.

27. *The Will to Power*, §493; cited from F. Nietzsche, *Werke in Drei Bänden*, ed. H. Schlechta (Munich: Hanser, 1966), III, 844.

28. "Where is the Place of Understanding," in *Essays in Hegel's Logic*, ed. G. di Giovanni (Albany: SUNY Press, 1990), 171-182.

29. An echo of I Corinthians 13.

# 8

# Hegelian Philosophy of Religion
# and Eckhartian Mysticism

*Cyril O'Regan*

The paucity of Eckhart reference in Hegel texts has not always prevented commentators and critics from being so bold as to suggest that Hegel's philosophy of religion, his philosophical enterprise as a whole, is nothing more than Eckhartian mysticism revisited.[1] With respect to this essentially 19th century charge Hegel may very well have been a witness for the prosecution, for he is reliably reported to have said after a reading of a particular Eckhartian passage: *das haben wir es ja, was wir wollen!*[2] Despite Hegel's own connivance with respect to the labelling of the theological intention of his work, it would be unfair to hoist him on his own petard, as it would be hermeneutically unwise, without further evidence of a substantive kind, to construe him as mandating a privileged reading of his own texts, understand him in a sense as authorizing the view that his philosophy of religion, arguably even the fundamental inspiration of his philosophy as a whole, represents a species of unconscious plagiarism.

Modern interpretation of Hegel has shown nothing like the 19th century consensus regarding Hegel's *actual* theological proclivities. Certainly, it was contended even by Hegel's detractors that there was something rescuable in Hegel's thought, provided, of course, its theological substance was submitted to "transformational criticism" (Feuerbach) or a "disfiguring displacement" (Marx).[3] By contrast, 20th century interpretations, such as those offered by Lukacs, Kaufmann, Solomon, White, etc., do not so much suggest that Hegel is rescuable from his theological commitment as deny the existence of the commitment altogether.[4]

The importance of Hegel's philosophy of religion, and his view of the intrinsic relationship between Christianity and philosophy, have, of course, continued to be recalled. Where full-blown theological readings of Hegel have been proposed, however, they have most often signalled themselves as belonging to one or other of two quite distinct camps, i.e., apologetic defense of Hegel's well-disguised Protestant orthodoxy or spirited attack against his ill-disguised demythologizing intention. Mystical interpretations of Hegelian philosophy and Hegelianism in general have been much less common (e.g., Ernst Benz, Albert Chapelle, Frederick Copleston, *inter alia.*), their voices not particularly noisy.[5] Still such interpretations establish a link both with 19th century interpretation, and the parameters of the Christianity of Hegel's own day, lacking in other kinds of interpretation, whether anti-theological, a-theological, or properly theological. Not all who agree on the mystical approach agree that Eckhart represents the privileged point of entry. Other mystical options are regarded as viable. Figuring high on the list is that peculiar variety of speculative mysticism instanced in that figure whom Hegel called "the first German philosopher" (Jacob Boehme).[6] Joachimite mysticism has also been proposed as a possible descriptor of the peculiarities of both Hegel's rendition of Christianity and its sublation into Hegelian philosophy (de Lubac, Dickey).[7] But the Eckhartian-mysticism hypothesis has also been retrieved, but, it is important to point out, not without considerable revision in a hermeneutical field that displays considerably more scruple and circumspection.

Acknowledging the less than substantial relation between Hegelian texts and definite Eckhartian sources, commentators have still found it important to insist that: (a) at various periods of his career (e.g., 1798-9, 1823-4) Hegel engaged in something like a serious study of Eckhart; (b) a general link between his own philosophy of religion and the speculative mysticism of the medieval Dominican monk is openly avowed by Hegel; (c) a definite rapprochement of construal can be demonstrated concerning the God-man and God-world relations respectively, as well as the understanding of the proper nature of the theological enterprise.[8] No startlingly big claims are advanced, but on the positive side all unsupportable claims are avoided. In particular it is not claimed that (1) Eckhartian mysticism represents the, or even a, determinative historical influence,[9] nor (2) that sustaining the thesis of significant connection between Eckhartian mysticism and Hegelian thought logically implies that Eckhartian mysticism is the only or best means of taxonomically identifying the religious and theological tendency on the surface of Hegel's texts.[10] Nevertheless, the modesty and caution of this more modern approach is not such as to lead to a thorough-going hermeneutical attenuation, the running of huge interpretative wheels for trivial results. Even within the modern coordinates of reserve, to suggest that Eckhart throws considerable light on the kind of Christianity recommended by Hegel and on important onto-theological proposals embraced by him is decidedly non-trivial, its demonstration worthwhile.

At the outset it is worth noting that there is but a single Eckhart citation in the entire Hegelian corpus, and in the texts published in Hegel's own lifetime none at all. Moreover, as a number of scholars have observed, the Eckhart citation is far from pure, representing in fact a condensing of passages from different texts.[11] Now, while none of this is especially encouraging, of the passage it can at least be said that it is far from being insignificant, touching as it does, either implicitly or explicitly, important themes in Eckhartian mysticism that not only are whole-heartedly embraced by Hegel but recapitulated in some measure when the German Idealist attempts to establish the precise contours of that form of Christianity amenable to what Fackenheim has called "speculative transfiguration."[12] The passage is to be found in LPR I E:

> The eye with which God sees me is the same eye by which I see him, my eye and his eye are one and the same. In righteousness I am weighed in God and he in me. If God did not exist nor would I; if I did not exist nor would he. (LPR 1824 I G 248 / E 347-8)

Exegesis of the passage discloses a threefold signification. The first two elements are visible and on the surface, the third implied and supplied by the context. The visible elements of signification are the two related but analytically separable themes of the passage, the first ending with the word "same," the second beginning with the word "in." While the first theme centers on human beings' quite extraordinary gnoseological capacity in a recall that presents and amends the New Testament mysticism of knowing as one is known, the second more nearly corresponds to what Hartshorne has christened the "transcendental relativity" of the finite and the infinite. The third element is suggested by the context in which the passage is embedded, a context determined largely by Hegel's appeal for a more speculative or "scientific" approach to religion in contradistinction to the fideistic model Hegel perceives as threatening hegemony. The kind of Christianity espoused by Eckhart becomes the norm by which modern renditions of Christianity, indeed onto-theological proposals in general, are to be judged. We turn now to a more detailed analysis of each of these three elements. Our focus will be mainly on the first and third elements, with the second element receiving a fairly sketchy treatment. Discussion of the first two elements make up the first section, discussion of the third element the second.

## I.

Though the "eye" passage in the Eckhart citation quite obviously reprises a New Testament mysticism of knowledge, and might also plausibly be read as an illustration—albeit a more than usually dramatic one—of a gnoseological position typical of the high Christian mystical tradition, the fact is the "eye" passage suggests a level of radicality found in neither. Eckhart seems to be implying more than the possibility that we may come to know as we are known in the graced love of God, more than the possibility of the real existence of a mode of cognition neither reducible to sense knowledge nor any modality of knowledge touching on time or matter. Indeed, it can fairly be said that the clear connotation of identity of vision (and/or consciousness) of the human and the divine goes beyond anything actually sanctioned or sanctionable by the Christian mystical tradition even in its most exaggerated deification thrust.[13] In recalling the "eye" passage, therefore, Hegel should not be thought to be engaged simply in approving and recommending an uncontroversially standard Christian mystical avowal, even if it is likely that the earlier as well as later Hegel would support mystical renditions against their contraries. Hegel in fact seems to be taking his stand with a peculiarly radical gnoseological mysticism eccentric to the mainline tradition. That Hegel fully embraces the identity implication in the Eckhart passage and finds its affirmation unproblematic is corroborated by other Hegelian texts where Eckhart is not explicitly recalled. For example, while there exists a dynamic narrative suggestion in the following justly famous passage, in broad respects it is undoubtedly of Eckhartian vintage:

God is God only in so far as he knows himself: this self-knowledge is, further, a self-consciousness in man and man's knowledge of God, which becomes man's self-knowledge in God. (E §564)

Nor is Hegel particularly shy about teasing out the implications of the essential identity of human and divine consciousness and self-consciousness. In the concluding reflections on philosophy at E §§572-7, as well as elsewhere in the text (e.g., E §440z), human consciousness and/or self-consciousness is said to transcend time. Moreover, the eternal dimension of consciousness is pointed to in other Hegelian texts. The eschatological appearance or parousia of absolute knowledge in the *Phenomenology of Spirit*, for instance, connotes the arrival of a form of cognition whose aspect is more than temporal. Similarly, the articulation of the divine logos "before" the creation of nature and finite spirit points to a dimension of being onto-logically prior to time and human temporality.[14]

If the Eckhart-Hegel gnoseological overlap only stretched this far, this would still be a matter of sufficient significance to merit commenting on. But it is possible, perhaps even probable, that an implicit Eckhartianism is even more pervasive in Hegelian texts. Taking Franz von Baader's presentation of Meister Eckhart to his Idealist contemporaries as inscribing the limits or horizon of knowledge of Eckhart in the early 19th century, it is clear that a somewhat more ample profile of Eckhart is culturally available. Proceeding from an understanding of axial Eckhartian ciphers such as the *Gottesgeburt* and the *Fünklein*, Baader can recommend to his contemporaries not only a general religious thinker superbly confident in the human power to know God, but a theologian in the strict sense with quite distinctive recommendations as to how Christians are to understand important biblical symbols such as "son of God" and "image of God."[15] The Eckhartian species of divine sonship and image, championed by Baader, do not, however, appear to be traditional without remainder. The quality of divine sonship, suggested by Eckhart as being a general human prerogative, appears to be more than adoptive, and the theology of image shows evidence of being more than a simple recrudescence of mainline Christian theologies of image with their insistence on the finite character of the image. The *Gottesgeburt* points to a divine action that constitutes the human self as son in the same way as the eternal logos; the *Fünklein* names the real self as co-eternal with the divine and always and already participating in it. For Baader the technical ciphers of Eckhart's theology of sonship and image are mediated by a pair of other less heteronomous sounding terms. Of these terms, one, that is, *Hauchs* or "breath" is still essentially biblical, the other, that is, *Vernunft* or *Vernunftigkeit*, in Eckhartian use names a form of cognition superior to sense or categorial knowledge. In construing *Hauchs* as more or less synonymous with *Geist* or spirit, and fully comprehending the post-Kantian meaning of *Vernunft*, Baader effectively provides Eckhart with a discursive transformation which renders him more assimilatable by Baader's Idealist contemporaries. Given such Baaderian translation, it would obviously be unfair to cavil with Hegel that nowhere is notice provided of the technical ciphers undergirding Eckhartian articulation of sonship and image. It is interesting to observe, however, that Baader, the theist, becomes quite uncomfortable with the radical implications of Eckhart's theology of sonship and image. In fact in recommending the thought of the medieval German monk, Baader appears to be simultaneously engaged in an ameliorative operation in which Eckhart is brought into the fold of mainline option and construal. The brazenness of Eckhart's theology is greatly trimmed in Baaderian presentation by assertion of the qualifier that divine reason or *Vernunft* can only be said to be represented or reproduced in human being (*die göttliche Vernunft sich in ihm nur repräsentirt oder gleichsam reproduciert*),[16] while the non-traditional appearance of Eckhart's theology of image gets corrected by means of the stipulation that the mystical theology of sonship is regulated in the last instance by the specifically Christian axiom of the unbridgeable difference (*unüberbruckbare Differenz*) between the divine and the human.[17]

A brief glance at those texts in the Hegelian corpus where Christianity is made thematic discloses a Hegel who seems to adhere to something like an unexpurgated Eckhartian rendition of a theology of sonship and image. For example, in "The Spirit of Christianity and its Fate" (1799)—written during the period of Hegel's first presumed non-casual encounter with Eckhartian material—the "son of God" symbol not only surfaces in the text, but surfaces in such a way as to recall a peculiarly Eckhartian reading in which the central religious role is displaced from Christ as "Son" unto his "sons" who constitute the Christian community or realize the kingdom of God.[18] Thereafter, this act of pneumatological displacement becomes more or less a fixed move in Hegelian texts, surfacing in the *Phenomenology of Spirit*, LPR, and even in the *Encyclopaedia*.[19] What is especially interesting in the "Fate" essay is that this displacement occurs, as Michel Henry has pointed out, via a reading of John 16.7 in which Jesus insists on the necessity of his going away on the grounds that his sheer physical presence is a screen hiding the divine sonship of human beings.[20] LPR can hardly be claimed to renege on this early christological view. Christ's importance, as the 1824 lectures have it, lies not in himself but rather in his role as mediating the recognition and recuperation of the divine sonship of human beings (LPR 1824 E 222 / G 152). Thus, for the later as well as earlier Hegel the uniqueness of Christ is functional rather than ontological. This being so, "sons of God" represents nothing less than the ontological exegesis of "Son of God." The latter point is, perhaps, most graphically made in a text from his *Lectures on the Philosophy of History* where Hegel is attempting to determine the essential historical significance of Christianity:

> It was through the Christian religion that the absolute idea of God, in its true conception, attained consciousness. Here man, too, found himself comprehended in his true nature, given in the specific intuition of "the Son" (*die in der bestimmten Anschauung des Sohnes gegeben ist*). (Sibree Edition, 333)

The immediately following sentences suggest that this non-traditional theology, effected by the displacement from the "Son" (singular, unique) unto "sons" as essentially constitutive of the "Son," is conjoined to an equally non-traditional theology of image:

> Man, finite when regarded from itself, is yet at the same time the image of God and a fountain of infinity in himself (*ist zugleich auch Ebenbild Gottes und Quell der Unendlichkeit in ihm selbst*).

While it is undoubtedly true that Hegel often proposes a more dialectical view in which human being is considered a *coincidentia oppositorum* of finitude and infinitude—this is especially true when Hegel focuses upon human being and culture under the auspices of development and becoming—the unequivocal embracing of the notion of the essential infinity of human being is far from untypical.

Collateral asseverations are made elsewhere (e.g. LPR 1821 III G 45 / E 109; LPR 1824 G 139-142 / E 207-11; E §441z). The jointure of image and infinity in Hegelian texts effectively disturbs, or to use the term of the literary critic, Harold Bloom, "swerves," the image theology which has been the staple of the Christian West. Specifically, it disturbs or swerves the principle or axiom that regulated all and every theology of image, what Kierkegaard writing after Hegel rendered as "the infinite qualitative difference between the finite and the infinite." If in terms of radicality Hegel's theology of image surpasses anything found in the Augustinianly determined West, it also goes beyond any position legitimated by the *theosis* tradition of the Greek East. For despite a palpably more relaxed attitude to the possibility of human divinization, the Greek East, too, was careful to protect the difference between the finite and infinite and not suppose that commerce went beyond certain strict limits. When the union attained in *theosis* becomes thematic in the theology of the Greek East (e.g., Cappadocians, Pseudo-Dionysius, Maximus) an "insofar as is possible" clause is almost invariably implied when not announced. No such modesty is exemplified in Baader's undomesticated Eckhart, nor in Hegel's Eckhart citation. Similarly, no such modesty is exemplified in those texts where Hegel has Christianity either as the proximate object of analysis or where it is the embedded but transformed configuration in the milieu of philosophy.

There is just one further point I should like to touch on by way of concluding treatment of the first line of sigification extrapolatable from Hegel's Eckhart citation. Whatever the limits of Hegel's knowledge of Eckhart, both structural and personal, it is of no little moment that it is Hegel rather than Baader who draws very Eckhartian conclusions from Eckhartian premises concerning the status of knowledge. Two analytically separable but intimately related corollaries from Eckhart's insistence on the eternity of knowledge or mystical vision are especially worth commenting on:[21] (1) such knowledge represents not simply a privileged anticipation of the eschatological state, but an actual prehension such that the qualitative distinction between the pre-eschatological and eschatological horizon collapses, and the mandated privilege of the "afterlife" vis à vis the mystical state—a staple since Augustine (*De Trinitate*, Bk 15) in the West and the Cappadocians in the East—is subverted; (2) such knowledge, now substituting for immortality, has no durational properties. That the above two-fold swerve from the mainline Christian tradition is repeated in Hegel is clearly in evidence in LPR. Two passages, the first from LPR III, the second from LPR I, are especially important. The first passage clearly seems to be engaged in dismantling the pre-eschatological-eschatological distinction by linking immortality and knowledge:

> The fact of the matter is that humanity is immortal only through cognitive knowledge (*dass der Mensch unsterblich ist durch das Erkennen*), for only in the activity of thinking is its soul pure and free rather than mortal (*sterbliche*) or animal-like. Cognition and thought are the root of human life, of human immortality as a totality within itself. (LPR 1827 III G 227-8 / E 314)

The second passage challenges the traditional durational characterization of immortality, which in Christian representation, Hegel seems to think, is indifferent to the pre-eschatological state-eschatological state distinction. Hegelian departure from mainline Christian construal, including mainline mystical construal, is symptomed by his use of the distancing "to begin with."

> This absoluteness and infinitude of self-consciousness is represented in the doctrine of the immortality of the soul. To begin with, the outstanding characteristic of the latter is duration in time; and in this way immortality, the fact that spiritual self-consciousness is itself an eternal, absolute element, is represented as a sublimation or elevation, a being snatched up out of time. (LPR 1821 I G 105 / E 195)

Starting with the gnoseological signification of the Eckhart citation we have been able to map in a tolerable degree of detail the considerable measure of overlap between Eckhart and Hegel regarding the intrinsic commensurability of the human and the divine. Restrictions of length militate against an equally ample treatment of the second element of signification in Hegel's Eckhart citation. This second element, which involves God and world in a relation of co-implication, for Hegel, validates a position which Hegel had arrived at early in his philosophical career. That the infinite and the finite mutually require each other, each being absolutely necessary for the other's definition, is asserted already in the Difference essay (1802) and thereafter becomes a constant. Traditional philosophical and theological practice of immunizing the infinite from contaminating and "unholy" contact with the finite is condemned by Hegel. On the conceptual level the challenge is made that the practice is inherently self-contradictory, for on the one hand the intrinsic separation of the infinite and the finite manages to finitize the infinite by having something outside it which limits it (a Spinozist point),[22] and on the other the intrinsic separation deprives the finite of an ultimate horizon which is its condition of meaning.[23] On the more nearly representational level that surfaces in LPR and in the comments in the *Encyclopaedia*, Hegel opines that neither the figuration of a worldless God or godless world makes Christian good sense given the centrality of revelation, indeed the centrality of a self-revelatory divine which in turn implies the theophanic character of the world. That Hegel is aware of, and engaged in arguing with, rival interpretations of the infinite-finite, God-world, relation, is disclosed by his sometime recourse to the Platonic Christian trope of the non-enviousness of God (e.g., LPR 1827 I G 23 / E 104).[24] Relationship is intrinsic and symmetrical. Eckhart, accordingly, plays a role in Hegel's rhetorical strategy, i.e., to establish the traditional Christian pedigree of an onto-theological view not shared by many of Hegel's Christian and philosophical contemporaries.

While Hegel was undoubtedly correct in assuming the congruence between his view of the infinite-finite relation and that of Eckhart—however a quite definite echo of Angelus Silesius can be heard in the text quoted by Hegel[25]—it was not unreasonable of 19th century Hegel critics such as Staudenmaier to deny Hegel the legitimacy of his "transcendental relativity" construal. From Staudenmaier's point of view, and in this he probably represents also Franz von Baader's considered opinion, this view is not only constitutionally a minority opinion, it is thoroughly nontraditional or heterodox.[26] Conjecturally, the common "swerve" of Eckhart and Hegel from the presumed traditional standard theistic opinion of the assymmetry in the relation between the finite and infinite plays some role in Carl Schmidt's labelling of the Hegelian system as a form of "pantheism" of an Eckhartian kind.

## II.

While the enlisting of Meister Eckhart against the fideistic construal of Christianity is insufficient to establish the traditional warrant of Hegel's appeal to the necessarily "scientific" character of the theological enterprise, Eckhart does enjoy palpable advantages over other precedents Hegel in LPR and elswhere cites in his favor. For instance, in contrast to the medieval theology (i.e., scholasticism) to which Hegel also makes appeal in the 1824 lectures on religion, "scientific" form in Eckhartian mysticism is (a) tied directly and intrinsically to substantive theological proposals that Hegel finds congenial, (b) seen to imply an intrinsic unity of form and content such that it can be considered as unambiguous between *Verstand* (knowing as consisting of concepts applicative to the spatio-temporal matrix) and *Vernunft* (a mode of knowing transcending *Verstand*'s conceptual restrictions) in a way that the *theologia naturalis* of medieval thought is not. Comparatively speaking, therefore, Eckhart's *critical* ratio is exceptionally high, an opinion shared by, and arguably borrowed from, Franz von Baader.[27] However, this is not to suggest that there is anything like agreement either with respect to the religious thinkers who are the proximate objects of critique, or even the Eckhart who functions as an instrument of critique. For Hegel it is clear in a way that for Baader it is not that the group of religious thinkers most meriting critique (often turning to vilification) are the Romantic Intuitionists (especially Jacobi, also Schelling and Schleiermacher),[28] just as it is clear for Hegel in a way it hardly is for Baader that Eckhartian mysticism is pure kataphaticism, where this kataphaticism serves as the emblem of the "mystical" interpretation of Christianity which Hegel comes to consider normative. The word "irony" is probably too flat to capture the curious and paradoxical nature of an interpretative move in which Eckhart—for Baader a theologian in the last instance of the secret (*Geheimnis*)— becomes a stick with which to beat a degenerate negative theology.[29]

According to Hegel the group of thinkers who admit of being nominated Intuitionists are united by certain constitutive assumptions. One such assumption is that no knowledge, i.e., no discursive knowledge, of the divine is either actual or possible. Every and any form in which Intuitionism makes this claim excites Hegel's ire. Hegel's truculent reply in LPR I to the effect that the position that one can know nothing of God "is an empty standpoint" (LPR 1824 G 173, / E 266) is fairly civilized by comparison with his treatment of Jacobi in *Faith and Knowledge*. In LPR Hegel's main strategy of attack is the consistent attempt to marginalize Intuitionism by removing its putative Christian sanction. The fideistic posture of Intuitionism, Hegel argues, is in flat contradiction to the central thrust of Christianity which is to know God (LPR 1821 G 6-7 / E 87-8; also E §564). A central element of this marginalization strategy is the rendering anachronistic of this particular type of interpretation. Diagnosis of the anachronistic character of Intuitionism's construal proceeds along two fronts. Along one front, Hegel, both implicitly and explicitly, wishes to indicate the specifically modern pedigree of Intuitionism, the *fons et origo* of whose ancestral line is the Kant of the first *Critique*.[30] The rhetorical effect of charting the shallow genealogical line of what in any event is a thoroughly belated phenomenon is undoubtedly to deprive Intuitionism of the warrant that would or could be provided if its view could be shown to have connection with the older theological tradition or traditions (e.g., LPR 1824 G 203-4 / E 299-300; LPR 1824 I G 213 / E 309; LPR 1827 I G 48-50 / E I 131-4).[31] Along another and related front the Intuitionist view is not only diagnosed to be anachronistic in the above sense but *constitutionally* so. That is, such a view would always and ever have been anachronistic given that not only the development of Christianity but originary Christianity speaks against it (LPR 1821 G 6-7 / E 87-88). Constitutionally anachronistic, then, the fideism of Intuitionism betokens a mis-reading in which the "revolution" that defines Christianity is systematically ignored (LPR 1824 G 204 / E 300) and Christianity read in the light of a previous religious dispensation rendered passé in/by the appearance of Christianity. The constitutionally anachronistic (and essentially deforming) character of Intuitionist interpretation is the proximate target in the following well known passage that rivals in viciousness and tone of irritability some of the more offensive polemical expressions in *Faith and Knowledge* and the preface to the *Phenomenology*:[32]

> If it were needful to win back and secure the bare belief that there is a God, or even to create it, we might well wonder at the poverty of the age which can see again in the mere pittance of religious consciousness, in which its Church has sunk so low as to worship at the altar long ago dedicated to the unknown God. (E §73)

Eckhart in a sense plays a critical role which effectively links both aspects of the strategy of marginalization. On the one hand, however he may differ as a mystic from scholasticism, from Hegel's point of view he is a prime exemplar of the medieval dispensation in which theologians were supremely confident in their power to know and elucidate the divine. On the other, Eckhart is a faithful, indeed expert, witness concerning the essence of Christianity as aboriginally given. Hegel, however, does seem to have some sense that the dispute between himself and fideism is not immediately resolved by appeal to the "mystical" or "mystical interpretation" of Christianity, since the sense of "mystical," its intention and allegiances, can themselves become matters of dispute, further elements in the *agon* of interpretation. Thus, in an important sense the interpretative conflict is pushed one step further back.

In LPR I Hegel clearly signals his intention to rescue the "mystical" from its debilitating contact with negative theology and dissociate it from the peremptory legislation of a religious thinker such as Jacobi (also Schelling and Schleiermacher) who insists on the connection of mysticism with hiddenness and unknowability (LPR G 1821 162 / E 254). Hegel in LPR I is not above pure assertion (LPR 1821 G 6, 26 / E 88, 107), no more than he was in the *Phenomenology*. In what seems on the face of it a revisionary claim he had written in the earlier text:

> For the mystical (*das Mystische*) is not the concealment of a secret (*ist nicht Verborgenheit eines Geheimnisses*), or ignorance, but consists in the self knowing itself to be one with the divine being or that this therefore is needed.[33]

In LPR a similar recommendation is implied in Hegel's twinning of *mysterion* and the disclosive *act* of the divine. (LPR 1821 I G 7 / E 88).

As E §73 suggests, Hegel does not rest his case wholly on an assertion. If Hegel is offering what superficially appears to be a revisionary interpretation of the mystical, he wishes at the same time to suggest that this so-called revisionary claim is an ingredient in Christianity from the beginning. In assimilating Intuitionism to the mystery or secret of the unknown God, rendered passé by Paul's preaching of Jesus Christ as the open secret of God, Hegel in an ingenious move is suggesting that his sense of the "mystical" is the revisionary sense provided by Paul, and thus foundational for Christian understanding. Paul, therefore, becomes the agent depriving the connection of hiddenness and mystery of Christian sanction by stipulating the specific difference of Christianity and its qualitatively unique sense of mystery. All apophatic renditions of Christianity, thereby, become illegitimate, signalling regression outside of or "before" Christianity. While undoubtedly Hegel might plausibly have found considerable support for this reading in the Alexandrian tradition,[34] it is the case that the invalidation of the apophatic affects not only Romantic Intuitionism but a tremendously important current in the Christian mystical tradition. The invalidation of the apophatic in its broadest sense is a hermeneutical phenomenon worth commenting on in more detail, and I shall make some remarks presently, but it should be noted here that Eckhart is read as confirming, without any equivocation, the Pauline and, now, Hegelian sense of the mystical as the revelation or manifestation of the divine. Mystery is disclosure without remainder, knowledge adequate rather than inadequate. Thus read, Eckhart in particular and Christian mysticism in general can play the forensic roles they play in Hegelian texts.

Hegel's reading manifestly raises a number of interesting hermeneutic issues. Did Hegel simply misinterpret Eckhart in construing him to be thoroughly anti-apophatic? Is the misinterpretation innocent and based on Hegel's less than expert knowledge of Eckhart and other Christian mystics?

The first question admits fairly readily of answer. When Franz von Baader stressed that for Eckhart the divine was in the last instance a secret (*Geheimnis*), he was indeed registering a more accurate profile of the figure who translated Pseudo-Dionysian apophatic vocabulary into the German vernacular. For instance, in Eckhart's hands the alpha privative of the original Greek finds expression in a suffix like "los," just as the prefix "hyper," which connotes the necessary movement of discourse beyond the categorial frame, becomes the "über" of the German mystical tradition. Moreover, Eckhart, as is well known, does not stop short at recapitulating and translating the Dionysian tradition. Though arguably not without precedent, Eckhart can be said to radicalize this tradition by deigning to refer to the absolute divine by means of the extreme apophatic cipher of "Nichts."[35] Similarly, when Baader praises Eckhartian *Vernunft* he is rightly not maintaining that Eckhart ever insisted on full gnoseological transparence, no more than he is suggesting that *Vernunft* corresponds to any version of discursive knowledge. Hegel's reading of knowledge as trans-conceptual in the Kantian sense brings his view and Eckhart's view into relation, but the relation is one of ellipse. Hegel's view and Eckhart's view cannot coincide, since Eckhart's *Vernunft* more nearly corresponds to Schelling's *intellektuelle Anschauung* than it does to the Hegelian understanding of *Vernunft* as the self-presence of intellectual articulation. In the Baaderian reading of the "eye" passage that so impressed Hegel, the knowing implied is non-knowing, the eye that sees is—hyperbolically speaking—blind.

The second question does not admit of as straight-forward a solution. Hegel's relative ignorance of Eckhart in particular and Christian mysticism in general is a quite plausible explanation for Hegel's highly kataphatic reading. And certainly such ignorance would facilitate Eckhart's and the mystical tradition's enlisting against the much better known enemy, that is, negative theology. Yet certain evidences in Hegel's texts argue against innocence. In the Jena period (1804) in offering his onto-theological proposals, Hegel, as H. S. Harris points out, still does not disdain to use an apophatic vocabulary, a vocabulary which comes to him from the German mystical tradition via Schelling.[36] Words such as *Abgrund*, *Nacht*, and *Nichts* are in play as basic elements of his conceptual machinery. By 1807 constructive onto-theological use of this vocabulary has all but come to an end and the vocabulary as such cease to play a major role in Hegelian texts. Of course, the change of status of apophatic language is a reflection of Hegel's break from Schelling. But nowhere, thereafter, does apophatic language regain its pre-1807 status. Later uses of apophatic language typical of the Jena period in explicitly onto-theological contexts are by and large either purely descriptive or critical. This is certainly the case in LPR. For instance, in speaking of the "night" from which the gods emerge in the 1824 Lectures Hegel does not understand himself to be endorsing Hesodian theogony any more than he understands himself to be siding with Valentinian Gnosticism when the latter posits the "abyss" as arché of the divine and world (LPR 1824 II E 465; LPR 1824 III E 195-196; LPR 1827 III E 288). Though sympathetic to the basic questions of both, in the light of what Hegel says elsewhere he has to be construed as being at least implicitly critical of apophatic valorization of the beginning of divine process. In evoking the Valentinian myth of the primal "abyss" in LPR II and LPR III Hegel has to be read as implying a criticism he makes in the *Lectures on the History of Philosophy*. The language of "abyss" and attendant apophatic valorization is in truth not really mystical language so much as the symptom of the presence of the covert operation of the understanding which itself is responsible for positing the prius of what can be conceptually articulated. The negative of the concept is itself immanent to the concept. If Hegel can be understood to emasculate the onto-theological power of important apophatic ciphers like "night" and "abyss" by limiting their currency and critiquing their basic intention, such is also the case respecting the apophatic cipher "nothing." In LPR "nothing" or "nothingness" only elicits an anthropological register and, never, as far as I am aware, receives onto-theological employment, either positive or negative. Read in the light of Hegelian logic the German Idealist's silence regarding "nothing" and/or "nothingness" is quite eloquent. Indeed, *the logic of Being* could be regarded as containing Hegel's decisive argument against the hegemony in the negative theology and mystical tradition of "nothing" over "being." Hegel resolutely decides for the archeoteleological divine and against the anarchic divine.[37] Moreover, it is "being," or rather its exegesis, that can be understood; "nothing" provides no foothold for discursive articulation. Perhaps it is Hegel's treatment of another mystic, i.e., Jacob Boehme, which suggests most nearly the presence of a systematic operation of the repression and/or erasure of the apophatic in the mystical tradition. For a Hegel, who apparently read some of Boehme's later as well as earlier texts, it is surprising to say the least when in a belated discussion, which is quite detailed, absolutely no mention is made of the abyss *(Abgrund)* or nothing *(Nichts)* or the divine who is nameless *(ohne Namen)*, ungraspable or unknowable.[38]

## Summary

Moving out in concentric circles from the single Eckhart citation in the Hegelian corpus, the attempt has been made to construct a picture of the way in which this particular German mystic is seen to provide something like the authentic *Gestalt* of Christianity in a field of interpretation which obviously demands choice. This does not necessarily mean—Hegel's enthusiastic claim to the contrary—that Eckhart must or even can be understood as fully and adequately rendering the

Hegelian mystical interpretation of Christianity, an interpretation crucial if Hegel is going to legitimate the move from *Vorstellung* to *Begriff.* Hegel's rendition of Christianity is at once too disposed to the value of time and history and the presence of the divine in them, and too dramatic and narrative in its conception of the divine to be summed up in and by Eckhartian mystical rendition or inflection of Christianity. Acknowledging the truth of this, however, may not necessarily involve (a) surrendering really major claims in the "mystical" hypothesis, (b) ignoring the importance of the Lutheran tradition. It may not necessarily do so, since there are in Hegel's day two other important genres of mysticism, the one, i.e., the Joachimite genre distinguished by its *Heilsgeschichte* emphasis, the other by its dramatic, narrative and ultimately trinitarian figuration of the divine, i.e., the mysticism of Jacob Boehme. Thus, if the mystical hypothesis is to work with Hegel, it is plausibly the case that one might have to see his rendition of Christianity as complexly determined or "overdetermined" by not one but three mystical varieties, or in other words triply mystically inflected. This more nuanced hypothesis, moreover, need not put in brackets Hegel's confessed and sometimes sustainable Lutheran allegiance as if it were an embarrassing counter-claim. It would be possible to argue for instance, that in the final analysis the object "Christianity" selected and/or constructed by Hegel is nothing more nor less than Lutheran Christianity triply mystically inflected. Needless to say neither of the above hypotheses will be demonstrated here. Yet their very suggestion does place discussion of the Hegel-Eckhart liaison in a more ample and rich interpretative context, which at one and the same time illuminates both the important contribution made by Eckhartian mysticism for an understanding of Hegelian onto-theology and its limitations.

## Notes

1. This charge was made explicitly by Carl Schmidt in the 19th century. His and other similar 19th century interpretations are recalled by Wolfram Malte Fues in *Mystik als Erkenntnis?: Kritische Studien Zur Meister Eckhart-Forschung* (Bonn: Bouvier Verlag, 1981), 49-59.
2. Cf. Franz von Baader, *Sämtliche Werke*, eds. Franz Hoffmann et al (Leibzig, 1851-1860), Bd 15, 159. Both Wolfram Malte Fues and Ernst Benz assume the

authenticity of Baader's report. For Benz's discussion of the relation of Eckhart and Hegel, cf. *Les sources mystiques de la philosophie romantique allemande* (Paris: Vrin, 1968), 12, 27.

3. By using the locution "disfiguring displacement" I am deliberately trying to steer between two distinct interpretative options regarding the relationship of Marx to Hegel, i.e., between an opinion which suggests that Marx's dialectical materialism merely involves an inversion of the locale of operation of dialectics (from heaven to earth, or spirit to matter) but not a transformation of dialectics itself, and another opinion, represented by Louis Althusser, in which Marx radically rethinks dialectics, dismantles its univocity and comes to regard dialectics as the transformational possibilities inhering in complex fields of tensional force.

4. Cf. G. Lukacs, *The Young Hegel*, trans. Rodney Livingstone (Cambridge, Mass.: MIT Press, 1975). Walter Kaufman, *Hegel: A Reinterpretation* (New York: Doubleday, 1965); Richard Solomon, *In the Spirit of Hegel: A Study of G. W. F. Hegel's Phenomenology of Spirit* (Oxford: Oxford University Press, 1983); Alan White, *Absolute Knowledge: Hegel and the Problem of Metaphysics* (Athens, Ohio: Ohio University Press, 1983).

5. Albert Chapelle does not address in a systematic fashion the question of Hegel's relation to mysticism, but throughout his brilliant study, *Hegel et la religion* (Paris: Éditions Universitaires, 1964-1971), he reverts on a number of occasions to Hegelian recall of Christian mystics such as Eckhart. Frederick Copleston, of course, is not the only Anglo commentator who suggests the affinity between Hegelian speculation and mysticism. Stace obviously heads in this direction as does J. N. Findlay. Cf. F. Copleston, "Hegel and the Rationalization of Mysticism" in *New Studies in Hegel's Philosophy*, ed. Warren E. Steinkraus (New York: Holt, Rinehart, and Winston, 1971), 187-200.

6. Cf. Hegel's *Vorlesungen über die Geschichte der Philosophie*, Teil 4, Philosophie des Mittelalters und der neueren Zeit, ed. Pierre Garniron and Walther Jaeschke (Hamburg: Felix Meiner Verlag, 1986), 78-87, 273-288. While both Jean Hyppolite and Malcolm Clark have suggested the importance of Boehme, only Ernst Benz and David Walsh have attempted in any way to assess the depth of the theological and philosophical overlap. Cf. Ernst Benz, *Les sources mystiques*, 121-2; David Walsh, "The Esoteric Origins of Modern Ideological Thought: Hegel and Boehme," (Ph.D. dissertation, University of Virginia, 1978); cf. also, David Walsh, "The Historical Dialectic of Spirit: Jacob Boehme's Influence on Hegel," in *History and System: Hegel's Philosophy of History*, ed. Robert L. Perkins (Albany: SUNY Press, 1984), 15-35. H. S. Harris and W. Schultz might also be added to the list. Cf. H. S. Harris' *Hegel's Development: Night Thoughts* (Oxford: Clarendon Press, 1983), 184ff., 397-8; W. Schultz, "Begegnungen Hegels mit der deutschen Mystik," in *Sammlung und Sendung. Vom Auftrag der Kirche in der Welt* (Berlin, 1958).

7. Cf. Lawrence Dickey, *Hegel: Religion, Economics, and the Politics of Spirit* (Cambridge: Cambridge University Press, 1987); Henri de Lubac, *La postérité spirituelle de Joachim de Fiore, Tome 1: de Joachim à Schelling* (Paris: Lethielleux, 1979), 218-225. Cf. also the essay by Clark Butler included in the present volume.

8. This point is clearly made by Louis Dupré in his essay, "The Absolute Spirit and the Religious Legitimation of Modernity," in *Hegels Logik der Philosophie*, ed. Dieter Henrich and Rolf-Peter Horstmann (Stuttgart: Klett-Cottal, 1984), 221-233.

9. Most of the authors who connect Eckhart and Hegel in some way are careful not to overstate the historical case. In addition to the authors cited in note 2, cf. Ernst Lichtenstein, "Von Meister Eckhart bis Hegel: Zur philosophischen Entwicklung des deutschen Bildungsbegriff," in *Kritik und Metaphysik* (Berlin, 1966), 260-298; G. Ralfs, "Lebensformen des Geistes Meister Eckhart und Hegel," in *Kant Studien*, suppl. no. 86 (1966); W. Schultz, "Der Einfluss der deutschen Mystik auf Hegels Philosophie," in *Theologie und Wirklichkeit* (Kiel, 1969), 147-177.

10. That is, no claim is being made, for instance, that to the extent to which Hegel admits of a theological reading that Eckhart is taxonomically superior to Luther, nor that Eckhart has superior credentials to a number of other Christian mystical varieties as a descriptor of the kind of Christianity sublatable in *Begriff.*

11. Peter Hodgson makes this observation in a footnote to the English edition at LPR I E 347. Albert Chapelle, however, made the same point a number of years earlier.

12. Cf. Emil Fackenheim, *The Religious Dimension in Hegel's Thought* (Bloomington: Indiana University Press, 1967), 160-222.

13. While the deification tradition in mystical theology was stronger in the Greek East than the Latin West, yet with few exceptions mystical theologians were careful to insist on the natural "createdness" of human beings. Divinization intended a "graced" rather than natural transformation such that human beings could live in the presence of God. Divinization implied no claim of ultimate identity between the divine and the human.

14. The narrative *vor* of the autonomous realm of the divine logos in the *Science of Logic* (Jubiläumsausgabe 4:46) is understood by Hegel in an onto-logical and not in a temporal way.

15. Cf. Franz von Baader, *Sämtliche Werke*, Bd 3, 245; Wolfram Malte Fues, *Mystik als Erkenntnis?*, 44.

16. Franz von Baader, *Sämtliche Werke*, Bd 2, 454; also Wolfram Malte Fues, *Mystik als Erkenntnis?*, 35.

17. Cf. Wolfram Malte Fues, *Mystik als Erkenntnis?*, 36. As a number of Baader scholars have pointed out, Baader tried to avoid the pantheistic implications he found in the mystical varieties of thought he found congenial. It was also a marked difference between his thought and Hegel's, whom he did not believe had an adequate view of the difference of creation. For a good account cf. E. Susini, *Franz von Baader et le romantisme mystique*, in his *La philosophie de Franz von Baader* (Paris: 1942), vol. 2, 283-301, 509-516; vol. 3, 282-298, 344ff.

18. *Early Theological Writings*, trans. T. M. Knox (Philadelphia: University of Pennsylvania Press, 1948; paperback edition, 1971), 266-73.

19. Cf. *Phenomenology of Spirit* §781 (paragraph numbers in the Miller edition); LPR 1821 I G 78 / E 142; E §569. Emilio Brito, Hans Küng, and Dale M. Schlitt are three Hegel commentators who address this particular aspect of Hegel's theological thought. Cf. especially Hans Küng, *The Incarnation of God: An Introduction to Hegel's Thought as a Prolegomena to a Future Christology*, trans. J. R. Stephenson (New York: Crossroad, 1987), 212-220; also Dale M. Schlitt, *Hegel's Trinitarian Claim* (Leiden: E.J. Brill, 1984), 153.

20. Cf. Michel Henry, *The Essence of Manifestation*, trans. Girard Etzkorn (The Hague: Nijhoff, 1973), 438, 333-4.

21. The point here is not that Eckhart is the actual source of Hegel's view, but that he is the Christian thinker who most nearly anticipates a view that is expressed with considerable force in Spinoza. Spinoza has quite definite credentials here as Hegel's source. Cf. *Ethics* Bk 5, Propositions 34-38; Bk 2, Proposition 44.

22. Cf. E §74, §77z, §151z. Of course, Spinoza only goes so far. He too has to be corrected in a dynamic direction. Cf. also LPR I 1821 G 139 / E 230; LPR I 1824 G 211 / E 307.

23. Cf. E §§93-95.

24. Cf. also E §564.

25. Angelus Silesius is a probable popular relay of some of Eckhart's more brazen thoughts. For example Silesius writes: "God is the fire in me and I in Him shine; are we not with each other the most intimately entwined?". Cf. Angelus Silesius, *The Cherubinic Wanderer*, trans. Maria Shrady (New York: Paulist Press, 1986), 39.

26. Cf. Franz Anton Staudenmaier, *Darstellung und Kritik des Hegelschen Systems Aus dem Standpunkte der christlichen Philosophie* (Mainz: Kupferberg, 1844); reprint edition (Frankfurt am Main: Minerva, 1966).

27. Cf. Wolfram Malte Fues, *Mystik als Erkenntnis?*, 35-51.

28. For Hegel's critique of Jacobi, cf. *Faith and Knowledge*, trans. Walter Cerf and H. S. Harris (Albany, NY: SUNY Press, 1977), 97-153; cf. also E §§61-78.

29. Cf. Franz von Baader, *Sämtliche Werke*, Bd 5, 32; Wolfram Malte Fues, *Mystik als Erkenntnis?*, 35-51.

30. The charting of a genealogical line in which Kant is perceived as the primogenitor is most perspicuously rendered in Hegel's foreword to H. W. F. Hinrich's *Die Religion in innern Verhältnisse zur Wissenschaft* (Heidelberg, 1822). For a convenient English translation, cf. the appendix to *Beyond Epistemology: New Studies in the Philosophy of Hegel*, ed. Frederick G. Weiss (The Hague: Nijhoff, 1974), trans. A. V. Miller, 227-244; esp. 235, 242.

31. It should be noted that in LPR 1 Eckhart is viewed as just one example of medieval Catholic theology.

32. Cf. *Faith and Knowledge*, 97-153; esp. 110-120. Schelling, of course, is a major target in the preface of the *Phenomenology* (cf. §16 for an example of Hegel's sarcasm).

33. *Phenomenology of Spirit* §722 (Jubiläumsausgabe 2:550 / Miller translation, 437).

34. Cf. Louis Bouyer, "Mysticism/An Essay on the History of the Word," in *Understanding Mysticism*, ed. Richard Woods (New York: Doubleday, 1980), 42-54; esp. 46.

35. Eckhart's precursor here is in all likelihood Eriugena. For an account of Eckhart's apophatic vocabulary cf. Ernst Benz, *Les sources*, 17-23.

36. Cf. H. S. Harris, *Hegel's Development: Night Thoughts*, 186.

37. Hegel reasons that if "nothingness" is posited as arche, then a mediated beginning becomes impossible. And only a mediated beginning avoids anarchy.

38. Cf. *Vorlesungen über die Geschichte der Philosophie*, Teil 4, 78-87, 273-288.

# 9

# Hegelian Panentheism as Joachimite Christianity

*Clark Butler*

## Joachim de Fiore

I f the forms move and potentiality actualizes itself, Hegel's reputation cannot fully rest on being either the Plato or Aristotle of the
modern world. I shall argue that his originality, if not his reputation,
largely consists in developing the tradition of deplatonicized,
historicized Christian Gnosticism founded in the twelfth century by
the far more obscure figure of Joachim de Fiore. This originality only
secondarily lies in redating the descent of the kingdom of the spirit to
1789. It primarily consists in extending a Joachimite *philosophy of history*
into a Joachimite *philosophy of the history of philosophy* in the *Science of Logic.*

The connection between Hegel and Joachim was noted by von
Windischmann in a 1810 letter to Hegel,[1] and more recently by theologically conservative and liberal scholars alike such as Henri de Lubac
and Michael Murray.[2] My intention is to develop their insight by
showing how Hegel's logic extends the Joachimite philosophy of
history into a philosophy of the history of philosophy.

The logic, which is the soul of the history of philosophy (E §86a),
encapsulates world history (and the philosophy thereof) on the level
of pure thought.[3] Sophoclean tragedy enters Christian theology in the
Joachimite philosophy of history:[4] God himself, as the Father, tragically falls away from the *unspoken* truth of his oneness with nature as
spirit. Yet the tragedy of the fall of God is only episodic, a prelude to
God's epic reconciliation with nature as the resurrected Spirit.

The history of Western philosophy repeats this same movement of
world history. Beginning with the Oriental reduction of the finite to

131

the infinite being of nature among the Milesians,[5] it moves to the Hebraic infinite transcending nature and the finite, and finally to the Christian inclusion of the finite in the infinite of nature as spirit. This same movement is reconstructed in Hegel's logic—the philosophy of the history of philosophy.

## The Individual Determinability of Universal Determinates

I shall attempt to confirm this view by book three of the *Science of Logic*, the logic of the concept. This logic vindicates speculative metaphysical theology against metaphysical skepticism in the logic of essence. It does so by revising the meta-metaphysical assumption of metaphysical theology to read: "The true, infinite universal. . . . *determines* itself freely [non-deductively] . . . *it is creative power.* . . . in particularity . . . the universal is not in the presence of an other, but simply of itself."[6] Restated with W. E. Johnson's distinction between determinates and determinables,[7] it reads: the absolute is definable, not merely under an abstract determinable description, but under a determinable description which necessarily overreaches a logically independent more determinate description.

Each determinable description of the absolute is directly given to one who has followed the logical deduction thus far, while some still more determinate description is given only indirectly, independently discovered by observation, not deduced. The description of having color is determinable as that of having this or that determinate color, which it overreaches but does not logically imply. Of course every general conceptual definition of the absolute (except the first) differs from being colored by resulting from a dialectical construction. Yet it is similar, being true only if necessarily determinable by some more particular description which it does not in particular imply. Being in general implies being determinate, being something, etc., but all that it is in particular cannot be deduced. An object which is colored without being of any particular color is not colored at all. Likewise, if the absolute is defined under one description alone (however complex), it lacks "creative power," self-defining objective being-in-itself. Posited merely one-dimensionally and for us, it cannot surprise us by undeducible self-particularizations.

## The History of Philosophy as Patricide against Plato

Classical Platonism is a theological age of the Father. The great conflict in the history of speculative philosophy, bordering on the tragic when a world-historical nation is fixated on a contradictory assumption in that history, is between (a) the Platonizing thesis that the absolute is fully intelligible under a single exhaustive attribute immediately given to intellectual intuition and (b) anti-metaphysical skepticism. This skepticism correctly denies the reductionistic definability of the absolute under a single such attribute, and thus denies the absolute is intelligible in *abstractly* rationalist terms. If the thesis of the total immediate intelligibility of the absolute is the only recognized form of rationalism, its denial denies metaphysical rationalism generally. The absolute cannot be known as mere pure being because it is *also* something in particular.

If every particular characteristic, as Duns Scotus surmised ("univocity only pertains to general characteristics"[8]), is unique in its individuality, every determinate quality is falsely attributed unless it is individually (non-universally) determinable and thus not open to multiple instantiation. As Nicholas Lobkowicz shows,[9] it is not easy to save Hegel from nominalism. Hegel agrees that universals are contradictory, at most demurring that contradictions truly exist! Occam's insight is at once Hegelian: "This does not follow: `I promise you a horse, therefore, I promise you this horse or I promise you that horse.'"[10] But if I promise a horse in general, the abstract determinateness of what I say I promise is non-deductively and individually determinable as promising this horse, that, or the other horse.

The nominalism of taking the absolute to be indefinably individual, knowable intuitively but not discursively in the historical Jesus or in a purely transcendent Lord, may be called the age of the Son in the history of philosophy.

The absolute, it is perceived, has no merely abstract Platonic essence, such as absolute immediate being or the absolute power of the Lord. Scotus, Occam, Luther, Hume, and Kierkegaard represent this reversal of Platonic rationalism. The logic of the essence defines the absolute as patently contradictory (e.g., mere abstract force *and* its expression, too), and thus points to the absolute's indefinability in the skeptical and nominalist tradition of modern philosophy.

Hegel's *concrete* rationalism ushers in a philosophical age of the spirit. It undercuts metaphysical skepticism by reconciling intelligibility with ever further mediation, denying the immediate intellectual visibility of all descriptions by which the absolute is defined. The metaphysical theology of the concept, however, does more than define the absolute as determinable and self-determining. Otherwise it would not escape the *objective* logic of being and essence. The *subjective* logic of the concept attributes to the absolute not only being-in-itself but being-for-itself—and not only objective but subjective being-for-self. Being-for-itself is not only posited objectively but is actualized in and by speculative thinking. The absolute is self-identical under different ever more particular descriptions. Among them is the description of being-for-itself. The absolute is not simply identical under different attributes like Spinoza's substance; it also *identifies itself with itself* across differences of description.

The transition from objective to subjective logic is complete only when as a speculative logician one recognizes one's own subjective agency in the objective description of the absolute as being-in-and-for-itself. The transition from the objective to subjective logic, from substance to concept, occurs within the logic of essence through the logician's self-reflection. The logician identifies with objective being-in-and-for-itself, whose act of being-for-itself is his own act:

> the actual substance [the absolute as objective] as such, the cause, which in its exclusiveness resists all invasion, is *ipso facto* subjected to necessity or the destiny of passing into dependency: and it is in this subjection rather where the chief hardness lies. To think necessity, on the other hand, tends to melt that hardness. For thinking means that, in the other, one meets with oneself. (E §159)

By the logic of the concept, thought comprehends the dialectical process of world history as autobiographical, the epic story of itself. It identifies with the world in process, and the world through the thinking self thus attains awareness of itself. One reason for translating *Begriff* as "concept" rather than "notion" is that "concept" refers to the self-concept which arises when thought melts the hardness of necessity and becomes "free", "just the ego or pure self-consciousness."[11]

Persons and only persons, Kant held, ought be treated as ends in themselves. The *Logic* adds that the final good, the end in itself, cannot remain a mere "ought". It cannot remain contradictorily finite, internally limited by a world of alien things and impulses. It must be an all-embracing metaphysical absolute *expressed* in the phenomenal world, not limited by it. Infinite goodness cannot belong to what has only finite transient being. Personality has infinite value only if undergirded by the force and might of the cosmos. The essence of religion is this faith that one's deepest aspiration is supported not merely by one's own meager efforts but by the force and might of the cosmos. Might external to right does not make right; but the real possibility of right's coherent actualization—the might of right—puts right to the final test. Though the absolute is not mere power, the good must, as such, have the power to actualize itself:

> The absolute idea [of oneness between the subjective self-concept and the objective world] has now turned out to be the identity of the theoretical [idea of oneness through the cognitive conformity of subject to object] and the practical idea [of oneness through shaping the object into conformity to the subject]. Each of these by itself is one-sided and contains the idea itself only as a sought after beyond and unattained goal. . . . The absolute idea, as the rational [self-]concept [or person] which in its reality coincides only with itself, returns to life in this immediacy of the objective reality; but on the other hand it has equally transcended this form of its immediacy, and contains the highest opposition [of the ideal and the real] in itself. The concept is not only soul but also is free and subjective concept, which is for itself and therefore has personality—the practical and objective concept, determined in and for itself, which as person is impenetrable and atomic subjectivity. Yet at the same time it is not exclusive individuality, but is, for itself, universality and cognition, and in the other has its own objectivity for object. Everything else is error and gloom, opinion, striving, caprice, and transitoriness. The absolute idea alone is being, imperishable life, self-knowing truth, and the whole of truth.[12]

## Personality

Infinite personality, which has its own other for its being, is "being, imperishable life, self-knowing truth, and the whole of truth." The absolute is truly defined as personal. "Everything else is error, gloom, striving, caprice, and transitoriness." Here is the *Logic*'s metaphysical vindication of the infinite value of persons, affirmed from the moral point of view by Kant. Our thought of the absolute is the absolute's attainment through us to the thought of itself. For us, as finite persons, to concretely and truly think ourselves—whether in art, religion, or philosophy—is to tie ourselves in our finitude, in our atomic separateness or "exclusive individuality," back to the infinite.

If we take ourselves to be essentially finite we thereby take ourselves to be *internally* self-limited by an infinite being which lies beyond us. We thus appear to ourselves under an essentially contradictory description, which like all contradictions cannot be maintained and ought be transcended. "Personality lies in the fact that in all my aspects—inner caprice, impulse and desire, as also external determinate being—I this [being] am perfectly determinate and finite and yet am still pure relation to myself, knowing myself as infinite, universal, and free even in finitude."[13]

The last three stages of the philosophy of spirit—of the absolute's self-awareness in humanity—are great art, higher religion, and speculative philosophy. In each the infinite thinks itself in and through finite human agents, enveloping the finite artist, worshiper, and philosophical inquirer. Only persons create art, religion and philosophy, and on this fact are based civil and other human rights necessary to the creativity of absolute spirit. In the context of world history, the logic of the self-concept justifies the central ideological notion of the contemporary world. The *Logic* is the epic reconstruction and metaphysical vindication of our post-1789 identity.

The *Logic*, the most abstract branch of speculative philosophy, is not the philosophy of spirit, and contains no developed account of human rights. Yet it provides the basis for a justification of human rights. For "a free state and a slavish religion are incompatible. . . . Principles of civil freedom can be but abstract and superficial . . . so long as those principles in their wisdom mistake religion so much as not to know that the maxims of reason in actuality have their last and supreme sanction in the religious conscience in subsumption under the consciousness of 'absolute' truth" (E §552).[14] But religion is philosophical truth accessible to all; the content of religion and philosophy is the same (E §573).

Different naturalistic descriptions under which the absolute is found are concealed expressions of one's own inner subjectivity, to be overreached and embraced by that subjectivity—to be comprehended, *begriffen.* To grasp the other conceptually is to identify with it as one's own self in a different form, to embrace it within oneself. This means to find it comprehensible. As speculative philosophers we maintain personhood even by thinking ourselves under the description of being the cosmic substance. "The truth of personality lies precisely in winning it by such submersion, this being submerged in the other" (LPR II E 286). The absolute is endowed with personality. Not finite exclusive personality, but the infinite personality of a person who loses and finds him or herself in the entire objective world. "Everything else is error, gloom, opinion, striving, caprice, and transitoriness."

Kant asserted that there is nothing absolutely good except the good will of persons. Kantian ethics is based on the infinite value of persons as ends in themselves. Hegel shows that a person can have infinite value only if he or she is infinitely actual. Hegelianism is a metaphysical personalism.

## Pantheism to Panentheism

In the history of philosophy the logic of being is pantheistic. It is the pre-Socratic reflection, on the level of pure thought, of the pre-historical age of innocence and oneness with the substance of nature seen in Eastern religion.[15] The logic of essence is theistic in intention but theologically skeptical in result. It is the Joachimite age of the Father—of the Platonic separation of the divine logos from the world, and of the logos made flesh from the departed Jesus of Nazareth. Yet in the logic the age of the Father is raised in the logic to pure imageless thought, despite Hegel's rhetorical use of the *image* of patriarchal lordship.[16]

For Hegel as for de Fiore, the age of the Son does not annul that of the Father. The eternal Son in general is not merely with the Father manifest to pure thought, but exists under the disguise of not being the Father, of being creation, the alien sensory other of pure thought.[17] The individual incarnate Son in his historical contingency, *sent* by the father, prolongs the age of the Father, of the division speculative philosophy heals. The historical Son perpetuates the external authority of the Father, even if with a human face. I must go that the spirit may descend on you, said the Son.[18]

The logic of the self-concept is panentheistic. It reconciles by pure thought the finite and the infinite. Pantheism (e.g., Parmenides) asserts that the absolute is intuitively present in everything. Theism (e.g., Augustine) claims that the absolute is not intuitively present in things but can be thought negatively as beyond things. Panentheism asserts the One in the all and the all in the One. The absolute beyond things is present in them, englobing their process. Spinoza is properly a panentheist, since finite things—the intelligible modes and attributes of the infinite substance—are not illusory; they are contained as finite in the infinite, which they reveal.

Though Hegel did not use the term "panentheism", as Robert Whittemore and Raymond Williamson have seen,[19] it is apt in characterizing the logic of the self-concept or personality vs. being and essence in the history of philosophy. Pantheism and theism deny that finite things as finite provide any positive disclosure of the absolute. Panentheism asserts they provide such a revelation in the developmental process through which the absolute realizes itself.

Since the attribute of thought is not analytically contained in that of extension, the extended substance as such is not spiritual. Yet in fact it shows itself to be spiritual. The substance as extended or material is, in Hegel's reformulation of Spinozistic panentheism, substance in itself; while this same substance as thinking is particularized and developed for itself.[20] In thought, the absolute, nature, comes to exist for itself as the "intellectual love of God," a love by which the absolute loves itself: "the intellectual love of the mind towards God is that very love of God whereby God loves himself, not insofar as he is infinite, but insofar as he can be explained through the essence of the human mind regarded under the form of eternity."[21] Further: "There is nothing in nature, which is contrary to this intellectual love, or which can take it away."[22]

True description of the absolute by its universal character as cosmic substance does not logically imply its particular description as self-knowing in and through us. Yet *some* particular description of the absolute is as necessary to a true definition of it as its universal character. In its particular aspect the absolute develops in a manner not logically necessary given its universal character, and yet which satisfies the logically necessary condition that it develop. Particularization differs from the mutual reference of correlates in the logic of essence: the determinate particularization of the universal, though logically independent of it, is yet embraced within it (E §161).

The progression from being through essence to the logic of the concept can be recapitulated as a progression from tautological identity through non-tautological identity to tautological identity conditioned by non-tautological identity: a=a, a=b, a=a only if a=b. In its abstract universal character, the absolute is tautologically identical to itself under the same universal description: being is being, force is force, the cosmic substance is the cosmic substance, etc. It is, as Hegel says, "free equality with itself" (E §163).

In its abstractly particular character the absolute appears as self-identical under a second description which particularizes the first. For example: force is expression. The particularity of a thing preserves its universal character precisely by giving it a logically independent contingent determination necessary to the truth of its universal character. Force is force as expression. It is only as particularized in such and such expressions that force is confirmed as force, and that what has force exists objectively or in itself.

The absolute as universal is non-tautologically identical with the absolute as particular. The absolute substance = the ego which thinks itself. But such a particular concept is already implicitly the concretely universal concept which integrates both particular and universal concepts.[23] In its concretely universal character the absolute is tautologically self-identical insofar as it is not self-identical merely tautologically: the cosmic substance = the cosmic substance under the more particular description of being self-thinking. Or, as Hegel put it: substance is substance insofar as it is subject.

If the above interpretation is correct, Hegel is a Christian, but not an orthodox one by the Nicene Creed. He denies the precedence of the Father, from whom the Son and the Spirit proceed. He denies that lordship is the meaning of divinity, so that Christ manifests divinity only as the risen Lord. The true definition of divinity is Spirit. But Hegel is not an *ancient* Gnostic like Marcion or Valentinus. He does not denigrate the body as the kingdom of the devil. He affirms the incarnation and construes nature as the logos made flesh, as spirit, i.e., the infinite Christ. He is a modern, Joachimite Gnostic: world history is the story of the logos making itself flesh in the rational state and human rights.

# Faith

I conclude by a definition of faith in the religion of Spirit. Towards the end of his life, as Hegel had completed his life work as a philosopher, his concern turned to greater rapprochement with Christianity. He had never done philosophy in the medieval tradition which proceeded *from* Christianity, but reason had nonetheless spontaneously moved *towards* Christian faith.[24] Kierkegaard made current the notion of an either/or choice between faith and total knowledge (Hegel). Yet Hegel argued not for rejection of faith in favor of knowledge, but for their reconciliation.

This reconciliation is best expressed in Hegel's 1829 review of C.F. Göschel. As William Wallace noted, "after 1827 this religious appropriation of philosophy becomes more apparent, and in 1829 Hegel seemed deliberately to accept the position of a Christian philosopher which Göschel laid out for him."

In this review Hegel epitomized the relation of reason to faith in St. Paul: "I know whom I have believed"— *Ich kenne in wen ich glaube.*"[25] Knowledge and faith for Paul concern the same individual, whose existence is not in doubt. The emphatic object of faith is not anyone's *existence*, but the future *reliability* of someone. Yet Paul's knowledge is knowledge of God under a different description from that under which he refers to God in faith. He knows God under a past description, while he believes in him under a future description. He has knowledge of God's past works in history, and faith regarding his future works.

But this faith is grounded in this knowledge. Because you know your spouse, parent, or child from past behavior you have faith in their future behavior. Because Hegel knows limited actual historical achievements of spirit he has faith that those achievements will be equalled and surpassed. To have faith that spirit is capable of overcoming contradictions remaining in the present is to have faith that it has the power to do so in the future, and will do so. To deny that spirit has this power is to deny that it is the absolute.

Applying Hume's dilemma to Hegel's theory of the absolute, either the absolute will actualize its aspiration for coherence, or it lacks such aspiration, or it lacks the power to actualize it. Definition of the absolute as spirit before the end of history contains an element of faith beyond knowledge.

Scientific knowledge for Hegel is of the past, of the present as a dialectical product of the past, but not of the future. Yet reasonable faith about the future is possible. Because I know spirit to have pursued a past course of progress in the story of freedom, I may believe in new and unprecedented progress. Faith can sustain one in the darkest moments of oppression.

It is of course possible to endorse Hegelian knowledge of past negation of the negation and to be a pessimist, to think that the age of dialectical progress is over, that history will not vindicate the absolute as spirit. But no one with Hegelian knowledge yet lacking Hegelian faith could accept the definition of the absolute as the infinite spirit. For Hegel knowledge issued in faith. People differ notoriously in the degree to which, based on an individual's past behavior, they are trusting. Yet knowledge at least sometimes engenders faith.

Actual reason has redeemed many a finite self-will in the past. Rational faith is a presentiment of the possible reason of the future. It is self-trusting reason, faith in the future work of reason. Salvation by reason is visible in past salvation by the negation of individual absolutization of the finite self. Faith anticipates a future salvation by reason based on knowledge of the past, and it knows the spirit in which it believes.

In conclusion, what von Windischmann, de Lubac, Murray, Whittemore, and Williamson together point the way to is a modern-Gnostic and panentheistic Hegel-interpretation which is still philosophically alive, and which is still Christian even if not orthodox. To be a heretic one must after all first be a Christian.

## Notes

1. *Hegel: The Letters*, translated by C. Butler and Christiane Seiler with commentary by C. Butler (Bloomington: Indiana University Press, 1984), 558 (Hoffmeister letter no. 155).

2. Henri de Lubac, *La Spiritualité de Joachim de Fiore* (Paris: Sycamore, 1979-81), Vol. 2, 359-77; Michael Murray, *Modern Philosophy of History* (The Hague: Nijhoff, 1970), 89-113.

3. *Philosophy of History*, translated by J. Sibree (New York: Dover, 1956), 56. (*Werke*, edited by H. Glockner, Vol. 11, 92.)

4. Christoph Jamme, "Hegel and Hölderlin," *CLIO* vol. 15, no. 4: 361-64, 368.

5. *Werke*, Vol. 17, 19-91, 208. (*Lectures on the History of Philosophy*, Part One, "Introduction" and "Philosophy of the Ionians.")

6. *Logik*, edited by G. Lasson (Hamburg: Meiner, 1963), Vol. 2, 244-45 / *Science of Logic*, translated by A. V. Miller (London: George Allen & Unwin, 1969), 605.

7. W. E. Johnson, *Logic* (Cambridge: Cambridge University Press, 1921), Part 1, Ch. 11.

8. Duns Scotus, *Oxford Commentary on the Four Books of the Sentences*, Book I, in *Philosophy in the Middle Ages*, ed. A. Hyman and J. Walsh (Indianapolis: Hackett, 1986), 605.

9. Nicholas Lobkowicz, "Abstraction and Dialectics," *Review of Metaphysics* Vol. 21, No. 3: 482-83.

10. William of Occam, *Commentary on the Sentences*, Book I, in *Philosophy in the Middle Ages*, 668.

11. *Logik* 2, 213-20 / *Science of Logic*, 577-83.

12. *Logik* 2, 483 / *Science of Logic*, 824.

13. *Philosophy of Right*, #35.

14. From the William Wallace translation (Oxford: Oxford University Press, 1971).

15. See *Lectures on the History of Philosophy*, Section B.1, Introduction.

16. E §112a. Hegel uses "lord" rather than "father" here. Yet patriarchal fatherhood is a form of lordship, and is arguably the genetically first human concept of lordship over human bondsmen.

17. Cf. LPR 1827 416. Joachim himself writes that the age of the Son is ambivalently poised between a "service" which recalls "slave bondage" under the Father and a "grace" which only anticipates the age of the Spirit. Delno West and Sandra Zimdars-Swartz, *Joachim of Fiore: A Study in Spiritual Perception and History* (Bloomington: Indiana, 1983), 17.

18. John 16:1-13.

19. Robert C. Whittemore, "Hegel as Panentheist," *Tulane Studies in Philosophy* 9 (1960): 134-63; Raymond Keith Williamson, *Introduction to Hegel's Philosophy of Religion*. (Albany: SUNY, 1984), 251-94.

20. Thought "separating itself from extension" is a "determinative and formative activity," a "movement which returns to and begins from itself" (*Logik* 2, 164 / *Science of Logic*, 536-37).

21. Spinoza, *Ethics*, Part 5, Proposition 36.

22. *Ethics*, Part 5, Proposition 37.

23. "[P]articularity is immediately in and for itself also *individuality*." *Science of Logic*, 611.

24. G. W. F. Hegel, Review of *Aphorisms* by Göschel, *Werke* 20, 310 / translated by C. Butler, *CLIO* vol. 17, no. 4: 390-91. The second part of the translation was published in vol. 18.

25. Review of Göschel, *CLIO* vol. 18, no. 4: 384; 2 Tim. 1.12.

# 10

# Particularity not Scandalous: Hegel's Contribution to Philosophy of Religion

*Stephen Dunning*

## I.

One of the major contributions of the new critical edition of Hegel's *Lectures on the Philosophy of Religion* is that it demonstrates unequivocally something many have long believed: Hegel himself was constantly reworking his ideas. The notion that he devised a system in which he pronounced the final word on each and every aspect of religion can no longer be legitimately maintained by any serious scholar. We certainly are all indebted to Walter Jaeschke, Peter Hodgson, and the translators of the new edition for the skill and industry which they brought to their task. But, precisely because they have done their work so well, we are confronted with a new problem. For now we must choose which lecture series we shall emphasize, knowing very well that none of them can give a truly comprehensive picture of Hegel's thought on the subject. I agree with Hodgson's choice of the 1827 series for the one-volume edition, although much of Hegel's influence on later thinkers was no doubt through the more derogatory remarks he made about some traditions in the earlier series. I like the 1827 series especially for its clear emphasis upon the particularity, not only of each discrete tradition but also of the truth of religion itself. Given how much Hegel has been castigated as one who sacrifices the particular or the individual to the universal, it is important for us to see that, at least in some of his thinking, particularity received a very important place indeed.

Of course, that is not to claim that Hegel no longer expresses serious reservations about particularity in the 1827 lectures. He is obviously distressed that Tibetans would identify God with anything so specific as the Dalai Lama (LPR 258), and he treats the Hindu pantheon of particular deities as so many bubbles rising out of what he condemns as "the depths of an unethical life" (LPR 291). Rather than taking Hegel to task for these judgments, I want to set them in a context that will hopefully shed some light upon why he reaches the conclusions that he does.

There are a great many dimensions to Hegel's analysis of the problem of particularity, but three are especially important, both in general and in terms of Hegel's concentration upon the issue of our knowledge of God in the 1827 lectures. For the sake of clarity, I shall refer to these as the dimensions of motive, method, and meaning. In each case, Hegel repeats critical remarks that are already familiar from the *Phenomenology* and other earlier works. But in each case he also demonstrates a more balanced position than is often acknowledged, one that does not simply reject particularity but rather affirms it in terms of what Hegel takes to be its proper role.

First, the question of motive. Hegel is convinced that those who claim to know God through their feeling of participation in a particular relationship with Him are simply exploiting the idea of God for their own self-fulfillment. When we claim to know God in feeling, we are so mired in subjectivity that "we take pleasure in ourselves, i.e., in our own fulfillment with the thing" (LPR 138). Having said this, Hegel goes on to connect feeling with bodily existence, a psychological state that amounts to nothing more than agitated blood and a vague warmth in the region of the heart. This is clearly aimed at Schleiermacher's theory that religion grows out of the feeling of absolute dependence. Hegel's antipathy toward such subjectively particularistic claims to knowledge of God finds expression in his comments on Pietism at the end of the 1827 lectures:

> Pietism acknowledges no objective truth and opposes itself to dogmas and the content of religion, while still preserving an element of mediation, a connection with Christ, but this is a connection that is supposed to remain one of mere feeling and inner sensibility. . . . The result of this subjectivity is that everything fades away in the subject, without objectivity, without firm determinacy, without any development on the part of God, who in the end no longer has any content at all. (LPR 486)

The second dimension in Hegel's critique of particularity is the logical question of the method to be used to attain knowledge of God. To focus upon particular predicates of God, argues Hegel, is a recipe for chaos and contradiction. On the one hand, such knowledge is incomplete, for it fails to grasp God as spirit, that is, as one whose is alive and "self-determining" (LPR 412). Hegel is loath to reduce God to an empty, passive center knowable only by its various appearances and external attributes. On the other hand, the predicates themselves will inevitably fall into contradiction with one another (LPR 419-420). Although he does not spell this out, it is easy to see in relation to three predicates that he does mention as examples, namely, the justice, goodness, and omnipotence of God. To say that God is just logically conflicts with belief in God's mercy; to insist upon God's goodness raises the question of God's role in the occurrence of evil; and to affirm the omnipotence of God is to contradict the freedom that God has given to human beings and is therefore bound to respect. In short, to conceive of God in terms of a list of particular predicates will inevitably lead to hopeless contradiction and confusion.

The third and most important dimension is that of meaning. Here the attack upon subjective feeling as motive and the criticism of a particularistic method of predication are united in Hegel's rejection of their concept of God as unworthy in an ethical sense: "Ethical life, love, means precisely the giving up of particularity, of particular personality, and its extension to universality" (LPR 427-428). What must be transcended is the consciousness focused upon "one's own immediate natural state (which subsists in the passions and intentions of particularity," in order to reach the true cultus or worship known as philosophy (LPR 194)! In a very significant passage, Hegel condemns feeling and particularity as the root of all evil:

> If feeling is the justifying element, then the distinction between good and evil comes to nought, for evil with all its shadings and qualifications is in feeling just as much as the good. Everything evil, all crime, base passions, hatred and wrath, it all has its root in feeling. The murderer feels that he must do as he does. . . . Undoubtedly the divine or the religious is in feeling, too, but evil has its own distinctive seat in the heart. This natural particularity, the heart, is its home. But that the human being's own particularity, egotism, and selfhood as such should be legitimated is not what is good or ethical. On the contrary, that is evil. The content must be true in and for itself if the feeling is to count as true. (LPR 143-144)

This reference to content may provide an important insight into just what Hegel is and is not claiming here. He is not stoically opposed to all emotions, for he even carries on from the passage just quoted to discuss the purification and cultivation of feelings. It is not feeling as such that is the target here. Rather, it is feeling that is centered upon particularity, and that refuses to transcend that particularity with the help of thought, that Hegel takes to be evil. When feeling is "purified and cultivated," then the heart wants to know "the genuinely true" which can be learned only "through representation and thought" (LPR 144). Indeed, the nature of thought is such that it can be said to produce "something universal, a universal content" (LPR 120). Whereas feeling as such can offer only an immediate sense of reconciliation, thinking "means reconciledness, being at home or at peace with oneself" (LPR 484).

The claim that feeling can be purified of particularity implies that the distinction between feeling and thought is not, for Hegel, as it often is for us, simply one of heart *versus* head. It is more a distinction based upon the content of the apprehension. If that content is merely something particular or finite, then feeling dominates. If, however, the content is universal, then thought is guiding us. In other words, the distinction between feeling and thought is less a distinction within the subject than it is a distinction between the objects that the subject apprehends. Knowledge, for Hegel, is neither a merely subjective mental state within the subject nor an uninterpreted datum of some allegedly objective reality; it is always a dialectical relationship between the subject and the object.

## II.

Having rehearsed these familiar Hegelian objections to particularity, I must now make good on my title. If Hegel really shows that particularity is not scandalous, how does he do it, and how does that denial relate to the problems of motive, method, and meaning that I have just described?

With regard to motive, Hegel's criticism is not so much a rejection as a qualification. He is happy to affirm particularity, subjectivity, and feeling, when the question is not that of knowledge of God but becomes rather the issue of the cultus, that is, the worship of God. Here the knowledge of God by thought has already been established, and the cultus plays the subsequent role of uniting that knowledge with the concept of God. In other words, here the subjective aspect of knowledge is sublated or *aufgehoben* with the objectivity demanded by the object itself. Rather than merely exploiting God for self-fulfillment, here one is able, through feeling, to participate in the larger truth of God's reality:

> The cultus involves giving oneself this supreme, absolute enjoyment. There is feeling within it; I take part in it with my particular, subjective personality, knowing myself as this individual included in and with God, knowing myself within the truth (and I have my truth only in God), i.e., joining myself as myself in God together with myself. (LPR 191)

Thus, while Hegel criticizes particularity in the knowledge of God as resulting in the subordination of God's truth to one's own pleasure, he understands worship as an activity in which the particular person is taken up into the life of God. Put briefly, in the cultus the particular transcends its own particularity, and thereby attains purification and universality.

The dimension of method may be the most obvious to those familiar with Hegel. As elsewhere in his writings, Hegel reminds us throughout the 1827 lectures that concepts are not merely static entities that reside in this mind or that reality. Concepts are dynamic: they are born, they develop, and they die, often to be reborn as aspects of larger concepts. The normal pattern of this development is described by Hegel as comprising three moments: first, a concept appears in philosophical thought as an abstract concept "in-itself," for example, the concept of religion. Philosophy must always operate on the basis of its own logical foundation, and Hegel believes that he has shown in *The Science of Logic* that this is the syllogism, which begins with a universal premise. The second moment consists in the appearance of particulars which represent the concrete or "for-itself" expressions of the concept. This is where he treats determinate religions, each of which is characterized by some particular concept of God and a corresponding elaboration of beliefs, rituals, and social or ethical values.

As we have already seen, to remain in this moment of mere particularity will consign us to an endless round of contradiction. Each religion will claim to be the true religion, and, since each has its own particular criterion for determining the truth, there will be no way in which to transcend those claims and bring them into a positive relation with one another. However, the moment of particularity does not exist in a static vacuum. It has emerged from the universal concept of religion, and it stands over against it as its negation. It is this contradiction between the universality of the concept of religion and the particularity of the discrete religions that drives the dialectic on to the third and final moment, one in which the universal moment is expressed in a particular, historical religion; and, conversely, particularity is raised to the universal. This third moment is designated by Hegel as the absolute or "in-and-for-itself" moment of individuality or singularity. It is represented in his philosophy of religion by the consummate religion, which he identifies with Christianity, and which he claims is the only religion in which the dialectical unity of the universal and the particular is fully revealed.

I have reviewed this familiar scheme in order to emphasize the logical place that particularity plays in Hegel's system. Without it, the entire dialectic collapses. For all his harsh comments on the logical contradictions and confusions of particularity, Hegel needs and respects it, and he knows that. All of those comments must be understood in their dialectical context, where they can be seen as protests against any effort to lift a given particularity out of its dialectical context and view it as something that, in its very particularity, has universal significance. To put this in religious language, we could say that Hegel is simply rejecting idolatry, that is, all alleged infinites that are really nothing more than exaggerated claims for something finite. But this cannot be taken to mean that he rejects finite particularities as such. They remain essential to the empirical intention of his entire philosophy.

The meaning dimension is the most difficult and intriguing of all. The priority of ethical life dominates the dialectic in the 1827 lectures. Here the darkly pessimistic complaints about the place of philosophers in the contemporary world (in the original 1821 manuscript and thus included in the Speirs and Sanderson translation[1]) are missing. Rather, this series closes with a discussion of the history of Christianity, a history that has passed from the apostolic period of immediacy through the medieval development of the church to its culmination in "the stage of ethical life" in the modern Protestant world. Here the opposition between religion and the world that has emerged and developed in the dialectic of determinate religion is finally overcome: "Thus it is in the ethical realm that the reconciliation of religion with worldliness and actuality comes about and is accomplished" (LPR 484). As we saw above, Hegel's comments on the ethics of particularity are very harsh, and so it should not surprise us that he offers no explicitly ethical antidote to those negative remarks. If we remain strictly within the realm of the ethical, then particularity is evil, a scandal that is no more defensible than sin itself.

But meaning, for Hegel, is not merely a matter of ethics; it is a question of the knowledge of God. The entire series of lectures is a sustained attempt to show how it is the concept of God itself that actually unfolds in the determinate religions, animating each one before moving on to a higher form. Ethical life may be the goal and consummation of all religion, but it is in no sense *a priori*, a mode of knowledge that is *sui generis* or independent of all other knowledge. That Kantian view, which then postulates the existence of God in order to support its moral philosophy, is emphatically rejected by Hegel. For him, it is God who creates and is the very substance of ethical life, and so ethical life is valid only insofar as it is based upon genuine knowledge of God.

Seen in this light, the question of ethical particularity can be transposed into the question of particularity in the concept of God. Does Hegel affirm it? And, if so, does he do so in such a way as to justify a firm denial of the famous scandal of particularity? The evidence in these lectures for maintaining such a claim is admittedly quantitatively thin; but, I believe, it is compelling in a qualitative sense. It is quantitatively thin in that there are really only a few texts that explicitly support my thesis. But the nature of those texts compels me to think that Hegel ultimately affirms particularity in the dimension of meaning every bit as much as he does in relation to motive and method.

The first text in the 1827 lectures occurs near the beginning when Hegel is outlining the abstract concept of God. There he assures us that:

> All through the development God does not step outside his unity with himself. In God's creating of the world, as tradition has it, no new principle makes an appearance, nor is something evil established, something other that would be autonomous or independent. God remains only this One; the one true actuality, the one principle, abides throughout all particularity. (LPR 119)

I suspect that many implicit applications of this notion—that God "abides throughout all particularity"—can be found in the chapters on determinate religion. I have located just one explicit application, one that occurs in Hegel's discussion of Persian religion, and consists in his claim that particularity or determinacy is posited by Zoroastrians "within the One itself" (LPR 299).

It is, however, in his discussion of the consummate religion that Hegel really affirms particularity in the very nature of God. The logical criticism he makes of knowing God through predicates is based upon his belief, as quoted above, that the "vitality of God or of spirit is nothing other than a self-determining," and that this self-determining is no empty abstraction but is "a self-positing in finitude" (LPR 412). These finite determinations of God do indeed fall into logical con- tradiction, but then they are immediately and continuously sublated into the ongoing life of God. As stated above, the problem with defining God by predicates is that it gives the impression that it is up to us to resolve the contradictions, whereas God's "creative energy" is what accomplishes that task (LPR 413). In a stunning, prophetic answer to Feuerbach and so much twentieth century criticism of knowledge of God, Hegel rejects all theories of projection and re- ductionist anthropomorphism:

> It would seem, then, that it is only our human particularity that comprehends specific, distinguishable aspects in God, and that these characteristics are rather just our own. *But the particularity does not merely belong to our reflection; rather it is the nature of God, of spirit, it is his concept itself.* In the same way, however, God is the one who resolves the contradiction—not by abstraction but in concrete fashion. This, then, is the living God. (LPR 413; emphasis added)

Here is the strongest possible affirmation of particularity: it is part and parcel of the very nature of God. If this is the case, then any ethical life based upon the knowledge of God will *de facto* have to embrace particularity also. Hegel does not work that out in the lectures on the philosophy of religion—for that we would have to turn to his *Philosophy of Right*, where the legitimate claims of particular persons within the ethical whole are examined. All that is established here is the foundation for that development, namely, that God is revealed in the particular and the finite as well as in the universal and the infinite.

There is, however, one more development of this idea in the 1827 lectures. That is one of Hegel's favorite theological subjects, the concept of the triune God, for the Trinity is the archetypical expression of his triadic dialectic. It would be a mistake to assume that Hegel affirms the Trinity simply because he is obsessed with triads. On the contrary, the depth and truth of the Trinity resides for him in the fact that it is not an affirmation of three numbers, but of three particular persons. Only a Trinity of persons can express the freedom and subjectivity of God, for "it is the character of the person, the subject, to surrender its isolation and separateness" (LPR 427). But to settle for the sterile opposition of two persons is not satisfactory either. Hegel's argument is that only particularity can make God concrete, and only the third person of the Trinity can sublate the particularities of the first two persons into a concept of God as living, subjective, and free. It is within this discussion of the Trinity that he continues with the comment quoted earlier: "ethical life, love, means the giving up of particularity" (LPR 427-428). But then he goes on to explain that what is given up is only the abstract personality, which is, by virtue of this very movement, won back as concrete: "The truth of personality is found precisely in winning it back through this immersion, this being immersed in the other" (LPR 428).

## III.

Particularity, then, is not scandalous. In Hegel's philosophy of religion, particularity is valid as the motive for worship, as a moment in the method of dialectical development, and as one crucial aspect of the meaning of God. But the question remains: is Hegel really attempting to tame religious particularity by making it rational in a way that betrays its true nature? Is he, like John Toland in *Christianity Not Mysterious*, merely reducing the Christian gospel to conceptual dimensions in order to make it seem palatable to rationalistic philosophers?

Not at all. As his constant—and in these lectures also concluding—remarks about the Enlightenment make clear, Hegel is no less opposed to a barren rationalism of the understanding than he is to the subjectivism of the Pietists. But this brings me to a point where I must severely qualify my entire argument up to this point. It is, I believe, entirely true to Hegel's intention and result. But it also presupposes his theory that reason is distinct from the understanding, a qualification that must now be examined in relation to the question of the scandal of particularity.

One of the themes to which Hegel frequently returns is the distinction between understanding and reason. Without going into his relation to Kant on this issue, let me simply say that he views the understanding as a faculty that is bound by the logic of non-contradiction. As he puts it, "For the nonspeculative thinking of the understanding, distinction remains as distinction, e.g., the antithesis of finite and infinite" (LPR 422). In contrast, the speculative thinking of reason realizes that the finite, as such, is "only a limit," and that "inasmuch as we know something as a limit, we are already beyond it" (LPR 173). In other words, our knowledge of the finite presupposes the infinite and the dialectical relation between finite and infinite. If there were no infinite, the concept of the finite would be meaningless. We designate as finite that which is not infinite, which is cut off from the infinite by its limit. Conversely, we call something infinite in order to assert that it is not finite. To Hegel, this opposition is valid as a moment in the dialectical process of knowledge, but it must not be thought to have the status of an eternal or static truth. (For him, of course, the phrase "static truth" is an oxymoron of the first order.) The error of the understanding is that it views both poles in any binary opposition as absolute, and thus the only relation possible between them is one of contradiction. It is this contradiction that reason sublates in a higher unity, a unity within which both poles are preserved only as moments; moreover, Hegel emphasizes that this unity will forever remain a mystery to the understanding (LPR 422).

From the perspective of speculative reason, then, the particularity of God is a moment within the spiritual unity that embraces also God's universality. For reason, this is not a scandal. But for the understanding, particularity and universality can have no other relation than that of contradiction. From the perspective of the understanding, the alleged unity of particularity and universality is what Hegel calls a mystery and what Kierkegaard will later describe as a paradox, an absurdity. One point that is illustrated by this analysis is that Hegel was a far more paradoxical thinker than Kierkegaard ever admitted; indeed, more than Hegel himself ever really admitted, perhaps due to his use of the rhetoric of speculative reason rather than that of paradox as such.

## IV.

I would like to turn now to the question of Hegel's contribution to the philosophy of religion. I am continually amazed by the impact he has had and continues to have, even upon thinkers who either criticize or try to ignore him. Kierkegaard is known as a prolific anti-Hegelian writer, and yet his own books and thought remain far more Hegelian in terms of their structure and often also their general thrust than he seems to have realized.[2] Karl Barth was both more laudatory of Hegel and also more critical[3]. I wonder to what extent Barth realized how much of his thought also takes the form of an Hegelian dialectic. (One example is the famous article 17 in the *Church Dogmatics*, "Revelation As the Abolition [*Aufhebung*] of Religion,"where Barth posits universal human religion as that which is negated by the particular divine revelation, only to affirm that the end result is a third moment which he calls "true religion."[4]) Such politically oriented theologians as Wolfhart Pannenberg are more willing to admit their debt to Hegel, although sometimes that debt seems to me theologically less profound than in the case of Barth. I cannot develop this thought here. Let me simply suggest that it is one thing to take a doctrine or two from Hegel; quite another to receive from him a way of thinking, even while appearing to reject his doctrines.

There are many areas in which Hegel's belief that we can and must strive "to know the truth in particular things" (LPR 431) has important consequences for the philosophy of religion. I would like to focus upon three of these consequences, two of which seem to me to be challenging in a way that is ultimately helpful, while the third is simply problematic.

The first consequence: Hegel's affirmation of particularity within a dialectic of immediate unity, differentiation, and sublated unity provides a theoretical foundation for engaging in several important tasks. In very general terms, it is this dialectic which undergirds Hegel's entire philosophy of history.

The first task is to approach the particulars of history as an arena of truth and meaning. This insight is, in my view, one of the profoundest implications of the Judaeo-Christian vision. But it was not until Hegel that a major philosopher realized its truth. With him, philosophy came to understand itself for the first time as both oriented toward and determined by the unfolding dialectic of history. Since him, it has become much more difficult to dismiss the particular circumstances and events of history as mere accidents.

A second task follows from this. Hegel believed that the time was ripe for the ancient dichotomy between sacred and profane, between religion and secular culture, to be overcome. Insofar as that dichotomy implies a perspective in which religion is relegated to its own, limited field of activity, I agree with him completely. As Martin Buber put it so forcefully in his discussion of "the man of today,"[5] any religion that cuts itself off from the ordinary and from the relationships in which everyone must live results in a barren and truncated existence.

The third and most significant task is the challenge Hegel issues to us to take seriously all the religions of the world. If we make the dialectic of differentiation within unity our foundation, two things become impossible: one is the exclusivist position of some traditionalists who would maintain that, for example, Christian truth has nothing in common with that of other religions, and that therefore the *only* concern of Christians should be to convert others; the other is the equally one-sided conclusion of, for example, some so-called "perennial philosophers," that all religions are essentially the same, or should be, and that particular differences are merely embarrassing vestiges of the past. Hegel has demonstrated persuasively, I think, that it does make sense to think about the nature of religion in general, and that this can be done responsibly only by taking into account the extraordinary variety of religions.

The second consequence of Hegel's affirmation of particularity is that he, perhaps more than any other modern philosopher, has taught us to think contextually. The intimate connection between ideas and the cultures that produced them and are shaped by them is one that we are still struggling to understand in all of its many ramifications. I have often wondered if the social sciences could ever have developed into academic disciplines without the sort of analysis of societies as spiritual totalities that we see in both the *Phenomenology of Spirit* and the lectures on *The Philosophy of History*. (Hegel might note, of course, that the time was ripe, implying that if he had not come along someone else would have!) In the past twenty-five years, there has been a growing general awareness that social relations—whether between races or classes or the sexes—are not arbitrarily and accidentally related to ideologies, and this dialectic is also one that Hegel anticipated, at least in theory. He was, of course, a man of his times, and a somewhat conservative one at that. But he provided the tools by which we are able now to rethink many of the issues and problems that have bedeviled us for centuries.

I am well aware that Hegel's contextualism seems to imply an ethical relativism that can raise more problems than it resolves. But I really do not see how something of the sort can be avoided. I do not think that all contextualism leads to a situational ethics which can too easily lose the universal moment and thus cease to be an ethics at all. But I also insist, in agreement with both Hegel and Kierkegaard, that we are not in any position to assert absolute knowledge about particular ethical claims. Hegel overcomes the absolute as a discrete entity by identifying it with the whole, while Kierkegaard insists that the absolute is in fact the God who is beyond all human intelligibility. My personal preference is for the Kierkegaardian way of making the point, but one point is the same in either case: we do not have access to the total picture, or to the mind of God, in any simplistic way, especially when it comes to universal ethical problems.

I must now try to express as succinctly and as fairly as I can that third consequence of Hegel's commitment to knowing the truth in particular things, the one that I find so problematic. Here my emphasis shifts from the particularity of the objects of knowledge to the mode of knowing adopted by the subject. There are really two issues here that concern me, the question of religious experience and the matter of language.

As I argued above, Hegel understands feeling and thought not as merely subjective states but as different modes of relating to an object. However, he seems to assume that these two modes exhaust the possibilities. The resulting tension between feeling and thought runs right through the 1827 lectures, from the discussion of the knowledge of God early on to the remarks about Pietism and Enlightenment at the end. It is also a major feature of the *Phenomenology* and other works. It is true that feeling is distinguished from sense experience, and that thought can appear as either understanding or as reason; but the fundamental binary opposition still stands. The only possible unity of feeling and thought that Hegel suggests is to be found in self-consciousness, for there the one self in effect claims and takes responsibility for both feeling and thought. This self-consciousness is what Hegel means by *Geist*, which can be translated as either "spirit" or "mind." Thus the "spiritual" for Hegel is a putative dialectical unity, not a mode of experience that has its own integrity, distinct from both intellectual and emotional experience.

Yet it is precisely the distinctively "spiritual"—whatever that might mean—that makes religious experience so important and unique a subject for investigation. There is no question of denying that both feelings and thoughts play a role in religious experiences, shaping them as well as resulting from them. In that sense, the recent works by Wayne Proudfoot and Nicholas Lash are on solid ground.[6] But they both fail to deal with the fact that William James took so seriously, namely, the role of religious experiences in shaping the development of Christian thought.[7] Accounts of such experiences vary widely, but they seem to share the assumption that whatever happened cannot simply be identified with either the intellect or the emotions. In English, the word "spiritual" is frequently used to describe such experiences, and there are entire traditions of spiritual theology and mystical thought that build upon them. I cannot go into detail on this question here, but I do not think that it can be ignored, as Hegel does when he insists on treating all spiritual experiences as either incipient speculative thought in the manner of Cusanus and Boehme, or as merely subjective feeling, as exemplified (for him) by the Pietist tradition, Hamann, and Schleiermacher.[8] Hegel seems to assume that experiences of the Spirit were genuine enough in the apostolic church, but that subsequently they were formulated in doctrines which now suffice for the edification of Christians (LPR 475). It seems to me, on the contrary, that every generation and every individual must, as Kierkegaard would say, reduplicate in their own existence the ideas that they wish to espouse.[9] And, to take a further step that is often only implicit in Kierkegaard, such reduplication would seem in many cases to involve experiences that cannot be classified as ordinary, whether of the intellectual or emotional variety.

My final question concerns Hegel's treatment of language. His theory of representational language (*Vorstellung*) can be stated briefly, for it is in fact the corollary of his theory of feeling. Both presuppose a dichotomy between the knower and the known, but, whereas feeling exaggerates the subjective side in the knower, representation, like the understanding, over-emphasizes the objectivity of the object known. In myths and religious histories, no less than in universalizing philosophy, consciousness knows its own truth only as other. As Hegel had put it in the 1824 lecture series, representation fails to see "the particular in the universal," but, "in so far as it thinks, thinks only abstractly, thinks only the universal."[10] Thus there can be no dialectical advance to self-consciousness until both feeling and representation, both the particular and the universal, are sublated in speculative reason and the language of philosophy proper.

Now, it is my opinion that Hegel is not being very fair or insightful where narrative is concerned. To assume that the only point of narrative is to illustrate some universal point for thought is, I think, to miss the very magic that the stories of many traditions hold for those who delight in telling and retelling them. The beauty of narrative is its concreteness, the way in which particulars are shown to reveal the universal. It would seem to me that narrative is an ideal candidate for the very sublation of particular and universal—in which each is necessary to the other—that Hegel was seeking. Indeed, has not Hegel himself turned all of philosophy and history and religion into long, breath-taking, narratives? To extract from any of Hegel's texts only the theoretical formulations would be to state his concepts in an utterly abstract and empty way. In the *Phenomenology* and the lectures on religion, history, and philosophy, he is, it seems to me, a brilliant story teller. That is how and why he can affirm particularity as he does. I do not believe that Hegel's program of demythologizing does real justice to his own thought any more than it does justice to the religious narratives to which he applies it. Just as his antipathy to Pietism led him to ignore or downplay experiences of a religious or spiritual nature, that same antipathy made him suspicious of all efforts to express the truth in biblical images or stories. But, by insisting that those images and stories can be fully translated into conceptual language, Hegel risked losing that very dialectical depth—the interplay of universal and particular—that he was trying so passionately to grasp and to express.[11]

## Notes

1. *Lectures on the Philosophy of Religion,* translated by E. B. Speirs and J. Burdon Sanderson (New York: Humanities Press, 1962), vol. III, 151.

2. I have argued this point at length in *Kierkegaard's Dialectic of Inwardness: A Structural Analysis of the Theory of Stages* (Princeton: Princeton University Press, 1985).

3. See Karl Barth, *Protestant Thought from Rousseau to Ritschl,* translated by Brian Cozens (New York: Simon and Schuster, 1959), 268-305.

4. Karl Barth, *Church Dogmatics I, 2,* translated by G. T. Thomson and Harold Knight (Edinburgh: T. and T. Clark, 1956), 280-361.

5. Martin Buber, "The Man of Today and the Jewish Bible," from *On the Bible,* ed. Nahum Glatzer (New York: Schocken Books, 1968), 1-13.

6. Wayne Proudfoot, *Religious Experience* (Berkeley: University of California Press, 1985); Nicholas Lash, *Easter in Ordinary: Reflections on Human Experience and the Knowledge of God* (Charlottesville: University Press of Virginia, 1988).

7. *The Varieties of Religious Experience: a Study in Human Nature* (New York: Collier Books, 1961).

8. I have examined Hegel's criticisms of Hamann in *The Tongues of Men: Hegel and Hamann on Religious Language and History* (Missoula: Scholars Press, 1979).

9. This is a frequent subject in Kierkegaard's writings. For one particularly rich discussion, see *Works of Love,* 261-262.

10. *The Christian Religion,* ed. and trans. by Peter C. Hodgson (Missoula: Scholars Press, 1979), 192.

11. I am grateful to Profs. John Carman and Gordon Kaufman for the invitation to deliver the first version of this paper at Harvard University in May of 1989; and also to Uwe Ritter for his very helpful criticisms and suggestions of that early version.

# 11

# Evil and Dialectic

*William Desmond*

## I.

W hat is the relation of dialectical thinking and evil? Can dialectics explain evil? Certainly Kierkegaard will say no.[1] What about Hegel? Hegel might arguably be called the greatest of dialectical thinkers. It seems to me that evil is both an extremely important issue in Hegel and also a supreme test of claims made for dialectical thought. Below I will look at Hegel's discussion of evil in the *Lectures on the Philosophy of Religion*. But first let me underline the issue's importance. A central reason Hegel is often dismissed relates to this. Hegel's dialectical holism is subliminally identified with something like the rational optimism parodied in Voltaire's Dr. Pangloss. Hegel is Dr. Panlogos who will always see or anticipate a silver lining in the dark clouds of every world-historical turbulence.

Reason rules the world. When this is uttered by Hegel a reactive howl of disbelief goes up. Why? Partly because a brief moment of reflection brings us back to the horror of history and its unrelenting blood and evil. A common picture of Hegel sees him as covering up this recalcitrant reality by dialectical sorcery. But, the claim is, this dialectical sorcery loses the power of its magic spell once we advance from the circle of pure concepts and confront face to face the concrete horror of real evil.

Is this a caricature of Hegel from which he can be freed? Are there deeper complexities in his dialectical interpretation? The crucial question is: Is there something about evil that repeatedly resists all our rationalizing, an otherness recalcitrant even for dialectical reason that puts before all philosophy a limit or boundary to its own discursive rationalizing? In his *Negative Dialectics* Adorno implied no poetry after

Auschwitz, but also no speculative philosophy. Does speculative dialectic then have no future and only a questionable past?

Hegel rejects the view that philosophy should prescribe how reality ought to be. This can be read in a number of ways. It might be read as a canonization of the status quo—social and political, as well as ontological; or as articulating a philosophical contempt for those dissatisfied with reality as it is. To be dissatisfied with the real is to see being as an evil, and to will it to be *other* than it is. By contrast, not to prescribe is to be complacent with the *same*, to refuse radically to think otherness, to rest satisfied in a mystifying quietism. Recognizably this line of interpretation informs the Marxist critique: Hegel's ontological reconciliation blinds us to the evils of social and economic exploitation. If the real is the rational, evil seems to have been blinked. Hence the implicitly *ethical* dimensions of many protests against Hegel. The persistence of such protests is rarely explicable in purely epistemological or metaphysical terms.

Hegelian reason offers a comprehensive and systematic rational account of what is. Can one offer such an account of evil? By the logic of Hegel's claims, we must expect him to offer such an account. The question is: Is there something about evil, is evil a certain other to reason, that subverts every claim to conceptually comprehend it? Is there anything about evil that always remains radically perplexing, radically enigmatic for human minds?

A philosopher significantly reveals or betrays himself in how he responds to this question. In my view Hegel deserves careful consideration. He is not without ambiguity, as we will see. He does not completely shed the propensity to rationalize evil in a manner which raises suspicions of dialectically domesticating it. Still he does this, not by running away from evil, but by trying to incorporate its negative otherness within the dialectical life of reason itself. Properly understood, there can be a fundamental honesty and seriousness to this. Whether it risks neutralization of evil is less clear—I think there is this risk.

There is also the following problem specific to the Hegelian system. Without exaggeration one can say that the place of evil is crucial in the definition of Hegelian philosophy, indeed wisdom. Consider how in the *Phenomenology* Hegel is in search of the standpoint of philosophical science: thought thinking itself in its other and in complete self-transparency to itself. How do we get to this end of absolute knowing, the real beginning of *Wissenschaft?* To get there we have to cross the terrain of evil. Evil names a fundamental alienation, an active antithesis, a hostile opposition between the self and itself, the self and the other, the self and the whole of being. Absolute knowing must surmount such estrangements.

Hence a crucial turning point in the *Phenomenology* occurs in the well-known discussion of evil and forgiveness. I find this discussion ambiguous for the following reasons. One is not always sure whether for Hegel it is the *same one* Spirit that is *both* the evil consciousness and the moral consciousness, or whether there is a real *duality* of consciousnesses here, the one irreducible to the other, such that the forgiveness of one is irreducibly the forgiveness of an *irreducible other.* In the first interpretation, evil would be the evil that Spirit as a *one,* as a dialectically self-mediating unity, inflicts on *itself,* and hence all forgiveness is self-forgiveness. In the second interpretation, evil might be inflicted on an other as genuinely other, and not on just the self in its own otherness; hence forgiveness here would also be a radical gesture of acceptance of the other as radically irreducible to the self. One is unsure if it is the one Spirit that is divided into two extremes at war with each other, or two spirits in extreme war with each other.

Before the end of Hegel's discussion, the second interpretation seems plausible in that we seem to have a genuine duality of "I's." But at the point of forgiveness and subsequently, Hegel speaks, not of a plurality of spirits, but of Spirit as an "I" that has expanded itself into a duality and now in the act of reconciliation has brought back to itself its own alienated extremes.[2] The difference in these two possibilities has serious implications. As we shall see below, Hegel understands evil and hence also its forgiveness in terms of the *dialectical self-mediation* of Spirit; hence also undercutting the radical duality of the other interpretation.

Whichever of these two we accept, only subsequently to this breakthrough in forgiveness can we advance to absolute knowing. Only on the condition of the forgiveness of evil can we be released for genuine philosophical knowing. Hence philosophical science is itself impossible without passing through what looks like radical evil and its overcoming. If this is so, and if we cannot make sense of evil and its overcoming, we cannot make sense of philosophical thought, certainly as Hegel conceived of it. The old adage has it: to understand all is to forgive all. Hegel seems to reverse this and say: to forgive all is to understand all. Only having forgiven the evil other is philosophy as absolute knowing possible.

Hence the question intrudes again: How does dialectical thought help us understand evil and such reconciliation? Is there room, not only for radical evil, but for a radically evil *other*? This, I suggest, is a Hegelian version of Descartes' malign genius. The power of dialectical thinking to acknowledge and deal with radical otherness itself is at issue. We are close to the heart of Hegelian philosophy where dialectical thought, as it were, shakes the foundations of being and mind. Does dialectical thought itself begin to shake? Some of Hegel's most daring claims stand or fall on how we respond here.

The question is not simply the traditional question about theodicy, but the implication of evil for philosophy itself. Hegel did not want there to be any radical other that reason could fail to comprehend. If Hegel refuses any radical other, and if evil is a radical other, albeit a negative otherness, has he finally failed to deal with evil properly? Perhaps dialectic will show or want to show that evil is not a radical other? Or if evil is said not to be a radical other, hence essentially comprehensible, has not Hegel framed evil within a certain conceptual space which serves to neutralize its aweful challenge?

## II.

Let me examine what Hegel says about evil in his Philosophy of Religion. To my knowledge this offers his most extensive discussion of evil, though scattered throughout the large systematic works one finds repeated reference to the issue. This will be my major point: we do not find a simple Hegel, but a double, and I think in the end, ambiguous Hegel. We will see a strongly *existential* side to his treatment. At times one shakes one's head at the Kierkegaardian echoes reverberating in his discussion. But then one remembers Luther and the ancestry of both Hegel and Kierkegaard in Lutheran Christianity, and the echoes become less startling. But this "existential" side coexists with what we might call a "logicist" side. The latter shows Hegel articulating evil in terms of the same rhythm of *dialectical self-mediation* that pulses throughout the system as a whole. From this logicist point of view, evil becomes one moment in the dialectical self-mediation of the concept.

These two sides, the existential and logicist, do not coalesce in a seamless harmony. Perhaps they cannot, and hence their tension cannot be taken as an easy point against Hegel. It would be a point against Hegel, if he were concerned to gloss over the tension. But the drift of his thought is less to gloss over, as to want dialectically to pass through the tension. This means that, teleologically understood, the tension becomes subordinated in the final reconstitution of harmonious accord. Does Hegel so insist on a reconciling telos as to diminish the recalcitrance of evil?

This question will come home to roost in what I see as a third strain in Hegel's account: namely a vision of evil in *world-historicist* terms. Hegel's vision is teleological. Hence as *Geist* deepens its self-knowledge through its own historical unfolding, so also it deepens its sense of evil as a logical constituent of its own dialectically self-mediating concept. This means that the world-historicist strain, in situating evil relative to the panorama of world history, displaces our concerns from the existential side, with its inevitable emphasis on the particularity of the concrete individual, towards the logicist side, with its more insistent emphasis on universality and logical wholes more encompassing than any particularity. The world-historicist strain points to the historical concretion or embodiment of what the logicist strain stresses in its universality. This third strain, then, emerges from the tension of the other two, but in tilting us predominantly towards the universal, it finally underplays the existential side and its recalcitrance to dialectical incorporation in the concept.

Let me briefly outline some main points in the *Lectures on the Philosophy of Religion.*[3] There are three consecutive sections where evil is the major theme. I will underscore Hegel's insistence on the logical necessity of evil. To my question whether dialectic can comprehend evil, Hegel answers: dialectic does not first comprehend evil; rather evil embodies the logic of the concept that dialectical thinking itself comprehends; dialectic comprehends evil only because evil itself is first a concretization of what is necessitated by the self-unfolding of the Idea.

Hegel first takes up the issue in relation to finitude and the natural goodness of humanity. His account follows a discussion of the second moment of the divine life, understood in Trinitarian terms. His treatment is wedded to a focus on the necessity of the finite as such

(LPR III G 218 / E 293). The second moment of the Idea—finite determination in particularity—is logically necessary to the full unfolding of the absolute process, whether we name this the divine life, or the Idea. The emphasis on evil's necessity also applies to the human being. Hegel says that there is a sense in which the human subject exists in a state of untruth. Those who say the human being is good by nature are correct at one level, but they do not attain the deeper conception of man as spirit. For Hegel man as man is spirit, and so is given over to difference and otherness. The human being as spirit is necessarily given over to estrangement from the immediacy of natural being (see LPR III G 222 / E 297-298). Properly speaking, the human being is neither good nor evil by nature; it is simply innocent, in so far as good and evil refer to categories of spirit, and not of nature.

Hegel puts the point by saying that *cleavage* is within the subject. (It is interesting that Hegel uses the word *Entzweiung* here: this is the same word he uses to explain the *origin of philosophy* in the *Differenzschrift*.[4] Recall my remarks above on evil and philosophy.) The human subject is cleavage and to that extent its being is simply contradiction. There is a necessary disjunction between the being of the self as particular and its concept. By a necessity the human being does not initially live up to its concept, and hence lives in evil. The evil which is necessary is simply an ontological structure inherent in the being of the human self, namely, that a sense of internal difference or rupture necessarily defines that being.

Thus Hegel's insistence on the ontological structure of cleavage makes him different, say, from Nietzsche who naturalistically accounts for "bad conscience" in terms of the violence of the animal man on himself. For Hegel I think any naturalistic account fails to get to the point. The ontological structure of cleavage is not static, but ingredient in a dynamic process of differentiation and development. Here the affirmative side of the negative begins to make its appearance. For one is not immediately born an ethical being; one becomes an ethical being; the internal cleavage of evil is necessary to the affirmative realization of this ethical self-becoming.

In the next section, Hegel turns to the religious representation of evil in terms of the *Vorstellung* of the Fall.[5] Hegel refers to the Fall in many places of his corpus (most notably at E §21z) using it to illustrate the logical and ontological necessity of differentiation. The main points to note are: Hegel strongly rejects any interpretation of this representation as historically literal. Further he insists on the importance of *knowledge*. Evil is deeply connected with knowing; the *knowledge* of good and evil is central in the self-development of humanity. Cognition itself proves to be the source of cleavage, the source of evil. Animals lack the self-relation, the free being-for-self in the face of objectivity that marks the knowing human. Hence animals have no sense of ethical evil and good.

Thus Hegel wants want to universalize the implicit meaning of the Fall by freeing its representation from the particularity that is necessarily associated with any *Vorstellung*. For him the issue is original humanity itself, that is, implicit humanity *according to its concept*, not some historical or individual Adam or Eve. Hegel even grants the truth of inherited sin, not in terms of some quasi-biological inheritance but in terms of the implicit concept of humanity. What binds humanity together across a span of temporal becoming is that every human exhibits the ontological structure of cleavage. As Hegel says: all humanity as humanity enters into this cleavage (LPR III G 226 / E 302).

Hegel's emphasis on knowing and necessity is thus also linked to a *dialectical elevation* of the human being through evil. Hegel delights in pointing out that the story of the Fall promises that human beings will become like God in eating of the tree of knowledge. He is at pains to say that this is not contradicted by God who says: look they have become like us. Hegel says: it is *knowing* that makes us gods. The transgression, precisely as necessary, must dialectically be interpreted, not as a transgression that might not have been, but as an absolute necessity that had to be, if the human being were to become the spirit it implicitly is. So this dialectical conception amounts to a radical rational justification of the necessity of evil. What or who rules the world or world-history? *Vernunft*, or *Geist*, or God? Or is it the Prince of Darkness, the serpent Hegel now dialectically exonerates?[6]

The stress on knowledge is also evident in his hermeneutic of the tree of life. The question of *individual* immortality disappears as Hegel relates immortality to cognitive knowledge. Only in thinking and in cognition is humanity immortal. Thus he says: "Cognition and thought are the root of human life, of human immortality as a totality within itself" (LPR III G 227-228 / E 304). This is a conceptual transposition of the religious representation that the religious consciousness might not itself completely accept. There is a dialectical switch of horses in mid race, and the Hegelian horse of universal knowing comes home as the winner, but wearing the number of the religious horse of personal immortality.

In more general terms, we see a tension between a more existential and logicist stress. The existential strain emphasizes the particularity of the will and its living internal cleavage; the logicist strain stresses the dimension of universal structure that is tied up with a cognitivist interpretation of evil. Thus the above sense of universal cognitive immortality is consistent with a noticeable displacement throughout Hegel's discussion in the notion of the will. There is a displacement from will as individual to cognition as implicitly universal; and from immortality as personal perpetuation to the abstract, general immortality of humanity as such. The *this as this*, the singularity somehow at the source of evil, is really only a subordinate moment of the dialectical story or rather dialectical logos, of a whole.

Turning to the next section (LPR III G 227ff / E 300ff.), we have what is, in some ways, the most interesting discussion. Again we see the tension between existential and logicist strains, but now the tension adds a certain dynamic richness. We are forced to qualify the impression that Hegel only reduces evil to a merely abstract cognitive condition. What Hegel means by a condition of knowing is also a condition of being—an ontological condition, not just an abstractly logical one. This should not be unexpected, given that the logical for Hegel contains its own necessary reference to being: the Hegelian concept is onto-logical.

So when I say there is a logicist strain in Hegel's discussion there is no intent to reduce the Hegelian concept to a merely abstract generality. In this third section *being known* implicates a reference to developed *inwardness*. The logical as ontological has an existential reference. In some respects, the result joins Hegel to Kierkegaard, in that Hegel shows himself deeply attentive to the anguish we experience in knowing evil. When we become aware of the living cleavage of contradiction that constitutes evil there is produced the condition of anguish. "Anguish is present only when there is opposition to what ought to be, to an affirmative" (LPR III G 229 / E 305).[7]

But once again a dialectical displacement begins to take over. Now we discover the emergence of the *third strain*, mentioned above. Hegel does not dwell with the inwardness of anguish as an inwardness. Out of the tension of existential particularity and logicist universality, we discover a dialectical displacement towards the stage of *world-history*. Indeed this *world-historicist* strain seems necessary if Hegel is to redeem the promise of his own *teleology* of evil. Were he to have only the existential strain, there would remain something about evil that as pure particularity resists dialectical comprehension, and hence resists dialectical teleology. Were he to have only the logicist strain, Hegel might not completely shake the suspicion that evil as concrete is betrayed in terms of a merely abstract structure. The world-historicist strain intends to rescue Hegel's dialectical account from the imputation of abstract logicism, while at the same time claiming to meet the requirement of concreteness on which the existential strain insists.

Hegel speaks of different ways in which the anguish of knowing evil is registered in terms of a series of historical gradations of inwardization, starting with the Parsee religion which keeps the cleavage external. Thus while the emphasis on the inwardness of evil might seem to align Hegel with the existentialist, the case is more ambiguous. Certainly anyone who speaks as Hegel does must speak from intimacy with the thing itself; there is nothing abstractly objective in his account. That said, one cannot blink the fact that there is a turning away at the level of *content* from individuality as individuality in Hegel's decisive turn to *history*. Let us say that though the tone is "subjective," the content now becomes "objective." The effect is to produce a discourse in which we detect significant tension between the inwardness of evil as experienced in its concrete intimacy and the more public arena of world-history where forces always more universal than the individual play out their dialectic. The individual himself becomes seen in the light of the way different *epochs* understood the antagonism and cleavage and anguish. This emphasis on a world-historical dialectic of evil is not Kierkegaardian.

Hegel notes two forms of the cleavage: one in relation to God; the other in relation to the world. The first is the absolute cleavage, the most radical of all, the one with the greatest depth. It can generate not just a particular or finite anguish; it can generate infinite anguish concerning oneself. Hegel powerfully puts its: "anguish is precisely the element of negativity in the affirmative, meaning that within itself the affirmative is self-contradictory and wounded" (LPR III G 229 / E 306). There is no escape from this, nor from the consciousness that one is not what one ought to be. "And thus the contradiction remains, no matter how one twists oneself about . . . my lack of correspondence to my essence and to the absolute remains; and from one side or the other I know myself always as what ought not to be" (LPR III G 230 / E 307).

When Hegel now invokes the second opposition of evil, namely our antithesis to the world, he refers to the unhappiness (*Unglück*) of this separation. This unhappiness is again dialectical in that its sense of opposition has the effect of pressing the self back into itself. Within itself it finds the demand that the world be rational, a demand that the world in its externality does not seem to satisfy. Here Hegel invokes the Jewish people and their sense of good and evil. Then he turns to the universal unhappiness of the world in the Roman period. The Roman period contributes world-historically as a crucial epochal expression of the antithesis and cleavage in which the self is driven back into itself. The formal inwardness that we find here (LPR III G 232 / E 308; this is also reminiscent of Legal Status in the *Phenomenology*[8]) is not unrelated to Stoicism and Skepticism. These reveal both the sense of humiliation, and the absorption of self in itself. In the Stoic and Skeptic sage the self is supposed to find itself at home with itself. In fact "here antithesis is at its height, and both sides embrace the antithesis in its most complete universality—in the universal itself—and in its innermost essence, its greatest depth" (LPR III G 232 / E 308).

Thus Hegel outlines a sequence of historical instantiations of the sense of cleavage which are dialectically related and ostensibly play out the plurality of possible relations between the self and what is other to itself. The dialectical point is, I suggest, to bring the dynamical cleavage to its most radical expression. This point has just been implied in connection with Stoicism and Skepticism. A reader even cursorily familiar with the *Phenomenology* will detect a markedly similar unfolding in the philosophy of religion. The case often has been made that a turning point in the *Phenomenology* occurs just as this point where also the antithesis is developed to its most radical antagonism. The violent antithesis of master and slave is internalized in the divided consciousness of the Stoic and Skeptic and reaches its most extreme form in the Unhappy Consciousness. In the *Lectures on the Philosophy of Religion* Hegel does not explicitly mention the Unhappy Consciousness but everything that he says fits this figure, as his borne out by his word "*Unglück.*" In his discussion of the cleavage, it is as if the Unhappy Consciousness is not concentrated in *one particular figure* of consciousness as in the *Phenomenology*, but distributed more *universally* in a manner applicable to a plurality of different interpretations of evil in different historical epochs.

In any case, Hegel is very insistent that here we come across the center of evil and anguish, of self-absorption and alienation, of the sense of humiliated finitude and agonizing longing for salvation in a beyond (see, LPR III G 231-233 / E 308-309.) In the *Phenomenology* the theme of the death of God appears at this point. In the Philosophy of Religion the same issue emerges in connection with Jesus Christ and the reconciliation of man and God. Again I suggest that the dialectical rhythm of the concept is Hegel's primary organizing focus in his presentation of the world-historical panorama of evil. Relative to this rhythm, the thought of absolute opposition, while a moment of anguish in itself, is a moment in transition, for it is also the deepest moment of dialectical *reversal.* When we think the absolute opposition through to its extreme, the opposition itself turns around into its opposite—absolute reconciliation.['']

So even on the stage of world history evil, when developed to the extreme of radical rupture, proves to be the penultimate moment of the good, dialectically conceived as the achieved coincidence of opposites. At this point, when the antithesis has been developed to its most universal, its most inward and its most extreme, Hegel brings in the concept of reconciliation. Evil is evil but also it now seems dialectically good.

I do not have space to say anything extensive about reconciliation. Hegel speaks in Christian terms, first in terms of Jesus Christ, and then in terms of the community of spirit. I note this tension between individuality and universality. On the one hand, Jesus is acknowledged as a unique I. On the other hand, Jesus serves as representative of the universality of the unique I which all humans are. The historical Jesus as a unique I is also an individual embodiment of the divine process which is eternal, universal, hence more than merely particular. Inevitably with respect to this second side, the first side, namely, Jesus as a unique I, stands in need of being *aufgehoben* by the philosophical *Begriff*. Thus there is a like tension (between existential particularity and logical and world-historical universality) in Hegel's account of reconciliation, as in his discussion of the Fall.

The same question can be put to both. Is Hegel guilty of having it both ways in first insisting on the unique I but then undercutting that stress by even more strongly insisting on the need of its philosophical universalization? Is this Hegel's duplicity or is it an ineradicable *doubleness* in the matter itself? I find Hegelian doubleness in the striking ambivalence with respect to the putative radical singularity of Jesus. On the one hand, Jesus is said to be irreducibly singular; his singularity is not a singularity in general. Yet this singularity is identified with sensuous immediacy, for Hegel a necessary moment in the appearance of the absolute, the self-particularization of the Idea. Thus on the other hand, despite this ambiguous emphasis on singularity, Hegel later will more explicitly bring out what is here veiled: thus in the third moment of the community/holy spirit, the singularity of Jesus as an historical this is done away with, and the universal holds undisputed sway once again.

In sum: Hegel does offer an extremely complex discussion. I have not exhausted it by any means. His dialectical account of evil essentially follows the logic of the concept as a kind of existential unfolding from the innocent unity of immediacy through the cleavage of conscious-ness and self-consciousness, through the mediation of this cleavage in consciousness itself up to the most radical antithesis, to the third moment of the dialectic when the absolute radical extremes turn towards each other and become reconciled in a dialectical *coincidentia oppositorum*. But this dialectical account inevitably leads to a philo-sophical displacement from existential concerns to logicist and world-historicist perspectives. The question is whether the "reality" of evil in its singularity is subordinated to a larger universal structure. Overall perhaps the best summary might be: Hegel's dialectical account of evil stands between the intimacy of existential pathos and the objectivizing neutralism of world-historical necessity, though the logical necessity of the concept to supersede singularity seems finally to win out.

Hegel says about *Geist*: the hand that wounds is the hand that heals. One asks if this now becomes: Is the Hegelian hand that gives irreducible singularity also the Hegelian hand that takes it away?

Which of these two Hegelian hands is the one that heals and the one that wounds? Is it completely clear which hand offends and which hand reconciles? Are they always the same hand? Must we come to terms with, live with *both* hands? If so, is this an ambiguity, a doubleness in Hegel, or is it essential to dialectical thought? If so, what is the status of a doubleness that seems essential to dialectic, and that also seems ineradicable? If it is thus essential and ineradicable, can dialectical thinking remain solely dialectical when it thinks through its own nature more deeply? Can dialectic then comprehend completely one of the hands: the this as this of evil in the existential intimacy of its inwardness; the *idiocy* of evil in the Greek sense of *idios*, its otherness to the public universal? Can the saving dialectic of Hegel restore to vigor a hand withered to a stump by its own deforming iniquity?

## III.

What of the question put at the outset? Can dialectic explain evil? I think, in fact, that dialectic does not completely comprehend evil, particularly with respect to the inward thisness of the individual will as evil, the idiocy of its negative otherness. Let me offer a few remarks, taken from a more thorough treatment elsewhere.[9]

In Hegel there is the danger of a confusion of being logical with being ethical, to the extent that innocence becomes identified with the logical category of immediacy, and evil with the category of otherness. I am not objecting to the use of those categories to make sense of evil. Hegel's use of these categories is helpful in many ways. The issue is the discontinuity of the category and being evil, whether in that discontinuity something basic escapes the category. The category mediates our understanding of being evil, but the mediation becomes a conceptual blindness when it becomes oblivious to what in evil cannot be mediated, when it forgets what is other to conceptual mediation.

Consider. When I commit an evil act, I can be told, or can tell myself that what has happened, or what I have done, reflects the universal structure of being. This may be true. But it bypasses what I call the *inward thisness or inward otherness* of the evil act as mine. I did the evil act. Neither being nor the concept did the evil act in pursuit of their own inherent rationality. I did the act. I may refuse to own up to this act; but the refusal is my refusal. I may agonize in remorse about the act as mine and seek forgiveness; but it is I who agonize and am sick at heart for having done an irrevocable evil. I may even use Hegelian philosophy to rationalize my act, but the ambiguity, even duplicity of this strategy is already borne by the word "rationalize." There is no consolation in any genuine sense in the claim that evil conforms to the rhythm of rational, dialectical, necessity, for the evil act as mine, I cannot escape myself into any more universal structure. To so escape is in fact to diminish this irreducible otherness of the evil act as a this, between which and all universal structures there is a gap.

The I that confesses "I did that" does not speak as an instance or representative of a universal humanity (which is not at all to deny that the I may share in a universal, communal humanity or that in some respects I may even be representative of humanity). There is about such a confessing I an absoluteness in singularity or a singularity that is absolute. Singularity is absolute in a sense of being *ab solo*: from itself alone. The I that confesses must speak for itself alone. This is the burden and grandeur of such an I. It does not confess as the representative of something other; one cannot confess for another, nor another for one (perhaps one might apologize for another, but that is a different matter). This confessing on one's own behalf is, as we say, literally "to own up to the deed"—no one but the I as singular can own up in this sense. This is what ultimate ethical responsibility means. There is a myness that is irreducible—in the sense of not simply being an instance of a more universal structure or condition.

This is not to say that the I, in the full range of its being, is not also implicated in a whole host of mediating relations which articulate and concretize its relatedness to others. This is entirely consonant with what elsewhere I call a metaxological sense of community.[10] The singularity of the responsible I as confessing and the essential relatedness to others of the being of the self are not antithetical. Indeed without the absolute responsibility of the I as singularity, it is hard to see how the relation to the other can be realized as a properly ethical relation.

Again this is not to deny that often one only becomes a singularly responsible I with the help of the ethical support of the others, that is, because the ethical other has welcomed the articulation of the ethical promise of self-being. I cannot see that we have to choose between this responsibility of the singular individual and deep acknowledgment of the bonds that tie the individual to others. In radically owning up to one's deeds, one may do this before oneself, one may do it before the other.

The singularity of the confessing I is not an inarticulate monad but is internally complex: acknowledging the rupture in itself, the rupture between itself and being that is other, willing to renew its bond with the deeper ethical energies of its own being and the other. It is double in the metaxological sense I have developed elsewhere. A double mediation is at work in the confessing I: its own dialectical self-mediation, and its metaxological intermediation with what is other to itself. Thus too the absoluteness of the confessing I is evident in considering the word "absolute" from another aspect: the absolute singularity of owning up can be experienced as absolving, as freeing, as releasing. Let us say that one owns up in absolute singular responsibility, not only in order to accept the deed as mine, but to ask for release from its evil, to be absolved, to be forgiven.

Consider the following story relative to what I called the idiocy[11] of evil: I read in the newspaper about a child so badly battered by his father that the coroner said that the injuries were more severe than could be sustained were the child run over by a motorcar. The death of this child has no effect on world-history. I read further that the father had left his 3 year old son to die for 3 weeks just before Christmas, after first inflicting the injuries. The boy actually starved to death in his broken body. When I read this report, all I could do was put down my head on the table. A crushing weight descends upon me, like a night of the spirit in which I swoon or black out or go blank. Alternatively, I shudder as if a dark abyss had opening up and swallowed all sense and my sense. My being and mind undergo a liquefaction in which all determinate sense seem to be reclaimed by a malign formlessness. I think that this is the natural response to the enigma of evil. This is the agony of evil.

I can give many psychological, sociological explanations and so forth, for the behavior of the father. He had a deprived childhood, lived in intolerable social circumstances and so forth. These "explanations" help us situate the evil in a more or less determinate context, and to that extent certainly aid us in making it intelligible in some measure. The necessity of our seeking as comprehensive an understanding of such a determinative type is not to be denied. We *must* try to understand to the utmost possible. But such "explanations" become obscene, if they take away from the particularity of the evil suffered as suffered. That is its idiocy as lived from within the intimacy of this horror. True understanding ought to bring us to the limit of this intimacy, not talk its way around it or away from it.

This intimacy of horror is something at the limit of sense or meaning, and our response to it is itself at the limit of sense and meaning. We ought not to fake our metaphysical helplessness here with the bustle of pseudo-explanatory discourse. That is why all I can do is put down my head, crushed under the burden of something that in the end would be obscene to try to rationalize. The evil suffered by this child is an obscene surd, and no rationalization will ever do away with that obscenity. The weight that descends is the night in which the light of spirit is extinguished; but this very night of emptiness and horror is the very sinisterness of evil itself. The response is to be crushed. But being crushed: there is no logic to being crushed; there is no dialectical structure; it is other to logos, other to structure. It is a destructuring indeterminacy, a negative otherness that resists total recuperation in the logic of dialectical concepts.

Do not simply say about evil and being crushed: Where is the argument? Ask: What is that we must *acknowledge* about this recalcitrant yet revealing happening? Is there something elemental in a properly mindful response? Being crushed exhibits a lack of dialectical structure because it is a collapse or retraction of the energy of being, a metaphysical oppression that resist being reduced to any mediated account. As the collapse of the energy of being into an inarticulate void, there is no dialectical logos of being crushed.

The same point might be made from the other, affirmative side of forgiveness. Here there is a leap into trust, but there is no dialectical logos of this leap, if by such a logos we mean a completely mediated articulation. The directionality of the energy of one's being is reversed from being crushed, but is there a dialectical logos of this reversal of directionality? The first is a negative otherness on the edge of dialectical structure; the second is a positive, indeed agapeic otherness which, as leaping, is likewise at the edge of dialectical structure.[12] It is never a dialectical structure that forgives; it is the generous energy of the being of a particular human being, or a God. Dialectic may structurally *flank* these others but it can never be identified with them. In the end both being crushed and leaping into trust cannot be completely said in a discursive way. They are done, not said; they happen. There is no exhaustive logical account or explanation of either.

In so far as dialectical thinking tries to stay true to the living dynamism of things, Hegel is attentive to many of the complex tensions and strains that informs the "reality" of evil. Yet even despite this desire for fidelity to concreteness, the old power of the dialectic swells up and evil becomes annexed to the concept. Then the dialectical explanation of evil, especially in terms of the logical and world-historical universals, risks neutralization of what just previously was named in all its non-neutrality.[13] We find then an objectification of what cannot be objectified. The power of dialectic to stay true to a dynamic process is short-circuited, in favor of the determinate structure that is said to emerge in that process itself.

The concrete "dynamism" in its otherness to thinking has a dimension of idiocy, intimacy of the individual will as individual, that cannot be reduced to any structure, even when it does instantiate universal structures. The consolation of a logic of evil offers itself in place of the irredeemable ambiguity of good and evil as lived from within. My own sense is that if dialectical thought stays true to the dynamic process, there should come a point when, in respect of this process, it acknowledges that something is beyond its power: an other it has not, cannot subordinated to itself. The honest dialectical thinker then says: I cannot make sense of this, try as I may. . .

But you will say: What about the acknowledgment of forgiveness in Hegel himself? True. Hegel is to be commended for trying to think this through. But my point could be reiterated. I have already hinted that forgiveness too, if it is genuine, always exceeds complete dialectical structuring. There is never any rational necessity that one person forgive another; there is a *radical gratuitousness* about the act of forgiveness. This too is a kind of surd, but not the obscene surd of evil. It is, as it were, the benign or agapeic surd.

What I am saying is quite well-known in its elemental intimacy, though perhaps for just that reason it is not always properly made the theme of philosophical reflection. If one attends phenomenologically to forgiveness, one will have little difficulty discovering this gratuitousness. Consider: another has offended, hurt me; my whole being has been insulted by this offense. But the other is sorry and asks for forgiveness. I think we all have the memory, in response to such an appeal, of being able to provide a host of reasons why forgiveness is not reasonable. One says: I will teach him a lesson; this insult is too much and there can be nothing between us anymore; my refusal to forgive will be justice for the first slight and so on.

Reason can becomes extremely busy thinking reasons why forgiveness makes no sense. The matter can be approached from the other side too. Indeed one might marshal all the reasons why one ought to forgive, and yet one may be incapable of forgiving. For forgiving is a willing, between which and reason is a gap. It is a willingness rooted in the intimacy of being. It is in this gap, in this intermediate zone, between reasoning and willing that the gratuitousness of forgiving makes itself apparent.

Indeed, to the self in this between there is a sense in which forgiveness makes no sense. To the rationalizing mind the deeper willingness of forgiving, as rooted in the intimacy of being, may appear idiotic, and in the worst sense. The between creates a kind of ethical epochē. I cannot find an absolutely necessary reason to forgive, an absolutely necessary reason not to forgive. A host of reasons, formal, informal, dialectical, transcendental, might be adduced on either side. But then, perhaps in a sudden moment of softening, I cease to be obdurate and yield: I forgive. Phenomenologically speaking, I believe there is no smooth dialectical transition to forgiveness. It is a leap in the middle, and across a gap that from the standpoint of one side makes no sense, but once having being made, makes absolute sense.

So it is not that forgiveness is simply senseless—Hegel is right in that regard—but something central to its mode of making sense does not have a dialectical structure. Invariably we have to resort to *metaphors* like "I softened, I gave way, I warmed to the other. . ." These point to a leap of trust, of renewed trust in the offensive other. This leap of trust, bringing the energy of willingness to mind from a source of being itself beyond self-mediating mind, is an act of opening to the other that springs out of the intimacy of my being. Again here, the I as the willing I, like the I as the willful I, lives its own being with an inward thisness that is something idiotic—it cannot be included in a system.[14] It precedes any system and exceeds all system. Like the cry from the heart,[15] there cannot be a systematic science of forgiveness, for forgiveness is an act of assent whose most important concrete reality is its thisness as a this.

That we have to resort inevitably to metaphorical language means that the effort to think forgiveness dialectically in terms of the pure concept shows an unavoidable drift back to just that representational language Hegel claims to have overcome in pure philosophical discourse. Willy nilly, the Hegelian concept reveals itself as *continuing* to be in tension with the representational language it claims to sublate. The necessity of the representational language persists. You will say that Hegel takes care of this in so far as his dialectical *Aufhebung* is said always to have a moment of *preservation*. I know this, but this is not my point, not the kind of persistence I am talking about. This persistence is not just a moment of a dialectical *Aufhebung*, for it shows us the continued need of philosophy for its others, indeed the need of the dialectical concept itself for what is other than the concept, and in the concept itself.

This means that the philosophical concept can never be purely thought thinking itself in pure possession of the absolute content and in self-possession of the absolutely pure, that is for Hegel, non-representational form. The other of the dialectical concept is within the concept itself, but not as an other that has been completely *aufgehoben*, hence completely comprehended, but as an otherness than always threatens to explode the pretension to such complete comprehension, should we simply continue to think about this always persistent otherness. The putative sublation of the other carries into its own putative self-transparency a Trojan horse that threatens the viability of all claims to absolute self-sufficiency that pure thinking makes on its own behalf. The other of thought is within the thought that tries to think itself, not as the completely appropriated other, but as a recalcitrant inward otherness that shakes dialectic from within, an inward otherness that produces from within the liquefaction of every claim made by dialectical thinking to absolutely self-sufficient self-mediation.

Thus in forgiveness Hegel is dealing with a happening that is at the edge of dialectical thought. If he still wants to say that this is just what dialectic thought is, namely, as I put it above, that leap across a gap that makes no sense from one side but *mirabile dictu* does make sense from the other, very well. But then we have to clearly acknowledge gratuities, surds, discontinuities within dialectic itself, and so go against the general exclusion or overcoming or attenuation of these by the Hegelian system as a whole. I am not at all averse to the possibility of a kind of *open* dialectical thinking that is the akin other of forgiveness. But then dialectic will have to shed some of the identifying marks that the panlogist Hegel also ascribes to it. Dialectic would be other to dialectic, or be the power to open thought to its own other without sublation. But then I believe it would not be dialectic in the classical and strong sense that Hegel wants to retain.

The question of dialectic and evil is not only a matter of Hegel scholarship, but has a deep ethical and religious, as well as philosophical significance. It concerns an issue that perennially perplexes all thinking human beings and consequently has central importance for philosophy itself. The issue also concerns the ability of philosophical thought to honestly face up to questions that may finally resist its efforts to conceptually master them. This question of how philosophy is to relate to what is other to philosophy is one of the most debated issues in current discussion, since it touches on the very self-identity of the philosophical project, the limits of dialectic in relation to different forms of otherness, and also with the question of the limits of philosophy itself.

I mentioned Adorno when he famously said that after Auschwitz one could no longer write poetry. But he also implied there could be no speculative philosophy after Auschwitz, and this in the context of a development of negative dialectics, in contradistinction to the affirmative dialectics of Hegel. I sympathize with Adorno's efforts to raise the question of the non-identical, the other. I think, however, that he does not do enough justice to the non-identical in Hegelian dialectics itself. He is too impatient to paint Hegel as a philosopher of identity. We have seen sufficient subtlety, richness and complexity in Hegel's view of evil and dialectics to reject the imputation of a mere philosophy of identity.

Is there possible a speculative philosophy of non-identity, a philosophical thinking that lives in an uncompromising acknowledgment of the irreducible others of self-thinking thought? I think the question of evil and dialectic concerns the very future of philosophy and what form its thought can take in the light of this negative otherness. I side with Hegel against Adorno in rejecting the closure of speculative thought after Auschwitz, though I side with Adorno against Hegel in thinking that such speculative philosophy has to be the thinking of the other of thought. It seems to me that the thought of such otherness, in fact, implies the strongest rejection of any putative end of speculative philosophy.

To the extent that the thinking of evil has revealed aspects other to dialectical incorporation, to the extent that evil as an ontological perplexity brings back the old metaphysical insomnia, then speculative philosophy will never sleep easy and its future, as a thought that thinks not just itself but also its others, is not in doubt. If I am right, philosophy did not have to wait until Auschwitz to be made sleepless by monstrous evil. The horror of Auschwitz magnifies into public visibility, if you like into world-historical visibility, that to which we are oblivious in the intimacy of being, the sleeping monstrousness in inwardness itself.

The philosopher does not have to wait for an Auschwitz to ask about the limits of dialectic. Indeed *after* Auschwitz we will soon want to sleep again. As we saw in the father's murder of the son, all that is needed to devastate the pretensions of mastering thought is *one* instance of evil as qualitatively unconditional. The category of quantity has secondary application here, if it has any application at all. One instance of evil as qualitatively unconditional provokes thought in relation to an enigmatic absolute singularity that is not a substitutable, replaceable variable and hence not an illustration of a general thesis.

Suppose such evil only appeared once and once only. Once is enough. There is a break and we are in a different world of thought. There is no going back behind this radical rupture and the sleeplessness of mind it will henceforth always call forth. Once is enough. Once is enough to change everything, certainly enough to force philosophy to ponder its enigma. In fact, it is our forgetfulness of this "Once" that contributes to the precipitation and repetition of the Auschwitzes of world-history. Speculative philosophy henceforth will have to think such enigmas, be on its mindful guard against the oblivion of this "Once." And yet here, in a lesson very other to the Hegelian lesson of sense-certainty, since it is an uncertain lesson in the senseless, our lack of mastery shows itself once more. Why? Because this "Once" is absolutely singular, we are always, almost at once, forgetting it once more. We cannot stand too long the thought of evil. Mind must sleep, else it breaks. And yet, break it must. Without this break there is no idiot wisdom.[16]

## Notes

1. S. Kierkegaard, *Sickness unto Death*, ed. and trans. H. V. Hong and E. H. Hong (Princeton: Princeton University Press, 1980), 119. Kierkegaard is talking about the impossibility of explaining sin speculatively.

The present paper is a shorter version of parts of a longer study which will appear as "Evil and Dialectic: On the Idiocy of the Monstrous," chapter 4 of *Beyond Hegel and Dialectic: Speculation, Cult and Comedy* (Albany: SUNY Press, 1992). Some of the points made, especially in the last part of this piece, are more extensively treated there.

2. *Phänomenologie des Geistes*, ed. J. Hoffmeister (Hamburg: Felix Meiner, 1952), 473 ; *Phenomenology of Spirit*, trans. A. V. Miller (Oxford: Clarendon Press, 1977), 409; hereafter PhG and PS: "For this antithesis is rather the *indiscrete continuity* and *identity* of 'I'='I'; and each, through the very contradiction of its pure universality, which at the same time still strives against its identity with the other, and cuts itself off from it, *explicitly* supersedes itself within its own self. Through this externalization, this knowledge which in its existence is self-discordant returns into the unity of the *self*. It is the *actual* 'I,' the universal knowledge of *itself* in its *absolute opposite*, in the knowledge which remains *internal*, and which, on account of the purity of its separated *being-within-self*, is itself completely universal. The reconciling *Yea*, in which the two 'I's let go their antithetical *existence*, is the *existence* of the 'I' which has expanded into a duality, and therein remains identical with itself, and, in the complete externalization and opposite, possesses the certainty of itself: it is God manifested in the midst of those who know themselves in the form of pure knowledge."

3. I will refer in the text to the lecture series of 1827, unless otherwise stated.

4. See *The Difference Between Fichte's and Schelling's System of Philosophy*, trans. H. S. Harris and Walter Cerf (Albany: SUNY Press, 1977), 89.

5. There is a reversal of the second and third sections between 1824 and 1827; the story of the Fall is second in the 1827 series.

6. In PhG 538 / PS 468, Hegel says that "the becoming of evil can be shifted further back out of the existent world even into the primary world of thought (*Denken*). It can therefore be said that it is the very first-born Son of Light who fell because he withdrew into himself or became self-centered." Here we have

the emphasis on knowledge that distances us from the representation (*Vorstellung*) of evil. See also E §248z, where Hegel assents to Jacob Boehme's account of creation in terms of Lucifer as God's first born Son of Light. In LPR III G 218 / E 293, Hegel mentions Jacob Boehme with respect to the same point.

7. As translating *Schmerz* as "anguish" might be misleading, since we now readily think of *Angst* in Kierkegaard, Freud, Heidegger. In Kierkegaard *Angst* is bound up with sin and the leap from innocence to guilty possibility. See *The Concept of Dread*, trans. Walter Lowrie, second edition (Princeton: Princeton University Press, 1957). There are some interesting affinities with Hegel here.

8. See my "Hegel, Legal Status and Otherness," in *The Cardozo Law Review*, vol. 10, no. 5-6: 1713-1726.

9. See note 1 above.

10. See *Desire, Dialectic and Otherness: An Essay on Origins* (New Haven: Yale University Press, 1987), and *Philosophy and its Others: Ways of Being and Mind* (Albany: SUNY Press, 1990).

11. On idiocy in the sense intended, see *Philosophy and its Others*, index under "Idiot wisdom."

12. On goodwill and agapeic otherness, see *Desire, Dialectic and Otherness*, chapter 7; also *Philosophy and its Others*, 203-205.

13. On Hegel and "aesthetic theodicy" see *Art and the Absolute: A Study of Hegel's Aesthetics* (Albany: SUNY Press, 1986), 150-159. On world-historical exculpation, consider Stalin: you can't make an omelette without breaking some eggs—repeated by the worshippers of Realpolitik who have struggled with their consciences and lost, a loss confessed with a peculiar satisfaction. See Bertolt Brecht, expressing a common attitude on the revolutionary Left:

> With whom would the right-minded man not sit
> To help the right?
> What medicine would taste too bad
> To the dying man?
> What baseness would you not commit
> To root out baseness?
> If finally you could change the world
> What task would you be too good for?
> Sink down in the filth
> Embrace the butcher,
> But change the world: it needs it.

The excerpt is from "The Measures Taken," in *The Jewish Wife and Other Short Plays* (New York: Grove Press, 1965), 96-97.

Relative to Hegel's apotheosis of knowledge, consider the Nazi murderers as "desk killers"; see A. Rosenberg and P. Marcus "The Holocaust as a Test of Philosophy," in *Echoes of the Holocaust: Philosophical Reflections on a Dark Time*, ed. A. Rosenberg and G. E. Myers (Philadelphia: Temple University Press, 1988), 213-215. In his essay ("Holocaust: Moral Indifference as the Form of Modern Evil") in this book, Rainer Baum points out about the commanders of the SS (71): "Products of German universities, 43 percent with a doctorate, they were among the most highly educated of all the leaders of the Third Reich."

14. See *Philosophy and its Others*, 201-205 on the "wolfman" and the refusing will as a wild, lawless otherness.

15. Hegel does acknowledge the heart (LPR 1827 I G 285-291); but reduces it to the level of mere subjective feeling; as the mere feeling of self-particularity, it reveals the undeveloped indefiniteness of immediacy; Hegel says it is a source or "seed" only in this barest sense of implicit immediacy, with all the dangers of subjective caprice. Hegel reduces the heart to a moment of equivocal immediacy within a logic of explicit dialectical self-mediation. I do not disagree with Hegel's view that the "heart" may call for mediated articulation; the whole issue is the nature of the mediation, whether there are mediations other than the dialectical, whether an essential elemental remains recalcitrant to dialectical self-mediation. On the elemental, see *Philosophy and its Others*, e.g. 269ff.; on Hegel and the elemental, 367.

16. On idiot wisdom, see *Philosophy and its Others*, chapter 6. On the "once" and the "never," see also my "Being at a Loss: Reflections on Philosophy and the Tragic," to appear in a volume on philosophy and tragedy edited by Nenos Georgopoulis (London: Macmillan, 1992).

# 12

## Community in Hegel's Philosophy of Religion: From *Bestimmung* to *Verstimmung*

*Sarah Lilly Heidt*

F or Hegel, Judaism was the old wound of the modern age which needed to be healed. Judaism represented the alienated spirit, and the figure of Abraham, in particular, became emblematic for him. In his early defense of the positivity of the Christian religion, Hegel begins with a discussion of Abraham who was called away from his homeland, by God, to wander the desert throughout his life; thus, Abraham perfectly represents the problem of estrangement. The *Early Theological Writings* depict Abraham as harshly separated from his world—almost as a stranger on the earth, or a foreigner everywhere he went. In fact, the nomadic life of Abraham is a point that we must keep in mind. Hegel writes:

> With his herds Abraham wandered hither and thither over a boundless territory without bringing parts of it any nearer to him by cultivating and improving them. Had he done so he would have become attached to them and might have adopted them as parts of *his* world.[1]

As a nomad, Abraham made no ties with the people with whom he came into contact. He struggled against forming a stationary, communal life with others.

This discussion is intended to explore the concept of community in Hegel's *Lectures on the Philosophy of Religion,* and to draw some conclusions regarding the fate of community in modernity. Within this context it may seem a bit strange to reach back into the early writings and begin with the figure of Abraham. But this is necessary for two reasons: first, the alienation of Abraham becomes a model for Hegel's program of reconciliation which will work itself through on many levels, including the reconciliation of state and religion that is to take place through the realization of the spirtuality of the community. Second, I hope that my analysis of community as it appears in the work of Hegel (as well as community as it "disappears" in modern society) will reflect a return to the figure of Abraham in certain ways. As Henry Harris states:

> Through Hegel's speculative comprehension the cycle has closed finally by a self-consciously transcendental return to the historic point of origin of transcendental consciousness.[2]

This return to the historic origin must be explained more fully.

The reconciliation of the Jews with the world is given in Jesus Christ, according to Hegel; Christ overcomes separation through love. He is the mediating factor, and the antipode of Judaic separation which is embodied in the law. While the Jew is portrayed as never at home, always wandering, the Christian seems to be able to make a place for God. Importantly, the death of Christ leads to the transition to spiritual *presence*. The members of the community are supposed to feel the presence of God; the Holy Spirit becomes "real, actual, and present" within the members of the community, and it has its "abode" in them. In short, the community serves as the locus for the presence of God. We must keep in mind that Hegel wants reconciliation on many levels. The *Lectures* are intended to furnish us with the rational cognition of religion. In addition, he there envisions the community as a means to reconcile the ecclesiastical and the secular. Hegel's ideal would have been for religion to pass over into the realm of the state. As he states in the 1831 lecture: "A people that has a bad concept of God has also a bad state, bad government, and bad laws" (LPR I 452). On the other hand, the consummate religion, which recognizes God as Spirit, will necessarily grant to man his fullest freedom, which will express itself in the ethical life of the community. Hegel's 1831 lecture is explicit about this:

> When this cultivation of subjectivity and this purification of the heart from its immediate natural state has been thoroughly elaborated and made an enduring condition that accords with its universal purpose, it is then consummated as the ethical realm, and by this route, religion passes over into ethics and the state (LPR I 451)

For Hegel, religion must overcome the opposition of sacred and secular. As a result, the relationship of the Church to the state was a central focus of Hegel's political philosophy, and appears specifically when the concern is the idea of community. Peter Hodgson makes clear the role of the community in reconciliation: it must be actualized in the world "in the form of rational freedom" as well as within the individual or the church. "The community should not remain simply ecclesiastical, nor will it simply pass away; rather it is to become a world-historical community" (LPR 70).

Reconciliation in life comes to its fulfillment in the ethical realm. Charles Taylor contends that three main points are to be taken from Hegel's doctrine of the primacy of *Sittlichkeit*. First, this must mean that man's most important goals can be attained only within the life of a community and are unachievable on the part of the individual himself. Second, the community cannot be merely partial. This I take to be a very important point, in light of the early ending to the lectures (found in the *Werke* and 1821 Manuscript) which claims that the reconciliation effected by philosophy is "only a partial one, lacking in outward universality" (LPR III 162). Finally, the life of the state supposedly expresses norms that are not merely human creations or conventions. Instead, they represent the ontological structure of things. This fundamental expression of the Idea in the state means that community is necessary to the completion of Hegel's system.[3]

Thus the importance of the fate of community for Hegel's system cannot be overstated. We can see from all of this, that in the end the ethical consciousness of the whole state becomes a form of cult. But this is a big leap which brings to mind questions as to whether Hegel is advocating civil religion, or religion that expresses itself in civil behavior. Here we should remember Hegel's statement that although ethical life is the most genuine cultus, "consciousness of the true, of the divine, of God, must be directly bound up with it" (LPR 194).

But there is a problem here of universality; for it would seem that the ideal of bringing religion and state together as one has become impossible in the modern age. We can look back to Hegel for some clues as to why this had to become an impossibility. The issues of religion passing over into the state are raised in their most complete form in the lectures of 1831, but were certainly not expressed at all in the first lectures which were delivered ten years earlier. In fact, Hegel ends those lectures of 1821 with the "passing away" of the community, rather than its realization.

> But if now, after having considered the *origin* and the *existence* of the community, we see that in attaining realization it falls into a state of inner discord in its spiritual actuality, then its realization appears to be at the same time its *passing away*. But ought we to speak here of a perishing when the Kingdom of God is founded eternally, when the Holy Spirit as such lives eternally in its community, and when the gates of hell are not to prevail against the church? To speak of a passing away would mean to end on a discordant note.
>
> Only, how can it be helped? This discordant note is present in actuality. Just as in the age of the Roman Empire, because universal unity based on religion had disappeared and the divine was profaned, and because, further, universal political life was helpless and inactive . . . reason took refuge only in the form of private rights; or, because what exists in and for itself was abandoned, individual well-being was elevated to the rank of an end—so too it is now. . . .
>
> For us, philosophical knowledge has resolved this discord, and the purpose of these lectures was precisely to reconcile reason with religion. . . . But this reconciliation is only a partial one, lacking outward universality. Philosophy forms in this connection a sanctuary apart, and those who serve in it constitute an isolated order of priests, who must not mix with the world, and whose work is to preserve the possession of truth. How the empirical present day is going to find its way out of its discord, and how things are going to turn out for it, are questions that must be left up to it and are not the *immediate* practical business and concern of philosophy.[4] (LPR III 161-2)

At this point we need to ask: what exactly *is* "community" for Hegel? We know that Hegel attributed to the community some type of "subjective consciousness" which is implicitly universal, not exclusive. The members of the community are unified by their faith and by the fact that they each have a relationship with Christ. This relationship which they all hold in common brings them together intimately; the community is formed by the assemblage of these empirical individuals.[5]

In light of all of this, it seems obvious that when Hegel speaks of a passing away of the spiritual community there is cause for concern. The community has a very important task in that it must make explicit what has been established implicitly. And once again, we are confronted with the concept of place; remember that community is the locus for the becoming-concrete of Spirit. As Harris points out in *Night Thoughts*, the community "must 'keep house' in nature (and particularly on the surface of the earth) as a whole."[6] The subject can become spirit by virtue of the fact that the subject traverses the process by itself. Community, therefore, is necessary to create consciousness of the reconciliation. Finally, Hegel can say that the community itself is "the existing spirit, the spirit in its existence, God existing as community" (LPR 473).

Now we can see the difficulty that lies in the ending of the 1821 lectures. Some would argue that the passing away of the community applies only to individual members who die. The fact that the individual members must perish is undeniable, but I sense that there is more at work in this passage. First, if the "passing away of the community" refers *only* to the death of individual members, it seems that there would be no grounds for so drastically changing "passing away" to "realization" in the subsequent lectures; for there is nothing objectionable in interpreting it as applying only to individuals, and certainly the fact that members must die does not change. There must be more at stake; he must be referring to something other than just the death of individual members. Secondly, and more importantly perhaps, is the fact that even if the community as such does not perish or pass away, Hegel still admits to no universal reconciliation, but rather only a partial one. According to Smith (who was apparently using the second edition of the *Werke*):

> The concluding pages . . . are remarkable in that they strike a discordant note and contain a candid acknowledgement on Hegel's part of the gap between the state of civilization in his time and the Hegelian program of reconciliation.[7]

Third, it seems that Hegel's talk of the passing away of the community was brought on by what Hodgson calls "a rather frightful vision of contemporary Christian decadence and of the collapse of the very secular-religious world into which he believed the community of faith was in the process of being 'transformed'."[8]

The comparison of the present day to the time of the Roman empire seems to have little to do with the fact that individual members of the community must die. Instead, Hegel criticizes the mania for private rights and bemoans the fact the gospel is no longer being taught, i.e., the salt has lost its savor. These criticisms run deep and indicate that something larger than the individual is perishing.

Although his vehement criticisms of the modern age are toned down or eliminated in the following years, vestiges of his dissatisfaction can be found in his discussions of "the two extremes opposing each other in the further development of the community"; that is, the Enlightenment and Pietism. The major criticism of both of these modern phenomena is that they lack, or are said to "volatilize," all content. "The purely subjective standpoint recognizes no content and hence no truth" (LPR 487).

Hegel realized that there were forces at work in his age which paralyzed the development of the community. Seen in this light, the ending to these lectures cannot be but problematic. John Smith writes:

> Hegel was in fact ending his lectures by raising a problem that is far more complex than he could have understood, the problem, namely, whether, and in what sense there can be a Judaeo-Christian civilization or indeed any "religious" civilization. The events of the past several decades have taught us to appreciate both the severity and the urgency of this problem.[9]

Clearly, however, we are aware of what Hegel's eventual vision is for the community. Peter Hodgson puts it most succinctly in his editorial introduction to the lectures of 1827: "The 'community' should not remain simply ecclesiastical, nor will it simply pass away; rather it is to become a world-historical community" (LPR 70).

Nevertheless, the problems that plagued the community in the manuscript of 1821, as well as the problems that it faced due to the religion of Enlightenment and Pietism have not really been overcome. Why, then, should we be optimistic that the community will be realized as world-historical? The problem is formulated by Smith, when he states:

> The problem now concerns the community itself; on the one hand it appears to be involved in such inner disruption that when it becomes actual it also begins to disappear. On the other hand, it is difficult to speak of its destruction because the kingdom of God is said to be founded eternally, and the Spirit is to live forever in its community.[10]

## II.

My contention will be that in many respects Hegel's first analysis of the situation is correct, and that the fate of community in modern society is to pass away. Without citing a laborious amount of evidence disparaging the secularization of the present age, I would like to quote the following statement from Heidegger's "What Are Poets For?" in order to establish the proper mood of urgency to which, I think, John Smith alludes:

> Not only have the gods and the god fled, but the divine radiance has become extinguished in the world's history. The time of the world's night is the destitute time, because it becomes ever more destitute. It has already grown so destitute, it can no longer discern the default of God as a default.[11]

The problems that confront man in modern society are compounded severely when they are no longer even recognized as problems. In my opinion this fate has befallen the concept of community as well. In his book *The Unavowable Community*, Maurice Blanchot speaks of the present age as a time when even the ability to understand the concept of community seems to have been lost.

Let us return to the issue of inner disruption within the community itself, for the problem of what it means for community to "pass away" has not yet been resolved. And even though this is not considered to be Hegel's last stand on the matter, the issue of "passing away" should still be confronted because it does seem that, in actuality, this is its fate. It would be very easy merely to claim that the later version of the lectures which discusses "realization" of community is just restating the idea of passing away within the context of the absorption of the religious community into the state.

However, this interpretation, although it is perhaps valid on some level, cannot fully explain passing away because it would not make sense of the "inner discord" which seems to befall the community. Such disruption seems to break apart the community even before it has a chance to be appropriated by the state. It also seems strange to consider the inevitable death of individual members of the community as inner discord. What then, could it be? I want now to suggest that the disruption which occurs can be seen as a transformation from

*Bestimmung* to *Verstimmung.* Before turning to this directly, however, some preliminary discussion is in order.

My own exploration of the problems facing community in modern society draws heavily from Georges Bataille and Maurice Blanchot, both of whom respond to Hegel in their writings. Much of Bataille's writing and other activity in the 1930's was concerned with the social manifestation of the sacred and the manner in which communities are composed. He was greatly interested in Gnosticism and Christian mysticism, and indeed their influences on his work can be seen, especially in his book *Inner Experience,* the first lengthy treatise of his philosophical concerns in which he discusses rapture, sacrifice, and includes sections on Hegel. In 1932, he attended Kojève's lectures on Hegel, which no doubt influenced his interpretation. Unfortunately, Bataille has too often been regarded as merely a shadowy precursor of post-structuralism. But his critique of Hegel has been influential, largely because he attacks the System from within and argues that Hegel did not know to what extent he was right.[12]

Maurice Blanchot, on the other hand, has produced mostly works of literature and literary criticism. His book *La Communauté Inavouable,* which I am drawing heavily upon in this discussion, is a response to the contemporary French philosopher Jean-Luc Nancy's recent book *La Communauté Désoeuvrée*—a meditation on certain central themes in the work of Bataille.

Bataille's view of Hegel can be traced to two specific issues that when examined closely are intimately related: the inconceivability of absolute expenditure and the incomprehensibility of idleness or unemployment in Hegel's system. First of all, Bataille's criticism that Hegel did not know to what extent he was right has been understood to mean that Hegel was correct in recognizing the importance of the negative, but that he undermined his own insights by insisting that the negativity must be negated as well. Bataille prefers that the negative be allowed to remain, albeit "unemployed." This has been called a "Hegelianism without reserve"—negation cannot be negated. This basic disagreement was the starting point for a great deal of Bataille's writing, both "philosophical" (he would have refused the term) and literary, which made a theme of fruitless expenditure, one form of which is sacrifice. However, absolute expenditure as Bataille would have it would have made no sense to Hegel—it would have been inconceivable within his system.

Instead of fruitless expenditure or loss, the Hegelian system assumes that "work" is being done—one speaks of the "labor" of the negative, for example. Specifically, in connection with the community, Hegel states explicitly that there is a task to be done. He even refers to the eternal "vocation" *(Bestimmung)* of the individual as a citizen of the kingdom of God. Harris, in *Night Thoughts* refers to a life that is "embodied in the institutions which are the work *(Werke)* produced by the community as a whole."[13] The families which make up the community need to be genuinely and consciously involved in maintaining the structure. The activity of the citizens sustains the ethical life of the state, and, therefore, the people see its creation and sustenance as their work. Mark Taylor describes Bataille's survey of the Hegelian situation as follows:

> As Bataille points out, if philosophy is to work, there can be neither *désoeuvrement* (idleness or unemployment) nor *dés-oeuvrement* (something outside work or outside the work). Everyone and everything must work—work properly by working within and for the System. If something does not work, if someone merely plays, if nothing somehow works, the System collapses.[14]

However, the fact that Hegel's philosophy is one of work (something Hegel would no doubt readily admit) is not yet a criticism. What is important is that Bataille saw this as somehow fundamentally profane. Bataille, an avowed atheist, is charging Hegel, the "Christian philosopher," with producing a profane philosophy. There are many facets to this argument, but I will focus on the relation between sacrifice and community. The criticism that Hegel's philosophy is one of work and project means, according to Bataille, that "by taking work . . . for existence [Hegel] reduces the world to the profane world; he negates the sacred world."[15]

Bataille opposes project (i.e., work) to sacrifice, arguing that in project the result matters whereas in sacrifice it is the act itself which has value. Project merely puts off existence until a later point. How does this confront Hegel's view?

The role of the sacrifice of Christ in Hegel's analysis is fairly straightforward. His death allows for the transition into the religious sphere; Christ must die in order for the outpouring of the Holy Spirit to occur. The idea that God himself dies means that the human, the finite, and the negative are part of the divine and that otherness does not prohibit unity with God. The disagreement begins with the idea that death is for Hegel at the same time both a stripping away of the human and the negative, and *is* itself this negative. The finite human element is removed and "what-subsists-in-itself returns to itself." Finitude and negativity are, for Hegel, only a disappearing moment in God. The negativity is negated. "God" as he is in his immanence or his unity within himself, does not die. It is only Christ who dies. What, then, is *death*? It is certainly not taken to its extreme in Hegel's thought, as far as Bataille is concerned.

Bataille views death in a much more radical way by emphasizing the agony of the "lamma sabachtani"—the despair of God. Even the figure of the Father seems to have withdrawn in the final moments and Christ as God dies an absolute death, not just a bodily death. This is not to indicate that Bataille's interpretation would necessarily exclude resurrection. It is only to bring out the point that death and sacrifice are thought in a more radical way in Bataille's writing. He tries to explain (in a tongue-in-cheek fashion) what "death" must mean in the Hegelian scheme:

> The privileged manifestation of Negativity is death, but death, in truth, reveals nothing. In principle, death reveals to Man his natural, animal being, but the revelation never takes place. . . . For man finally to be revealed to himself he would have to die, but he would have to do so while living—while watching himself cease to be. In other words, death itself would have to become (self)-consciousness at the very moment when it annihilates conscious being. . . . Thus it is necessary for him to live with the impression of truly dying.[16]

For Bataille, however, the sacrifice is seen as an expenditure or loss that cannot be recouped, that cannot be put to work.

For Hegel, community and sacrifice are linked in several ways. As we have seen, the members interiorize the sacrifice in the form of repentance. But, additionally, the actual act of the sacrifice seems to found the community. This is fairly clear in the LPR in that the death, resurrection, and ascension of Christ are given a spiritual interpretation by the community which recognizes the reconciliation effected by Christ. Blanchot, in *The Unavowable Community* also refers to the "sacrifice that founds the community." Death itself is at the core of the community. But, as Blanchot explains:

> To remain present in the proximity of another who by dying removes himself definitively, to take upon myself another's death as the only death that concerns me, this is what puts me beside myself, this is the only separation that can open me, in its very impossibility, to the Openness of a community.[17]

This death, I take it, is absolute death, or radical negativity.

How then, does this later analysis of sacrifice (which serves as the ostensible figure for an investigation of death, and therefore for Negativity itself) affect the resulting "community"? First of all, in Hegel's "economy" the negation of negativity or otherness leaves us with homogeneity. The community as such will have no "other" because it will naturally be appropriated in the state. However, the community of which Blanchot speaks exposes itself to alterity—so much so, in fact, that the community "includes the exteriority"—a fate that Hegel also sensed, but was unable to capture.

Hegel spoke of the disappearing moment of negativity in God—the death of Christ that leads to the spiritual presence in community. But perhaps community does not allow that moment of negativity to disappear. In the movement of the life of the community which eventually produces the content for itself from out of itself, this community would inscribe within its proper content the radical negativity of the sacrifice and thus retain that moment. In the moment of sacrifice, for Hegel, the negative *works* and likewise the community has a job to do in that it must traverse the divine process in itself. Remember that when the community is first originated, the "content, the history and the truth of the community is distinguished from them and stands over against them" (LPR 471). Bataille, too, would agree to a certain extent that we must traverse the divine process, as can be seen by his reference to the advice of St. John of the Cross who said that in imitating Jesus we must also imitate his fall from grace, his agony, and his despair—the "lamma sabachtani." However, when such a community appropriates *this* content as its own, the results must be completely different than those which Hegel had both anticipated and questioned. Negativity in Bataille's description is "unemployed" so to speak, and so is the resultant community. It does not come within the province of the work, and does not allow itself to create a work. In fact, one could say that it withdraws from the work. Blanchot (and Jean-Luc Nancy via Blanchot) then takes this one step further to say that the community is involved in *désoeuvrement*, which has been variously translated as idleness, unemployment, and unworking. The Hegelian economy, on the other hand, assumes a "full employment." Nancy enumerates the vital aspects of this type of community when he writes:

> The community takes place of necessity in what Blanchot has called the unworking. Before or beyond the work, it is that which withdraws from the work, that which no longer has to do with production, nor with completion, but which encounters interruption, fragmentation, suspension.[18]

Does a community of this sort have any hope for survival? But even more importantly, does a community of this sort *know* itself as a community? For Hegel, as John Smith points out, the community has a distinctive being and knows itself as inwardly possessing a form of subjectivity. When this subjectivity is lost, so is the vocation or *Bestimmung*. The characterization just given presents community as realized in modern society as working only at an "unworking." Indeed, Blanchot even refers to it as a "non-place," quite in contrast to the description given above about the Christian community "keeping house" or providing some sort of "place" for the spirit to "inhabit" in its concreteness.

To take this analysis to its extreme, community now seems to signify a certain *de*-subjectification. It brings to mind all of the tones, discordant tones, that have sounded within and around Hegel's conclusions concerning the community and its fate. Hegel in fact ended the 1821 lectures on just such a *Mißton*. Later, when Hegel refers to the work that the members must do, he uses the word *Bestimmung* (translated by Smith as "vocation") which in either language has definite connotations with tones, chords, vocalization, and could be translated as a "calling." Unfortunately, the *Bestimmung* has no "place" in the modern community. Instead, as Blanchot points out, the community necessarily gives rise to "multiple speech." It is this multiple speech that I identify with *Verstimmung*.

Derrida, in his essay "Of an Apocalyptic Tone Recently Adopted in Philosophy", discusses the word *verstimmen*:

> *Verstimmen*, which Guillermin translates not without reason by *délirer*, to be delirious, is first of all to put out of tune [*désaccorder*], when we speak of a stringed instrument [*instrument à cordes*], or yet, for example, a voice. . . . Less strictly this signifies to derange, to put out of order, to jumble. One is delirious when one is deranged in the head. *Verstimmung* can come to spoil a *Stimmung*: the bathos [pathos], or the humor that then becomes testy. The *Verstimmun* of which we are speaking here is indeed a social disorder and a derangement, an out-of-tune-ness [*désaccordement*] of cords [*cordes*] and voices in the head.[19]

In addition, he mentions that *verstimmen* is said to indicate a sudden change of mood, a derailment. "It is the disorder or the delirium of the destination."[20]

Remember that *Bestimmung* can be translated as "determination" or "destination" as well. To this extent one could say that Hegel, in his change from "passing away" to "realization" exhibits *Verstimmung* as well within his own corpus.

With this exploration I have tried to refrain from making any subjective judgment as to whether community should or should not pass away, because the assumptions leading to each conclusion are so disparate. However, it does seem necessary to give some sort of justification (perhaps even a "Hegelian" justification) for why the modern destiny of the community is to dissolve itself into the *Verstimmung*. One possible recourse would be to address the issue of eschatology, which, of course, is unfeasible within the scope of this discussion. However, in the LPR it does seem to me that the apocalyptic issues and questions of the Second Advent are overlooked, especially in light of their relationship to the early church. The community which formed after the death of Christ seemed to be eagerly awaiting what they thought was his imminent return. This relation of the apocalyptic to the community is alluded to by Blanchot when he writes:

> Hence the foreboding that the community in its very failure, is linked to a certain kind of writing, a writing that has nothing else to search for than the last words: "Come, come, you for whom the injunction, the prayer, the expectation is not appropriate".[21]

The Revelation of St. John, of course, resounds with the word "Come!" The bride (the Church) is supposed to ask Christ to "come", to return to earth. Hegel, however, in ending with the kingdom of the spirit in which community peacefully works to sustain the ethical life of the state seems to disregard the eschatological altogether. Why would such a community say the word "Come!" when it is living in the complete presence of God? What is lacking? It seems that somehow the community of which Blanchot speaks is necessary if that "Come!" is to resound.

What, then, remains? What has this community become? Blanchot would say that in the end the community posits its own absence. Bataille speaks of the "negative community" or the community of those who have no community. But Bataille, in *Inner Experience* uses an odd image to represent the community: he speaks of an existence that "makes of man a multitude, a desert. It is an expression which resumes and makes precise the sense of a community."

But although he speaks of the "desert" as the continuation of ancient man and an abandonment of the concerns of present day man, he states that: "He is not a return to the past; he has undergone the consumption of the 'present-day man' and nothing has more place within him than the devastation which it leaves—it gives to the desert its desert-like truth."[22] This metaphorical return to the desert seems very important for understanding the course which community must take in modern society. In one sense, then, we have effected a return to what Harris calls the "historic point of origin" of transcendental consciousness, and along those lines, we have a return to Abraham, the nomad.

As a final point, I would like to suggest a connection with the work of the contemporary French philosopher Gilles Deleuze, who, with Felix Guattari has written an analysis of the nomad in the chapter of his book *A Thousand Plateaus* entitled "Nomadology." First, their explanation of the functioning of religion with the state:

> Making the absolute appear in a particular place—is that not a very general characteristic of religion . . . ? But the sacred place of religion is fundamentally a center that repels the obscure nomos. The absolute of religion is essentially a horizon that encompasses, and, if the absolute itself appears at a particular place, it does so in order to establish a solid

and stable center for the global. The encompassing role of smooth spaces (desert, steppe, or ocean) in monotheism has been frequently noted. In short, religion converts the absolute. Religion is in this sense a piece in the State apparatus.[23]

However, the nomadic relation to the state is very different, and in this sense a community which "returns to the desert" has little chance of being appropriated by the state in the manner in which Hegel envisioned. They write that

for the nomad the terms of the question are totally different: locality is not delimited; the absolute, then, does not appear at a particular place but becomes a non-limited locality; the coupling of place and the absolute is achieved not in a centered, oriented globalization or universalization but in an infinite succession of local operations.[24]

One is reminded of the storm god Yahweh who accompanied the band of nomads in the form of thunder clouds. I take this figure to be an example of the "non-limited locality" just mentioned. The Greek influence discussed above, which allows for the divine to make its appearance within the static enclosure of a temple, seems to have had enormous ramifications for the consummate religion and the community it is fated to engender. Each body has become a temple of the spirit, and that multiplication and *Verstimmung* has dis-placed us into a region topologically, but not historically, similar to that with which we began.

## Notes

1. *Early Theological Writings*, trans. T. M. Knox (Philadelphia: University of Pennsylvania Press, 1971), 186.

2. Henry S. Harris, *Hegel's Development: Night Thoughts* (New York: Oxford University Press, 1983), 318.

3. As Charles Taylor writes in *Hegel and Modern Society* (New York: Cambridge University Press, 1979): "In the final analysis it is of vital importance because it is one of the indispensable ways in which man recovers his essential relation to the ontological structure, the other being in the modes of consciousness which Hegel calls "Absolute Spirit," and this real relation through the life of the community is essential to the completion of the return to conscious identity between man and the Absolute" (93).

4. The cited text is from the older edition of the lectures, quoted by the editor of the new edition in a footnote concerning "the difficulty that lies in the ending of the 1821 lectures which concerns the passing away of the community. The information about what was said in these lectures comes from two sources: the second edition of the *Werke* edited by Bruno Bauer, and the actual manuscript of Hegel himself. There are some discrepancies between the two sources, which seem to be due to the fact that Bauer interweaves certain passages into the manuscript from the now-lost Henning transcript of the 1821 lectures."

5. John Smith explains more fully what community is *not*. For example, the members of the community should not be thought of as "mere individuals" or as "parts of some organism as yet to be established," nor do they "lose their individuality in some undifferentiated one." These ideas are alien to Hegel's thought. But somehow Spirit nevertheless does give the religious community a "peculiar sort of reality," because the community is more than just a collection of the individual members. It understands itself to be, as a community, in possession of the form of subjectivity. Cf. Smith's essay "Hegel's Reinterpretation of the Doctrine of Spirit and the Religious Community," *Hegel and the Philosophy of Religion*, ed. Darrel E. Christiansen (The Hague: Nijhoff, 1970), 164.

6. Harris, 338.

7. Smith, "Hegel's Reinterpretation," 157.

8. Hodgson's comments are in his edition of *The Christian Religion* (Ann Arbor: Scholars Press and American Academy of Religion, 197), 346.

9. Smith, "Hegel's Reinterpretation," 174.

10. Smith, "Hegel's Reinterpretation, 173.

11. Heidegger, in *Poetry, Language, Thought*, trans. Albert Hofstadter (New York: Harper and Row, 1971), 91.

12. Mark Taylor, *Altarity* (Chicago: University of Chicago Press, 1988), xxxi.

13. Harris, 331.

14. Taylor, *Altarity*, 223.

15. Georges Bataille, *Inner Experience*, trans. Leslie Ann Boldt (Albany: SUNY Press, 1988), 81.

16. Georges Bataille, "Hegel, Death and Sacrifice," trans. Jonathan Strauss, *Yale French Studies: On Bataille* 79 (1990): 19.

17. Maurice Blanchot, *The Unavowable Community*, trans. Pierre Joris (Barrytown: Station Hill Press, 1988), 9.

18. Jean-Luc Nancy, *La communauté désoeuvrée* (Paris: Christian Bourgois Editeur, 1986), 78-9.

19. Jacques Derrida, "Of an Apocalyptic Tone Recently Adopted in Philosophy," trans. John P. Leavy, *Semeia: Derrida and Biblical Studies* 23 (1982): 72.

20. Derrida, "On an Apocalyptic Tone," 84.

21. Blanchot, *La Communauté*, 12.

22. Bataille, *Inner Experience*, 27.

23. Gilles Deleuze and Félix Guattari, *A Thousand Plateaus*, trans. Brian Massumi (Minneapolis: University of Minnesota Press, 1987), 382.

24. Deleuze and Guattari, 383.

# 13

# Religion, Worldliness, and *Sittlichkeit*

*Michael Vater*

H istory is mercurial, but perhaps kind, in furnishing Hegel an illustration of what it might mean for religion, fulfilled as religious consciousness, to come down out of the clouds and take up residence in the city. For of all the surprising events that Germany witnessed in the East's silent revolution of Autumn 1989, few are quite as surprising as how the revolution that toppled a state started in a few Leipzig churches—in the weekly peace prayers at the Nikolaikirche and the Thomaskirche, where the DDR had brought Bach's corpse back for reburial in 1954 in an attempt to legitimize itself. On November 13, 1989, the eighth Monday protest and prayer service at the Nikolaikirche heard the preacher say:

> Seven days Joshua marched around the walls of Jericho, and by themselves the walls fell to the ground. Seven days Leipzigers have marched through the city and called out, "We are the people," and the wall came tumbling down.[1]

Most thinkers resist simplification; Hegel more than most, especially on the topic of religion. His seminary education, early programs for moral, religious and political renewal, his use of theological allusions in both text and lecture, and his explicit address of contemporary religious situation in the "Prefaces" to the *Encyclopaedia* all point to a lifelong deep concern for religion.[2] I shall argue in this paper that this concern was central to Hegel's vision of doing philosophy. Religion is introductory to and, especially as part of a shared tissue of life-forms, illustrative of humanity's spiritual conversation with itself. But it is not mere ornament, dumb-show, or picture. Whether it ranks in the last analysis as text or footnote is an open question.

For Hegel, the history of developed or Christian religious consciousness embodies three central moments of philosophy: (a) the transition from representation to thought, (b) the invalidation of finite categories in the infinitizing process of thought, (c) the emergence of concrete universality of ethical life from the opposition of the bare universality of the God-concept and the singularity of the human individual. I shall discuss each of these themes in turn, after some brief remarks on the relevance of religion to human life in general. My interest is on the third moment, the claimed emergence of communal ethical life from the abstract idea of God and the self-enclosed singularity of the individual human. If Hegel is right on that score, religion can rightly be seen as both a worldly and world-renewing force, as perhaps it was in the East's peaceful revolution.[3] If he is wrong, then perhaps it is merely the perennial gathering place for the dissatisfied.[4]

## Religion is for Everyone

Hegel repeatedly voiced his conviction about an essential interinvolvement of philosophy and religion. "Religion is for everyone," say the 1827 Lectures.[5] "Religion is the kind of consciousness valid for humans of every rank and calling, since it is truth for them all," says the 1827 Preface for the Encyclopaedia.[6] Religion was the one, perhaps the only, place in culture where Hegel surmised his students might have encountered the strictly conceptual content of philosophy. As a widely shared form of life, it also provided him a body of images and allegories useful for illustrating difficult conceptual paradoxes in the lecture hall. Thus the theological bent of the *Encyclopaedia*.[7]

But once the philosopher admits any identity between philosophy and religion, the "enlightened" spirit of the age insinuates itself into his study and politely requests that religion be played down as an external, narrative, or figurative form of truth. Religion may announce truth, our Mephistopheles concedes, but it speaks in *Vorstellungen* and thus disfigures what it says.[8] The fault is not that it re-presents, but that it presents, makes immediate, singularizes, makes a matter of constant presence what is structural, dispositional, thus both substantial and invisible. It is insistently literal about features that should fade into the background. Religion limps as a vehicle for truth because in its literalness it freezes the voices of spiritual conversation into a single text. Religion, says the objector, itself becomes idolatry, the mis-location of truth.

Hegel's own voice on the matter is not that of the Enlightenment disenchanter. He insists on the identity of philosophy and religion, and on the validity of religion as a form of spiritual life. *Geist* is Hegel's term for Aristotle's *Nous,* and has the same range of meaning: intellect, the proper characteristic of the divine, and that alone which is divine and invariant in the functions and capacities of the human animal.[9] Each domain, philosophy and religion, is a story about spirit, about the gap that opens up in a spiritual being, a question about the extremes of that gap, a questioning attempt to measure the distance established between the human and the divine in that act of chasm. Each extreme equally belongs to life of the being whose existence is mediated by thought. Each domain puts essential questions to the human about who she is. Thus religion is for everyone.

## Religion as Representation

Hegel repeatedly said very elementary things about religion in order to unmistakably locate it. A typical utterance is that humanity in its possession of thought is higher than the animals, who have no religion; freedom and reason are humankind's prerogative alone.[10] This simple utterance puts organic interdependence and its form of consciousness, feeling, on one side, and spirit with its *modus operandi* of thought on the other. Animate life is in touch with its being in feeling; its life is self-enclosed immediacy. Spirit lies at a distance from its being: it is shut out of the *Tiergarten* of immediacy.[11] It must come to itself, return to itself, thinkingly. Thinking implies duplicity, distance from oneself, having the agent-observer hear counsel from too many voices and see too many points of view.

The pietist religiosity of Hegel's time or the secular religion of self-esteem of our own offers much of animal warmth and consolation. It does not address specifically human needs, however, and does not challenge the intellect in quest of its place in the cosmos. For this task, thinks Hegel, are needed the ideal shapes of deity and humanity offered by the history of religions and the conceptual paradoxes enshrined in Christianity's dogmas of trinity, creation, atonement and reconciliation. We might now (500 years after Europe's colonization of "second" and "third" worlds) be tempted to ask: Why these shapes? Why not others? The point is not that these shapes are ultimate, but that they are shapes, starting points for thought, historically evolved items of content. Spirit cannot rest in mere feeling.

Hegel's dispute with the pietists is as interesting as any of his wrestlings with the angel of immediacy. Immediacy claims competence to deliver the whole of what is, in all its complexity, directly and without remainder.[12] The immediate religionist claims to find in the human affects a cognitive apparatus without specified object; it yields global reactions of well-being or woe not tied into the registering of any objective state. What a suitable messenger of the divine! No further need for dreams and prophets, miracles, proofs, or even examination of conscience. And what economy; no use of so-called higher faculties required.

Feeling and faith, sense-certainty, the deliverances of a plain understanding that says just what there is to say—all these have the structure of immediacy. Left to itself, this spirit of simplification would forego all mediation, thickness, depth, complexity. It would side-step the bothersome business of self-questioning and cling to the beauty of surface. Yet the sinner's sense of guilt, the penitent's remorse, the community's feeling of reconciliation are meaningless without a substructure of objective commitments and responsibilities. The feelings of moral persons, even those of aesthetes, are feelings about complex domains fully accessible only to cognition. They are meta-feelings, emotional commentaries on matters whose complexity is not wholly translated into affects, either simple or complex. After Hume (if not Plato) discovered the benign moral emotions and Freud their pathological counterparts, it is impossible to consider the information conveyed by human affects on the level of simple immediacy.

Immediacy does not lie unless it passes itself off as the truth, as what is real in a thick sense. An aspect is not an entity. The particular emotive and cognitive states of a human individual are not a matter of or for religion until the being that has them is a spiritual being. Kierkegaard was plainly a good Hegelian when he pointed out that spirit, as thinking, has a stance toward spirit as such, and is conscious, even if only in the interrogative form, of the tenuous relation between her being and the being of spirit as such. The subject of religious experience, the individual finite cognizer and actor, and the object of religious attention, spirit as such, both call for the translation of representation into thinking. This is nothing other than the classical description of theology's vocation given by Anselm: *fides quaerens intellectum.* There is no immediacy, thinks Hegel, no moment of simple cognition, without background or antecedent. There is no finite being, no simple entity that rests in itself or is understood in its self-enclosure. There is no synchronic structure, no essence, that rests in itself apart from the diachronic flow of an agent's actual cognition or a community's ethical life. Nothing is simple or self-contained save an abstraction, and an abstraction is a sample of and a point of view upon a rich, polymorphous, overdetermined content. Everything immediate is only seemingly simple; its being is adjectival to the thicker substantial core wherein every aspect is tied in every way to every other.[13] The view sounds existentially messier if expressed apart from the language of logic, but this is Hegel's view of the "syllogistic" substance of reality.

How does this view of the inter-involvement of immediacy and mediation bear on the uniqueness of religion as a form of life? Clearly it makes religion a more commonplace, worldly, and equivocal sort of thing than some of its proponents would like. If religion claims to speak in a unique or higher voice, that claim must be seen against a background of the ordinary voices directive of human conduct—economics and politics and morals—and its supposed 'uniqueness' must be reduced to the distinctness of one voice in thick polyphony. If it address its claims to a specific human faculty, e.g. emotion or imagination, then these capacities must be connected to the whole picture of human cognition and action.

All stories of wonders and miracles, feelings of desolation and consolation, of primal ages and "final days" to come must be adjusted to the total anthropological context, as best we can conceive it. 'Anthropological context' is a slightly agnostic term for Hegel's spirit. All religious truths are testimony given in spirit, to spirit, about what it means to be spirit. This implies that all *soi-disant* immediate items and aspects must be inspected for their connections, all limited contexts examined inspected for origins, ends, and wider frameworks. No "big picture" narrative suggesting ultimate meanings, ends, and norms can be accepted simply as offered.

The truth is not simple for spiritual entities. The so-called simple truths offered to simple feeling are most in need of translation to the mediating frameworks of understanding and dialectical reason, of community life and the life of a tradition over history. Because religion speaks to spirit about spirit, its voice must sound over history and its message become intertwined with the cultural patterns of human self-understanding which have come to light. "[T]he very nature of spirit is to develop itself, to differentiate itself even unto worldliness."[14]

The validation of religion's claim to a "higher" or "special" point of view must be its translatability to other languages, its connectivity with other domains. Hermeneutics and post-structuralist philosophy have reminded us how a canon of texts functions generally in this way within a cultural tradition. What is the conclusion a Hegelian could draw? Religion proves its claims to special significance and to privileged communication the more it permeates human culture as a whole and encroaches on other discourses.[15] The specificity of the religious point of view is its generality. Spirit's pre-eminence lies in its connectivity, its "networking" abilty.[16] Only that remainder of talk about the divine that cannot be translated into Babel's many tongues will stir the *Aufklärer's* suspicion.

## Religion as Thought

Hegel's speculative or 'thinking' treatment of religion typically comprised three topics: first came an extrasystematic analysis, often polemical, of the contemporary situation of theology. The Church's thought-elaborated dogma, which Hegel viewed as central to the Christian confession, was challenged by the religion of creedless feeling, on the one hand, and the abstract thinking of Enlightenment natural theology, on the other. Only thought, which has been at work and continues to work inside the doctrinal core, can reconcile rationalism and emotionalism and, at the same time, develop content inside faith. Second, Hegel explored the role traditionally assigned to reason in the elaboration of the faith inside the philosophical tradition of 'proofs of divine existence.' God is not an item for proof, and God's being is not 'existence,' but the thinking elevation of the mind to God effects an internal destruction of finite modes of thought and a subjective surrender of the attitude of 'reasoning.' Third, Hegel usually turned to the history of religions. In his view, the universal concept of religion became fully concretized in an inward and reflective way within the history of the Christian community, both in its philosophical and social-political dimensions. In some important ways these three steps mirror the essential stages of thought marked out in *The Science of Logic.* The first things a speculative treatment of reality must admit are a body of descriptions, superficial and extrinsic, lying ready at hand, the product of a historically delivered common sense. Then it must abolish them, and through a process of immanent critique attain the standpoint of the infinite or conceptual. The infinite or essential contents of thought are expressed in categories dyadic, correlative, and ultimately symmetrical. When, in a third or syllogistic phase, thinking proceeds out beyond the dyadic forms for the schematization of content and includes its own thinking as a third, the philosophical process becomes introspective and (purely) methodological. Hegelian speculative theology repeats this triadic pattern. (1) Historical content external to the situation of thinking, namely the positive content of religion, is appropriated.[17] (2) Its finitude is exploded; here the critique of the "proofs of divine existence" functions the way negative theology did in the robustly rational theological traditions. (3) The mode of appropriation or subjectivization of this content is explored in a meta-reflection on the relevance of absolute or Christian religion to the conditions of modern life.

In the first matter, the face-off between contemporary noncognitive (or at least non-speculative) theologies and the doctrinal development of the orthodox creeds, Hegel has little choice but to locate doctrinal debates and confessional decisions in the past of the community's life.[18] But just as little as the metaphysician is free to construct otherworlds anew in arbitrary disregard of transcendental critique, so little is the theologian free to begin anew to fashion Christian doctrine in arbitrary disregard of the psychologization and moralization which Christianity has undergone in modern times. Since thinking is always about the subject who thinks, it cannot progress if it fails to profoundly question that subject in the whole of her being, including circumstances historical and recent, conditions essential and contingent.

Thinking is tied to time, hence to a historical and communal past. The contemporary experience of the irrelevance of doctrine is thus a necessary starting point for theological reflection. The twofold lack of content which Hegel discovered in the religion of his time—a lack produced on one side by the self-enclosed emotion of pietism and on the other by the 'enlightened' understanding which destroys the specificity and detail of its object—dictated for him the task of speculative philosophy in his time. Philosophy is to re-establish the mean, heal the cleft of faith as an attitude and the Faith as a body of contents. It is to produce a justification of Christian religion in the rational and necessary knowledge of its contents.[19]

Doctrine is not the only surpassed item of positivity in Christianity's past. In the second phase of his treatment of religion, Hegel returns to the tradition of offering proof of the divine existence. With great dialectical economy, Hegel at once restores the thrust of Anselm's prayerful thinking to its spiritual context ("elevation to the infinite") while at the same making the moment of proof the occasion for the incorporation of negativity, the shattering of the finite upon its own nullity. Rationalizing understanding interprets the proofs as a demonstrative ascent from the secure being of worldly things, taken singly or as a whole, to the divine being. Such an 'ascent' would be blasphemous, if it could be consciously made. As an unconscious and frustrated mode of reasoning, it merely blunders into the double category mistake of thinking that finite beings *are*, independently and in their own right, and that the divine shares the same sort of generic "existence" finite beings have.

The 'proofs' effect a speculative raising of the mind to God because, earnestly attempted, they involve the sacrifice of finite modes of thought.[20] If there is "elevation" to the divine, its condition is the laying down of the prejudice of the substantiality of mere things. And when once substantiality has been anchored in the simple being of the whole rather than in the finite's existence, the understanding's tendency to see entities where there are only aspects is blunted and transformed.[21] So is its tendency to see paradoxes instead of processes, to see individuals and their isolated volitions instead of communities and patterns of action constrained by traditions and institutions. In the so-called proofs, philosophy begins in earnest.

Philosophy and religion both involve inducing a change of heart and mind in the individual. They effect a reversal of view and values as sudden as the biblical "kingdom of heaven." The living effect of the failure of the proofs of divine existence is the disproof of the reality and importance of contingent things. The step from categories of finitude to those of infinitude is the crucial one in thought's progress from insufficiently relational to fully reflective concepts. It is with some justice the Jena Logic makes the transition from the finite to the infinite thought's central deed: "This is precisely the true nature of the finite, that it is infinite, that it suspends itself in its very being. The determinate has no other essence than this absolute unrest: not to be what it is."[22] The static language I use to speak of a simple transit to the infinite belies the unrest, activity, and fondness for contrast which characterizes a spiritual whole. The work of thought must exhaust the whole vocabulary of grounding and existence, necessity and freedom, and push the concept of substance through a circuit of first objective, then subjective development before it can "get it whole."[23] And if logic attempts to think the whole in bare abstraction, philosophy of religion must do so in terms more spiritual, more directed to the relational nature of self-consciousness, and speak of inclusion, sundering, and reconciliation of particularized spirit as the life of this substantial whole.

Here of course Hegel's philosophy of religion attaches to the positivity of Christian religion in a way that seems either shockingly arbitrary or fortuitous. Perhaps the latter, for the mythic features of the Judaeo-Christian story of creation and fall as well as the dogmatic outlines of Christian concepts such as trinity, atonement, and church are abstract and logical enough to be the right sort of positivity for Hegel's conceptual reconstruction. At a suitable distance from scriptural narrative and theological decrees of Church councils, Hegel's consummate religion does not seem a bad fit with "Orthodoxy." He can still be accused of arbitrariness in his speculative take-over of Christianity's positivity, and perhaps also of chauvinism in his readiness to take Christianity as "definitive" religion. These are traits, however, which he shares with the earliest Church Fathers and every theologian after them. If the shape of spiritual reality emerges historically in an essential way, then it has to do so somewhere, to someone, in very particular (perhaps painfully particular) ways. "Spirit is only for spirit."[24] Perhaps only for a spirit, or a particular human community.

## Religion as Worldliness

Christianity has come to understand itself as a historical religion and one with a universal mission. It defined itself against the background of Israel's narrative encounter with deity, though its founder understood himself as either the messenger or the vehicle of a profoundly discontinuous interruption of that historical flow (the "reign of God").[25] But it also defined for itself a future process of outreach or universalization. As a definite and universal religion, Christianity is characterized by a paradoxical focus on specific temporal events (Jesus' preaching, death, the formation of the community by the presence of the Spirit) whose significance is to be seen only their in long range and nonlocal cultural manifestations. The meaning of Christianity is, for Hegel, to be read in the destiny or the fate of a Christian culture.

If that were Hegel's dry thesis, we could label his attitude toward Christianity mere historicism. Perhaps it bespeaks a relativism, an indifference toward the claims Christianity advances as the "consummate" form of religious self-consciousness. But the case is not so simple. Christianity's universality, spirituality, inwardness, and historicity all point toward a drive to disestablish religion as a special or separate sphere of cultural life and to integrate it into the texture of everyday life. Its spiritual impulse is to leave behind its founder (and also the outpouring of the Spirit upon the original community of believers, as well as the doctrines, institutions, and authority of that community's determinate form) and in its attainment of universality become worldly. "[T]he way in which the subject determines its goals in its worldly life depends upon the substantial consciousness of its own truth. This is the aspect under which religion reflects itself in worldliness."[26]

The truth of religion is the reconciliation of spirit with itself in the midst of its finitude and its time-bound form. The wholly universal vocation of the community in which spirit is present is to realize the freedom and rationality of the self-conscious subjects who make up the community. In its final form, the truth of religion is completely anthropomorphic: "Inwardness knows itself as subsisting with itself precisely in this reconciliation of spirit with itself; and this knowledge of being at home with itself is precisely thinking. Thinking means reconciledness, being at home or at peace with oneself."[27]

"Thinking!" The idea that thinking is a pre-ordained end of human existence, its highest capacity, and its intrinsic fulfillment might seem a bit of Greek nostalgia today, as irrelevant to the religious person as to the unchurched hedonist. But Hegel did not advocate an academic remake of the earth. Thinking is the species-defining mode of human existence; it is the genus of deliberative freedom and rational action. Historically few humans have emerged into the individuality required to exercise these powers to a significant extent. Modernity has informed us ever more pointedly of the factual constraints upon their efficacy. Religion and philosophy (in the perennial mode Hegel imagines its existence) have exhibited in idea these powers as the telos of rational existence. Yet the idea, religious myth and philosophical concept, is persistently misappropriated when it is concretized and located. Thus for Hegel it is no longer sufficient for modern individuals to intuit the totalized and reconciled world of their humanity alongside or over and above their quotidian activity. Religious story may mislead qua story, but religious truth is neither world denying nor world duplicating.[28] Religious truth must instead be world embracing, transformative.

So, Hegel claims, the end-point of the development of religious consciousness is the ethical life (*Sittlichkeit*) of modern communities, where moral, social, political concerns as well as religion fuse with the fabric of everyday activities and forms of existence. The ethical community is pervaded by thought; activities, forms of life, and values that are richly mediated structure the short-range concerns and the daily conditions of individuals. Freedom is realized, though of course realization means that it is partially truncated and obscured by appearing within the constraints of existing conditions. The subject enjoys rational life, though that life is a totality of pre-given conditions, objective and subjective. Grace, to speak poetically, perfects nature in manifesting freedom and reason resident within necessity and contingency.[29]

What happens to God, or to speak more carefully, to God-consciousness in this world-transformative realization? Hegel gives two answers, each carefully crafted, each equivocal. The first is that God (or the finite within God) is realized and dead:

The truth to which human beings have attained by means of this history, what they have become conscious of in this entire history, is the following: that the idea of God has certainty for them, that humanity has attained the certainty of unity with God, that the human is the immediately present God. Indeed, within this history, as spirit comprehends it, there is the very presentation of the process of what humanity, of what spirit is—implicitly both God and dead.[30]

The text suggests that religion, if still relevant in modern times, has become a wholly immanent affair. One can talk of the finite as a vanishing moment in the divine the way that Nietzsche talks of the human as a bacterial infestation on the crust of this planet. Apparently there is an other or higher frame of reference, but the true referent for all terms in the lexicon of values is the human fabricator and user of values. Since it is all about humans, religion is immanent discourse. Only in that it speaks of the creation of value is the subject of that discourse not just human but spirit.

Hegel's second answer seems to say the same, but a bit more dialectically. In contrast to the pietistic and enlightenment abolition of religious content, speculative Hegelian philosophy preserves the content. "The concept produces the truth—this is subjective freedom—but it recognizes this truth as at the same time not produced, as the truth that subsists in and for itself."[31] We make religious ideas, the text seems to say, but they are independently true.

It remains an open question whether Hegel's worldly Christianity rescues religion for modern consciousness and reinvigorates (as theology should) the content of an old form of life, or whether it effects the same vaporization of religious content that emotivist or rationalist reductions induce. History has given us a parable. A quiet revolution started under the guise of weekly prayer services for peace. It spilled out of the churches into the streets. One politician quietly ordered the troops not to fire on those chanting, "We are the people."[32] A wall tumbled. A state crashed. Was all this the phenomenon of religion becoming 'worldly'? Surely, but the churches in Leipzig are quiet and empty again. Is that what 'religion becoming worldly' also means? If in 1989 the churches were the "moral space" of the disaffected and dissatisfied, what is their function now that disaffection finds a public voice? Should religion survive as a space of sacred protest? Can it do so without content? Does the positivity of past religious experience suffice for content? These questions cannot be answered by a single writer. Following Hegel's ideas, we ought to look to the lives of peoples. But where is the testimony of spirit to be found, in the secular satiety of first-world societies or the yearnings of third-world societies where religions continue to suggest paradigms of liberation or of order?

# Notes

1. *Die Zeit* (November 24, 1989): 2.

2. In 1827 the pietist theologian Tholuck draws Hegel's attention to the equivalent emptiness of Enlightened and pious theologies (cf. the Preface to the *Encyclopaedia* [Frankfurt am Main: Suhrkampf, 1970], Vorrede 2, 26-27n). In 1830, theological wrangles at the University of Halle evoke reflections on the essential place of doctrinal development in Christianity (Vorrede 3, 34-6).

3. A Lutheran pastor explained the Church's role in nurturing the peaceful revolution in East Germany thus: "There was no other social force in the country that had independence both from the state and the party. And we had an understanding of the Christian Gospel as a message with political content" ("Church As Moral Authority in Peaceful Revolution," *The New York Times* [December 7, 1989]: A, 20:4).

4. "The weekly vigil had long been a gathering place for the dissatisfied." "March Gathers at St. Michael's [sic] Church," *The New York Times* (November 14, 89): A, 18:1.

5. LPR 106.

6. E, Vorrede 2, 23.

7. Schelling was the first commentator and critic to call attention to the logical and naturalistic awkwardness of the transition between The Logic and The Philosophy of Nature, modelled as it is on Christian accounts of Creation and the Fall (which were fused into one in Jaocb Boehme's poetic accounts). Schelling finds the transition the Achilles' heel of Hegel's system not because it is theologically motivated, but because the foregoing logic is too abstract and lacking in reality to motivate any move, dialectical or abrupt, toward something as real as nature. Hegel retreats there from the discovery he should have made of the difference between identity-philosophy and positive (or "empirical") philosophy. See "Zur Geschichte der neueren Philosophie. Münchner Vorlesungen" (1827) in Schelling's *Werke* 10, 152-155.

8. On Hegel's own view, the weakness of religion is not that it utilizes images and figures. Its weakness is one of thought, for it thinks judgmentally, in propositional mode. In a judgment, God (or spirit or nature) is presented or representatively named, but since the concept is separated off from it in predicate position, it is merely mentioned or tangentially related to the living core of truth. See Hegel's *Science of Logic*, trans. A. V. Miller (Atlantic Highlands: Humanities, 1989), 624-25. (Hereafter cited as SL.) An adequate "discourse" for conceptual thought would draw subject into predicate, essentially reflect the moments of the predicate among themselves, then unify their distinctions in a methodological or historical narrative.

9. Though Hegel might have quoted Aristotle's rigorous argument in *Metaphysics* xii, 9 which links the self-thinking nature of divine thought to the perfection of self-sufficiency, he chose instead as a concluding doxology to the *Encyclopaedia* and to the philosophy of spirit in particular the more anthropomorphic text of *Metaphysics* xii, 7. There the goodness, pleasure and very life of God are said to be due to its perpetual possession of the active intellection we sometimes possess. See *Metaphysics* 1072b 14-30. For Hegel as for Aristotle, the human and the divine are complements, not opposites.

10. "Human beings think, and they alone have religion." LPR 121. "If it is right (and well should it be) that humanity differentiates itself from the beasts through thought, then everything human is human solely because it has been effected by thinking" (E §1).

11. LPR 214.

12. Hegel disputes the claim to immediate knowledge of God which calls itself 'faith': "All conviction that God is, and regarding what God is, rests, so it is surmised, upon this immediate revealedness in the human being, upon this faith" (LPR 86). Under the explicit name of 'pietism' Hegel attacks an inward turned private spirituality that in its arbitrariness goes so far as to claim that "it is the master of what is good and evil" (LPR 486).

13. "Only slight experience is needed to see that where there is immediate knowledge there is also mediated knowledge and vice versa. . . . The true is their unity, an immediate knowledge that likewise mediates, a mediated knowledge that is at the same time internally simple, or is immediate reference to itself" (LPR 99).

14. LPR 482.

15. Similar accounts might be given of ethical discourse or serious literature. Hegel's use of various ethical voices and literary figures in the *Phenomenology* suggests as much, though there perhaps the point is that both directors of conscience and archetypal protagonists or heroes are irreducibly plural.

16. "God loses nothing when he communicates himself. Therefore this knowledge [of God] on the part of the subject is a relationship that issues from God; and as issuing from God it is the absolute judgment that God *is* as

spirit *for* spirit. Spirit is essentially a being for spirit and spirit *is* spirit only insofar as it is *for* spirit" (LPR 393).

17. See Hegel's extensive treatment of the positivity of religion in general, and of Christianity's founding and its doctrine in LPR 395-402. Hegel's solution to the problem of positivity is rather abrupt: "Only the concept on its own account liberates itself truly and thoroughly from the positive. For in philosophy and in religion there is found this highest freedom, which is thinking itself as such" (LPR 402).

18. The religious community that looks to doctrine for its knowledge of human reconciliation with God has the direct outpouring of God's spirit behind it as its past, a mode of divine action no longer effective. See LPR 475. Seen from the point of view of human consciousness, the positivity of religion is a vanishing moment. Revelation ceases, canons close, and work of thought and action begins.

19. LPR 485-87. Hegel enunciates a very nuanced position here on the relation of faith and speculative reason. Religion is not just assimilated to philosophy, annexed as a canceled domain to a secular search for truth. Philosophy and theology are identified in their common content, the moral-theological vision originated in Greece, Israel and Rome. This makes philosophy essentially theological. It also makes theological reflection essential to the content of religion.

20. See LPR 162.

21. "The sole import of this procedure is that *the infinite alone is;* the finite has no genuine being, whereas God has only genuine being" (LPR 172).

22. *Jenenser Logik, Metaphysik und Naturphilosophie* (Hamburg: Meiner, 1967), 31. Perhaps the finite and the infinite are related the way the plane surface (in its own frame of reference) and the Moebius strip (where the same has become both inner and outer) are. A "flatlander" would certainly undergo intellectual adventures discovering her world was Moebius-flat.

23. Hegel relates the following ladder of the forms of being or immediacy: being, determinate being, existence, ground and existence, actuality, substantiality, and finally objectivity (SL 708). The only higher form of being is idea, the coincidence of being and thinking (SL 757, 759).

24. LPR 393.

25. "This kingdom of God, the new religion, thus contained implicitly the characteristic of negating the present world" (LPR 460). This revolutionary attitude attacks existing ethical bonds as well. See LPR 461.

26. LPR 106-07 n77.

27. LPR 48.

28. It would follow for Hegel that genuine forms of realized spirituality are neither withdrawn from the world, as in early Christian asceticism, nor divorced from the robust activity of secular life, as in pietism's and

romanticism's cult of feeling. There is to be no schizophrenic division of a religious world from a secular one. See LPR 482-483.

29. "This vocation of the subject ought to be foundational in its relation with what is worldly. This freedom of the subject is its rationality—the fact that as subject it is thus liberated and has attained this liberation through religion, that in accord with its religious vocation it is essentially free" (LPR 482). See E §159 where the unification of freedom and necessity effected by the thinking through of necessity is described in religious terms: "This liberation, existing for itself, is called self; totally developed, free spirit; when sensed, love; when enjoyed, blessedness."

30. LPR 468.

31. LPR 487.

32. The turning point of the East Germany's peaceful revolution came on 9 October, 1989 when Egon Krenz, then security chief, quietly canceled Erik Hoenecker's order "to be prepared to open fire" on Leipzig demonstrators (cf. *The New York Times* [November 19, 1989]: A,1:3).

# List of Contributors

**John Burbidge** is professor of philosophy at Trent University in Canada. He is the author of *On Hegel's Logic* (1981) and *Hegel on Logic and Religion* (1992). From 1988 to 1990 he was president of the Hegel Society of America.

**Clark Butler** has taught at Purdue on the Indiana-Purdue Fort Wayne Campus since his doctorate from USC in 1970, with visiting teaching at Trent Polytechnic (Nottingham) and the Université de Strasbourg. He co-edits the journal *CLIO*, and has done co-translation and the commentary for *Hegel: The Letters*.

**William Desmond** is professor of philosophy and chair of the department of philosophy at Loyola College, Baltimore. He is the author of *Art and the Absolute* (1986), *Desire, Dialectic, and Otherness* (1987), *Philosophy and Its Others* (1990), and *Beyond Hegel and Dialectic* (1992). He is currently (1990-1992) president of the Hegel Society of America.

**Martin Donougho** is associate professor of philosophy at the University of South Carolina. He has published widely in German philosophy, and in the philosophy of art, and is working on books on Hegel's Aesthetics, on the genealogy of aesthetics, and on a translation of Hegel's 1823 lectures on the philosophy of art.

**Stephen N. Dunning** is associate professor and chair of the graduate program in Religious Studies at the University of Pennsylvania. He is the author of *The Tongues of Men: Hegel and Hamann on Religious Language and History* (1979) and *Kierkegaard's Dialectic of Inwardness: A Structural Analysis of the Theory of Stages* (1985).

**Louis Dupré** is the T. L. Riggs Professor in the philosophy of religion at Yale University. His published work is mainly in the area of social thought (*Marx's Social Critique of Culture*), philosophy of religion (*The Other Dimension; A Dubious Heritage*), and critique of culture (*Passage to Modernity*, in preparation).

217

**Sarah Lilly Heidt** is currently a graduate student in the Department of Philosophy at Yale University.

**Walter Jaeschke** was from 1974 until 1989 an associate at the Hegel Archive at the Ruhr University in Bochum. Since 1989 he has been at the Academy of Sciences in Berlin; he teaches philosophy at the Free University of Berlin. He has edited several volumes in the critical edition of Hegel's complete works, the *Science of Logic* and the lecture manuscripts, especially the *Lectures on the Philosophy of Religion*, which he edited together with Peter C. Hodgson and Ricardo Ferrara.

**David Kolb** is Charles A. Dana professor of philosophy at Bates College. He is the author of *The Critique of Pure Modernity: Hegel, Heidegger, and After* (1986), and *Postmodern Sophistications: Philosophy, Architecture, and Tradition* (1990). From 1988 to 1990 he was vice-president of the Hegel Society of America.

**Martin J. De Nys** is associate professor of philosophy and religious studies at George Mason University. He specializes in philosophical theology, metaphysics, and political philosophy.

**Cyril O'Regan** is assistant professor of modern Christian thought in the department of religious studies at Yale University. He is an Irish national with degrees from University College Dublin and Yale University. His primary interests are in modern religious and philosophic thought, and ancient and medieval Neoplatonism.

**Stephen Rocker** is a Catholic priest and associate professor of philosophy at Wadhams Hall Seminary College, Ogdensburg, N.Y. He received his S.T.B. and Ph.L. at the University of Louvain, and his Ph.D. at the University of Ottawa.

**Michael Vater** is associate professor of philosophy at Marquette University. He has edited and translated Schelling's <u>Bruno</u>, and authored articles on Fichte, Spinoza, and Hegel.

**Robert R. Williams** is professor of philosophy at Hiram College; he is the author of *Schleiermacher the Theologian* (1978), *Recognition: Fichte and Hegel on the Other* (1992), editor and translator of Isaac A. Dorner's *How God's Immutability Should Be Understood* (1992), and has published articles on Hegel, Fichte, and Schleiermacher.

# Index